Other books by

BEVERLEY NICHOLS

Fiction

SELF

PATCHWORK

PRELUDE

FOR ADULTS ONLY

CRAZY PAVEMENTS

EVENSONG

REVUE

MEN DO NOT WEEP

General

TWENTY-FIVE

THE STAR-SPANGLED MANNER

ARE THEY THE SAME AT HOME?

WOMEN AND CHILDREN LAST

CRY HAVOC!

THE FOOL HATH SAID

NO PLACE LIKE HOME

NEWS OF ENGLAND

GREEN GROWS THE CITY

Philosophical: Chronicles of Allways

DOWN THE GARDEN PATH

A THATCHED ROOF

A VILLAGE IN A VALLEY

Omnibus

OXFORD-LONDON-HOLLYWOOD

Drama

FAILURES

MESMER

VERDICT ON
INDIA

by

BEVERLEY NICHOLS

JONATHAN CAPE
THIRTY BEDFORD SQUARE
LONDON

FIRST PUBLISHED 1944
JONATHAN CAPE LTD.   30 BEDFORD SQUARE, LONDON
AND 91 WELLINGTON STREET WEST, TORONTO

BOOK
PRODUCTION
| WAR ECONOMY |
STANDARD

THIS BOOK IS PRODUCED IN COM-
PLETE CONFORMITY WITH THE
AUTHORIZED ECONOMY STANDARDS

PRINTED IN GREAT BRITAIN IN THE CITY OF OXFORD
AT THE ALDEN PRESS
PAPER BY SPALDING & HODGE LTD.
BOUND BY A. W. BAIN & CO. LTD.

CONTENTS

AUTHOR'S FOREWORD   ·   7

PART ONE

I   THE ELUSIVE INDIAN   9
II   POMP AND CIRCUMSTANCE   19
III   BELOW THE BOTTOM RUNG   30
IV   THE STORMY NORTH   42
V   LESSONS IN BED   55

PART TWO

I   SEARCHLIGHT ON HINDUISM   64
II   PAUSE FOR BREATH   80
III   GENTLEMEN OF THE PRESS   86
IV   HINDU HOLLYWOOD   95
V   IN SEARCH OF AN ARTIST   106
VI   MUSICAL INTERLUDE   122
VII   MUMBO-JUMBO   137
VIII   GAOL-BIRD   148

PART THREE

I   HEIL HINDU!   157
II   HATE FOUNDS AN EMPIRE   178
III   DIALOGUE WITH A GIANT   188
IV   HUNGER   198
V   WHITE AND OFF-WHITE   215
VI   LOOSE ENDS   227
VII   TO QUIT OR NOT TO QUIT   249

AUTHOR'S FOREWORD

THIS book is the record of over a year's intensive study of modern India. The accent is on the word 'modern'. It is an endeavour to trace the workings of the Indian mind not only in politics but — *inter alia* — in art, in literature, in music, in medicine, in journalism, in the cinema, and, of course, in religion.

It has involved journeys of many thousands of miles, on foot, by car, by bullock-cart, by aeroplane and occasionally on a stretcher. I have not attempted to describe these journeys except in so far as they illustrate the main theme.

There are two reasons for this foreword.

The first is to stress the fact that *Verdict on India* is, as the pavement artists used to say, 'all my own work'. It is not 'British propaganda'; it does not represent the 'official point of view', whatever that may be; it is not sponsored by the India Office. I have never met Mr. Amery, nor seen him, nor heard him, nor communicated with him or with anybody connected with him, unto the third and fourth generation.

It is necessary to insist upon this point because almost from the day I set foot in India the national Press chose to regard me, to my considerable astonishment, as ambassador of Empire, envoy incognito, armed with all manner of secret weapons of diplomacy and intrigue. It was fiercely asserted that I was in the pay of the Government — playing the role, presumably, of a sort of rococo Stafford Cripps. One paper so far lost its sense of humour and proportion as to announce that I had been offered the post of Viceroy.[1]

The facts, alas, are less glamorous. I came to India, originally, as a correspondent of Allied Newspapers; a long and serious illness interrupted this connection; I stayed on as an independent observer; and when I felt that I had observed enough, I wrote this book. It is a completely individual expression of a personal point of view.

The second reason for this foreword is to apologize, in advance,

[1] *Bombay Sentinel*, May 5th, 1943.

7

What was the man getting at? There must be something behind the question; he was not the facetious sort, and even if he had been, twenty years in Darjeeling would have cured him of it. You can't be facetious, living under the scrutiny of the eternal snows.

I began to think of some of the Indians I had met; they seemed to move before me in a pageant of astonishing diversity and colour.

At the head of the pageant, strange to say, were four murderers. They had been my neighbours in hospital at Peshawar. They were chained to their beds and you could hear the chains rattling in the night. A pleasanter group of murderers you would not find in a month of Sundays, mild of eye, soft of voice, gentle of gesture. Each of them had murdered for love or passion or honour, none of them for gold. That is the way of the North-West Frontier.

In the wake of the murderers — (for the dusk plays tricks with the mind, making it flicker from point like shadows in the valley) — marched three nautch girls. They had been the high spot in a religious procession at the palace of the Maharajah of Mysore, and once seen, they could never be forgotten, for they were so surprisingly unlike what one expected. For a whole hour we had stood on the steps, watching a turbulent river of colour; standard-bearers with palanquins of purple and jade, soldiers with rods of solid gold, shaped in the semblance of serpents, priests with many-pronged candelabras of silver, encrusted with jewels.

Then the sacred cows — elegant and coquettish, their backs covered with tapestries of crimson and azure, their great horns gilded, their faces touched with mascara and vermilion. Even their feet were tipped with gold and braceleted.

And at last the nautch girls.

'Look!' they cried. 'Here they come!'

'But where?' I leant forward with fierce impatience; after all, one's first nautch girl is an experience; no race of beings has been invested with a rarer aura of poetry and romance.

'Over there. One in gold, one in purple, and one in silver. Don't you *see*?'

I saw.

I saw Miss Zazu Pitts, Miss Haidee Wright and a lady who greatly resembled the late Duchess of Teck.

Now all these ladies, in their way, have shining qualities, but they would be the first to agree that they do not immediately suggest themselves as typical of the legendary nautch girl. Of course, it was not really these ladies who were dancing past, but their Indian doubles; and the reason why such comparatively mature persons were gyrating for our benefit was because the profession of nautch girl, in Mysore, is rapidly dying out. These were the best they could get.

But they were a shock, particularly the oriental Miss Pitts, who twisted her hips and wobbled her neck in a manner that may have appealed to the Hindu gods but was somewhat frightening to the Western observer.

II

This would never do.

It was nearly dark; soon my friend would come back from his snake-bitten coolie, and I had not even begun to answer his question.

'Have you ever met an Indian?'

Met an Indian? An *Indian?*

How many Indians had I met? To speak to . . . at least a thousand. But it would be hopeless to try to remember them individually.

Supposing we generalized? Supposing we looked at India, as it were, from a great height, dividing the broad masses of the population into separate groups, like those fascinating relief pictures which help the layman to grasp the outlines of a great battle? Maybe that would help.

Here goes.

First group. 180 million caste Hindus. They were Indians all right, the very core of India. But wait a minute . . . were they? What about the 60 million non-caste Hindus who were standing, or rather grovelling, in their dust? Were they Indians too? According to the caste Hindus, they were not even men and women! They were 'untouchable'. To drink from the same cup would be spiritual poison; their very shadow was pollution. Some of them were even 'unseeable', and must hide themselves by day, only coming out when there were clouds over the moon.

If these 60 million — (nearly equal to the total white population of the British Empire) — were regarded by their own brethren as a good deal lower than the lowest animals, how could they be described, by a Westerner, as 'Indians'? They could not *both* be Indians. Or could they? It was all very puzzling.[1]

Let us leave the Hindus for a moment and turn to the Muslims. How many of them? Nearly 100 million. And we do not have to ask them if they are Indians, for they are shouting it at the top of their voices. '*We* are India!' they cry. 'We are the *only* race, apart from the British, who have ever established a great Indian Empire! And we want our Empire back! It may not be an Empire of all India — (though some of us have our own ideas about what we shall do when we have the power) — but at least it will be *Muslim*. It will be as free as we can make it from the taint of Hinduism, which is not only a different religion, but a different culture, a different social system. And this Empire we shall call Pakistan!'

Pakistan! Pakistan! What does it mean — this strange unborn Empire that exists only in the form of a dream? Later on, we shall try to analyse it; in the meantime it is enough to note that the cry of 'Pakistan' threatens to drown all others in the Indian babel.

So if the Muslims are 'Indians', it would seem that the Hindus are not. And if the Hindus are 'Indians' it would seem that the Muslims are not. These vast bodies of men are so acutely conscious of their differences that they not only refuse to eat together or think together, or pray together, they refuse even to live in the same unit of territory. They want their own geography as well as their own history; they want their own earth as well as their own heaven. On the lips of the vast majority of them such a phrase as *Civis Indianus sum* would sound grotesque.

[1] In spite of the much publicized declarations of Mr. Gandhi and the strenuous efforts of their leader, Dr. Ambedkar, to say nothing of British legislation, the position of the Untouchables in India is still almost as deplorable as it has always been.

III

The light is growing fainter and fainter, and it would seem that with it is fading our chance of meeting the 'Indian' whom we are seeking.

But perhaps we are bemused by numbers; perhaps the roar of the millions is drowning the voice of the individual?

Let us therefore try a different method of approach; let us begin at the other end with India's smallest community, the Parsees. There are less than 90 thousand of them, and of these, nearly half are settled in Bombay. The world at large knows little of the lives led by the Parsees; it has been too busy concentrating its attention on the manner of their deaths. For it is the Parsees, the followers of the prophet Zoroaster, who carry their dead to the Towers of Silence, there to be devoured by the awaiting vultures. It is a dramatic way of leaving the world and — on first thoughts — a rather horrible one. But at least it is clean and uncompromising, if you really believe that the spirit is all and the flesh nothing. And it is the last gesture of charity which a man can make to the earth that has nourished him — to give his body to the fowls of the air, who, after all, are also God's creatures.

However, this is not a book of the dead but of the living, and if we judge them by the achievements of their lives the Parsees immediately assume a position of importance on the Indian scene, out of all proportion to their numbers. And with this thought, our hopes rise again, for if we are seeking 'Indians' we should surely find them now.

Wherever there are riches in India you will find the Parsees — not, let us hasten to add, in the role of vultures but playing a dynamic part in the creation of wealth. To give only one example: the vast network of Tata industries is entirely Parsee, in conception, in execution, and in present-day direction. The firm of Tata's *is* industrial India. Its steel works at Jamshedpur, employing 30,000 people, are the largest steel works in the British Empire. Its hydro-electric system, with a capacity of 250,000 horse-power, is the largest unit in the country. Its air-craft industry, in a few years time, may challenge the biggest combines of the West. Tata's make everything, from gliders to golliwogs, from corkscrews to eau-de-Cologne.

Wherever you find culture in India, you will find the Parsees. They are almost the only patrons of art. They are the only people who have apportioned anything like an adequate part of their wealth to the social services, founding hospitals and libraries, establishing parks and playing grounds. Theirs are the only figures that stand out from the vast desert of mediocrity which is the Indian Press.

India without the Parsees would be like an egg without salt. And without a good deal of its yolk too.

But — and it is a very big 'but' — we cannot really call them 'Indians'. Even if they themselves claimed the title — (and a large number of them do not, preferring to regard themselves as a separate community, living on tolerance) — the vast majority of Indians would deny it to them. They say that the Parsees are really Persians, as their name implies. They always were Persians, and they always will be. And they say it in terms which are by no means polite. For the Parsees have aroused great envy; thousands of fingers are itching to get at their gold. 'Wait till we are free — you won't be able to see the Parsees for dust.' So runs the argument. It is an argument to which the Parsees would do well to pay heed.

I V

And now the darkness is almost complete . . . the darkness of the mountains and the valleys surrounding us, and the darkness of our minds in this search that leads to Nobody.

However, just as there are still a few gleams of gold in the sky so there are still a few rays of hope in our minds. For there are still large communities, running into many millions, which we have not yet considered. For instance, we have not mentioned the Sikhs. Nor the Jains, nor the Buddhists. Nor, for that matter, the Christians. Maybe, among some of these . . . ?

So we make a last effort, beginning with the Sikhs. The Sikhs are among the true aristocrats of India; they are virile and clean-living, swift of brain and body. And in the teaching of Nanak,[1] their first Guru, they have a divinely inspired philosophy. Nanak scourged the Hindu Brahmins as Christ scourged the Pharisees, crying . . . 'Thou bathest and washest and worshippest stones, but without being imbued with God thou art the filthiest of the filthy'. In words of unforgettable force he trumpeted the power of God — ('He can appoint a worm to sovereignty, and reduce an army to ashes') — and the sufficiency of His love — ('If it please Thee, rivers flow over dry land and the lotus bloometh in the heavens; if it please Thee, man crosseth the terrible ocean; in Thee I shall dwell in peace, to dwell in Thee is all I wish.') He was a true mystic, but he was also a man of the people and his teaching, with its simple metaphors of everyday life, burned deep into the peasant heart . . . ('Evil-mindedness is a low woman; cruelty a butcher's wife; covetousness is a dog, food obtained by deceit carrion, anger the fire which burns.')[2]

But their very devotion to the memory of their great prophet makes of the 5 million Sikhs a race apart. They have never forgotten that they were persecuted by the Moguls, and that the treacherous Emperor Aurungzeb killed the ninth Guru for his refusal to embrace the faith of Islam. Their hostility to the Muslims makes them implacable enemies of the dream Empire of Pakistan, for if the dream were ever realized, the Sikhs, who nearly all live in the Punjab, would find themselves hopelessly isolated and outnumbered, a tiny island of the faithful surrounded by a sea of foes.

'If you grant Pakistan', they cry, 'we shall set up a separate Sikh State of our own. We shall call it Khalistan, and we shall defend it to the death.'

Civis Indianus sum . . . if we ever find any Indians who say those words with real sincerity, without hypocrisy and without any thought of self-interest, it will not be the Sikhs.

So shall we give it up? Shall we lie back and watch the fire-flies gathering in the branches of the tamarind, lighting it up with

---

[1] Born 1469, died 1546.
[2] *Thus spoke Guru Nanak*, compiled by Sir Jogendra Singh (Oxford University Press).

a thousand sparkles, till it looks like a gigantic Christmas tree?
But the associations of the word 'Christmas' reminds us that there
is still one faith which we have not considered.

Might this 'Indian' for whom we are seeking be a Christian?
Might there be something in the supreme teaching of Jesus which
caused him to forget these fratricidal hatreds, and to regard himself as a member of one of God's great families, the Indian family?

We can best answer this question by telling a story.

Not long ago I was sitting in a little Indian restaurant in Madras
waiting for a friend who was going to show me photographs of
some old churches which he had taken in Goa. Goa is Portuguese
territory, and it is very rich in churches of late eighteenth-century
baroque. They are frail and fading now, their jewels have long
been stolen, and two centuries of Indian suns have bleached the
last flecks of colour from their elegant façades; they stand like
ghosts on the sea-shore, their windows staring homewards. But
though they wilt and crumble they are still thronged with worshippers — Indian converts of long ago who have kept to their old
faith.

My friend arrived. His head was bandaged.

'Hullo! Where d'you get that crack?'

He grinned. 'In the best of places. In church.'

'In *Church*?'

He explained. He had been to mass. When the sacred wine
was being offered a Christian Hindu noticed that the cup had
been handed to a woman of a lower caste than his. He got up and
tried to snatch it from her. The woman screamed, the other
members of her caste gathered round to protect her, sides were
taken, and within a few seconds an unholy row was in progress,
with the struggling bodies of Indians reeling backwards and forwards over a pavement stained with blood and wine.

'You look shocked,' said my friend.

'Well, it isn't a very pretty story.'

'Oh — but it happens all over India, in every Christian church.
Why, down here in the south, the fights were so fierce that they've
stopped processions down the aisle. People used to tear the
banners out of each others' hands. It's worst during Holy Com-
munion. We've had to put up little brass enclosures for the

various castes. Even so, they complain that they're been polluted by drinking from the same cup.'

Pollution — from the cup of Christ!

Civis Indianus sum!

The search is off.

And now, it seemed a little less dark, for the stars were out and the fireflies were having a gala night in the tamarind; the whole tree shimmered as though its leaves had been dipped in liquid silver. To make it still gayer there was a slip of a moon hanging on the lower branches, like a gaudy toy.

Footsteps on the hillside. My host appeared, followed by a group of coolies. All of them had the pure Chinese cast of features which is typical of Northern Bengal. (Were *they* 'Indians'? But no — we've given up asking that question.) He gave the coolies some directions and they wandered up the mountain path, humming to themselves in a monotonous chant.

'Well,' said my host, 'we pulled him through — the snakebitten young gentleman. But it was a near thing.' He reached for the decanter. '*Chota* or *barra?*'[1]

'On the *barra* side, I think.'

'Your Hindi's come on in the last year.'

'You should hear my Tamil.[2] To say nothing of my Bengali.'[3]

'It's a strange country, isn't it?'

'Country, did you say, or countries?'

He smiled at me in the half-light. 'You sound as though you'd made up your answer to my question.'

'Yes.'

'And it's in the negative?'

'It is.'

'Well — you've learned something; and you've learned it sooner than most Englishmen.'

[1] 'Large or small?'

[2] The language of about 30 millions in the South.

[3] Spoken by 50 millions. These languages differ from one another, and from Hindi *in toto.*

B

'Maybe I have. But it's a damned unsatisfactory answer, when you come to think of it.'

'How do you mean?'

'Well, I want to write a book. And it's an exhausting business, writing a book on a negative note.'

'But supposing you have no alternative?'

He leant forward, and spoke very earnestly. 'Supposing you come to the conclusion that India is a whole series of negatives? You've already told me about your search for modern art . . . and how you found nothing. You've met dozens of leading personalities in the political world, and you yourself told me that none of them had any really creative proposals.[1] Isn't that another way of saying that their favourite word is 'No' when it ought to be 'Yes'?

'That's one way of putting it.'

'But isn't it *true*? Isn't India one gigantic series of No's, from start to finish?'

'I'm too tired to answer abstract questions like that.'

'But you'll have to answer them if your book's going to be of any value. What's more, you'll have to find the reason why.'

'Is there a reason why?'

'I think so. But it's not up to me to give it. After all, it's *your* book.

Yes, worse luck, it is.

So perhaps we had better begin to get on with it.

---

[1] This was before I met Jinnah.

CHAPTER II

POMP AND CIRCUMSTANCE

WE may as well begin at the top, by going to stay with the Viceroy.

It will not teach us much about 'India', but it is an instructive experience in other ways. Besides, it was my first port of call, and there is a faint hope that we may be able to keep to some sort of rough chronological sequence. This is desirable, not because we are unrolling a pictorial panorama but because we are tracing an intellectual development. India gets into your system all too soon; the first shocks wear off with astounding rapidity. The flaming blossoms of the golden mohur trees, which scorched your eyes when you first saw them, soon lose their glory; to-day you do not even ·turn your head whereas yesterday you stared and stared.

It is the same with the horrors. Indians are *not* deliberately cruel to animals, they have a natural feeling of kinship and affection for them. But their ignorance and poverty are indirectly responsible for appalling suffering. I had not been in India ten minutes before I saw my first typical skeleton horse, limping and staggering down the road, and eventually plunging into the gutter, a quivering mass of pain and sores. When you see that sort of thing for the first time you do something about it. What you do is usually very silly and quite useless, engendering heat, worrying the police, and in no way helping the horse. So you learn, out of bitter necessity, to harden your heart.[1] With the beggars too, you hold your hand. Your first visit to a railway station, the favourite rendezvous of India's beggars, is like a trip through the galleries of those waxen monsters that used to be exhibited by the showmen at the great Prater fair in Vienna. Here are lepers, and tertiary syphilitics, and blind children — not

---

[1] This need not prevent you from subscribing to the R.S.P.C.A., one of the finest bodies of men and women who are fighting the battles of the animals in any part of the world. Their address is 359 Hornby Road, Bombay, and every anna helps!

born blind, but blinded by their parents so that they may prove a source of future income in the beggar market. Here are the St. Vitus dancers, real and bogus, some of them fluttering to a ghostly music in their own brains which will never cease till they die, others twitching for profit; and here are the lunatics, with spittle on their chins, and the deaf and the dumb patting their flaccid lips as they lean into your railway carriage. To these too, in the first few days, you extend your charity. But the flock of dreadful beings that fly towards you, attracted by the clink of coins, is too great; they seem to appear from nowhere, to drop from the sky and the trees, gibbering, spitting, moaning, screaming, and pointing to their sores. You give it up. You know that the Hindi for 'go away' is 'jao'; you say it reluctantly, you say it louder, and still louder, till you find yourself shouting it. Then at last you have peace, and silence. But it is a queer sort of silence, that seems to be filled with reproachful echoes.

So let us arrive at New Delhi, where a very grand car is waiting for us at the station, driven by a giant in white and gold, with another giant sitting by his side. And as we are about to enter the car let us turn our heads slightly to the left, in order to say a word of thanks to a coolie who has been unusually efficient. As we do so, the words die on our lips. We have seen something . . . our first shock.

I I

QUIT INDIA

There it was, in letters a foot high, chalked on the wall a few yards away.

I blinked at it, growing rather red in the face, not through anger, but through a sort of social embarrassment — as though one had been found gate-crashing.

QUIT INDIA

The words seemed to have a personal application. Out of the corner of my eye I scanned the enormous chauffeur. Supposing he saw it too, and turned round and barked, 'Well, you know what to do about it, don't you? Get out and go home!' But the giant stared impassively ahead.

QUIT INDIA

Really this was a very extraordinary situation. Here was a flaming insult, an incitement to revolt, flaunted before the eyes of hundreds of people. But nobody was taking any notice of it. Were they blind? Or dazzled by the sun? Or not quite right in the head? Passengers hurried past, British soldiers with rifles on their sweating backs, business men carrying attaché cases, Indian women in sarees of green and silver, Brahmin priests, peasants carrying hens by the legs, Indian sailors lugging kit bags. None paid the least attention.

And then I thought of another scene, very far away. Grey trees, November mists, sooty railings ... Hyde Park and the mob orators. Their strident voices echoed in my memory, and they too were shouting 'Quit!' They were shouting it to the King and Queen, to the lords and ladies of England, to all those who dwelt in gilded palaces. And nobody paid any attention. The policemen grinned, the mob chimed in with coarse but affectionate interjections; the words were Robespierre's but the reaction was Robey's.

Had England, in India, performed another of her unconscious miracles? Was she once again shaming the volcano by ignoring its eruptions? It looked very like it.

Within a week or so QUIT INDIA ceased to shock, one saw it so often. One of the favourite pastimes of American soldiers was to get a piece of chalk and alter the slogan into QUIT INDIAnapolis. There were other variations by the British, but they were too impolite to be quoted here.

III

Shock number two came about an hour later, after we had made a rapid tour of the city of New Delhi and were heading for the Viceroy's house.

It was a negative sort of shock. I found myself checking a vast yawn and suddenly realized that I was excessively bored.

This was very odd. All these strange sights and sounds, the white and silver sarees of the women, the croak of the crows and the scream of the kites ... all these lovely flowers, trim beds of scarlet crotons, sheets of zinnias four feet high ... all these Hollywood crowds, hundreds of little Sabus sprawling naked on the pavements, long chains of girls carrying everything on their heads but the kitchen stove ... how could one be bored in one's first Indian city?

Glancing back through the window of the car I thought I guessed the answer. We were speeding up the slope of the Viceroy's drive and for the first time it was possible to see New Delhi as a whole. There it lay, far flung, spacious, spick and span, like a sort of Oriental Washington, coloured terracotta instead of white. There it lay, and it was all very imposing and eminently respectable; and it was about as Indian as Shepherd's Bush.

That was why I had been bored by our first Indian City, because in spite of the aforesaid crowds, whom it dwarfed and overshadowed, it was not an Indian City at all. It was alien, it had never taken root. It had less real life than the ghost-ridden ruins of the seven Delhis of the past, stretching all around it in the dusty plains. For at least, in those ruins, the ghosts were Indian. They 'belonged'.

New Delhi suggested a British matron in fancy dress. It tried, most painfully, to speak the native language, but the accent remained the accent of South Kensington. Sir Edwin Lutyens, who was largely responsible for it, had obviously made the most strenuous efforts to please, balancing a façade of Hindu pillars with a Moslem dome, offsetting a Saracenic arch with a decoration that might have come from a Hoysala temple, as though to say 'See how impartial I am!' — but he had ended by pleasing nobody. The result was a sort of architectural Esperanto; and Esperanto is not a language in which men make love, or soldiers sing to battle, or builders dream great dreams.

· If New Delhi had been coldly and consciously British, like the lovely Colonial buildings in Calcutta or the graceful old residencies of the interior, with their white colonnades and spacious verandas, the result would have been happier. As though we had said: 'Here we are, whether you like us or not; we are not in the least ashamed of ourselves. We represent an era of history which we have written ourselves; we have no desire to rewrite it'.

But New Delhi, in spite of its magnificence, has no such assurance. It is the child of compromise, and as a result it has never come to life. That is perhaps the most extraordinary thing about it, the fact that even in the throng and throb of war it remains, obstinately, an architect's print. One has a Lilliputian sense of having strayed into a model city, of strolling through a series of immense dolls' houses. Surely these walls are only made of cardboard, dyed terracotta? And these sentries — are they not stuffed, and animated by some ingenious sort of clockwork? The sky above — is it not really the lid of a glass case? And is it not inevitable that at any moment some god will come along, lift the lid, and sweep the whole pigmy contraption into limbo?

To ask the British to Quit India in New Delhi would be superfluous. They have never arrived.

I V

Shock number three was really a composite of many minor shocks, all caused by the Brobdingnagian nature of the surroundings. Nearly all my early Viceregal impressions must be prefaced by some such word as 'vast' or 'gigantic'. It was a vast distance from my bedroom to the A.D.C.'s room, where we gathered before dinner, and all the way down the lofty corridors there were groups of gigantic servants in white and gold, at intervals of about ten yards. As one appeared at the end of the corridor, the first group of servants — (there were seven or eight in each lot) — rose from their haunches, and stood to attention, gazing fixedly ahead till one had passed. Then they sank down to the floor again. By this time, the next group was rising, and so on . . . as it seemed . . . *ad infinitum*. It was a very pretty sight, as one walked on, and on, and on, with this perpetual rise and fall of the giants in white and gold; there was a strange sense of partaking in a sort of oriental Sylphides. I know some women — (they shall be nameless) — who would adore it; they would never stop walking up the corridors imagining that they were the Queen of Rumania, pleasingly thrilled by all this subservience. For me, it was an embarrassment — indeed, a penance. I can

never forget that servants, black or white, are also men, who fall
in love and like to sit in the sunshine, rather than crouch in
corridors waiting to salute bewildered authors. Besides, there is
the matter of expression. What expression *does* one assume on
such occasions? At the beginning of the journey down the
corridor I could usually summon up a fair imitation of hauteur,
but by the end of the first hundred yards the hauteur was wearing
a bit thin, and had degenerated into a sort of nervous twitch,
due to the fact that I suspected a button was undone, but did not
dare to look, in case the giants misunderstood.

Arrived at last at the A.D.C.'s room — far too early, because
one is terrified of being late, and is, indeed, in a state of acute
nervous tension — one steps out on to the terrace to look at the
gardens. These are as vast as everything else, and, in my opinion,
rather frightful. They are the sort of gardens that enrapture
everybody but gardeners. They are as formal as a chess board . . .
an endless series of small oblongs in the middle of a desert of red
brick. Each of the oblongs is packed tight with very brilliant
flowers — a bed of scarlet salvias, so overcrowded that they pant
for breath, a bed of dwarf anchusa, bursting with blueness, a
bed of crowded cosmos, like a block of ice-cream. Admittedly,
Lady Linlithgow made the best of a bad job; she arranged the
chess-board with the utmost skill, and achieved some exquisite
gradations of colour. And in the one and only part of the garden
which had real 'possibilities' — a miniature arena with a sunken
pool in the centre — she created something of real beauty. But
the general effect of those gardens, thanks to their designer, Sir
Edwin Lutyens, was profoundly depressing. They made a real
gardener long for a ragged old herbaceous border with an apple
tree at one end and a water butt at the other and oh . . . the
heaven in between!

Vast were the gardens, vast the swimming pool, vast the ball-
rooms and the halls of audience. But vastest of all were the
Viceroy and the Vicereine; they towered head and shoulders
above the crowd . . . and their intellectual capacity was not
unworthy of their stature.

V

Enter Their Excellencies.

You see them coming from a great distance, walking slowly through a series of ante-rooms. In front of them stalks an A.D.C. Always, during their term of office, the A.D.C. must precede them. One irrepressible ex-Vicereine once told me that after a few years she began to feel that she could not get into the bath unless an A.D.C. had jumped in first.

The guests stand in line, and as they are presented, the women curtsy, the men click their heels and bow. Their Excellencies sweep on. As we enter the dining-room we notice a fresh chorus of giants in royal livery, one behind each chair. The giants, for a brief and beautiful moment, cover their faces with their white-gloved hands. Whereupon, we sit down.

That is how it was in the Linlithgows' time. The Wavells, with whom I also had the honour of staying, have cut down the ceremony a little, and things are slightly more informal. It is worth noting that under each regime the food was of the utmost simplicity. Compared with the banquets offered by the Princes or by any of the rich Hindu merchants, it was Spartan.

The life of the Viceroy, too, was Spartan; it *had* to be, for there were always mountains of work to be done. The only time that Linlithgow ever relaxed was for twenty minutes after dinner, when he lay back in an arm-chair, with his hand over his eyes, listening to the news. As soon as the news was over, he rose to his feet, a little wearily. There would be curtsies and bows, and then he would disappear to his study, where a green lamp was shining, shedding its light over piles of papers and documents. The lamp went on shining till long after midnight.

He had the toughest and bitterest job that any servant of Empire ever had to tackle, and at the end of his seven years he had given all he had to give. He had a deep affection for India, and he knew its people far better than the average Indian. It was not his fault that his record was largely a record of 'might-have-beens'. Not all of those 'might-have-beens' were fruitless. If he had not used an iron hand in August 1942, when anarchy was abroad, the whole country would have run with blood, and the eastern ports would have fallen to the Japanese.

Hardly anybody said 'thank you' to Linlithgow. The Congress hated him because he was a realist, and he disdained to use the glib patter which might have endeared him to the liberal elements in England. How ludicrous was the popular picture of the Viceroy which is so often offered for our delectation — a peer on a peacock throne, fanning himself while the people starve!

V I

We come to shock number four.

I sat in my room at midnight, writing.

Outside, the jackals wailed and howled in weirdly human tones. (If any film producer ever decides to shoot Dante's *Inferno*, and finds himself in need of Lost Soul Noises, he would do well to hire a pack of jackals; they go on losing their souls, with the utmost gusto, all night long.)

I was trying to catch up with my diary. It was in a terrible muddle, and looked like the ravings of a surréalist. Thus . . .

'Green parrots on the telephone wires, cannot get over ridiculous feeling that they have escaped from cages . . . Peacock fans at railway stations, young Indian told me that the reason God gave the peacock its beautiful tail was to hide its ugly feet . . . Talking of feet cannot get used to bare feet of Viceregal servants, always afraid they will tread on drawing pins and create social crisis . . . Who was the Maharajah who came to dinner to-night and were those real pearls? Something very touching about drinking the health of the King Emperor . . . it certainly sounds well . . . "The King Emperor", with the candlelight flashing on the glasses and bringing out the lovely silver tints in the tuberoses . . . Of course the flowers are exquisite but nobody in India seems to have any idea how to arrange them and I cannot really approve of this business of hanging chains of flowers round one's neck; apart from the insects which crawl down one's back, hate to see flowers dying on a string, want to unthread them all and put them in water . . . Am learning Hindi faster than expected, and

had quite long conversation with woman selling betel nut ...
She told me Hindi for "to-morrow" is *kahl,* asked her Hindi for
"yesterday" and she said that was *kahl* too ... incredible as it
may sound this is apparently true ... feel there is probably some
deep psychological meaning behind this but far too tired to
unravel it at the moment.'

However, apart from this disjointed scribbling there was
something else which I wrote that night — namely, a straight-
forward piece of journalism describing some of the more picturesque details of the Viceregal entourage. It was an ordinary,
competent piece of reporting, whose only merit was — (I hope) —
that it was easy to read and was reasonably well-mannered.

This article was the cause of shock number four. As soon as it
was cabled back to India, after its English publication, it created
an uproar. Garbled versions appeared on the front pages under
scare head-lines; leader writers tipped their pens with their
bitterest acid. I was later to discover that this was the invariable
reception accorded to the most modest and banal generalizations;
one murmured a platitude and caused an explosion. At the time,
however, the uproar was startling.

What was the cause of all the trouble? It lay in a couple of
paragraphs in which I suggested that the splendour of the Viceregal setting was right and fitting, that it accorded with India's
history and that anything on a more modest scale would be not
only inadequate but artificial. After all, Indian history, until the
arrival of the British, was a record of unbridled despotism; India
had always been a land of glittering palaces, surrounded by masses
of human antheaps; there was never any middle class, and no
breath of democracy had ever stirred the Indian dust until we
came. We were changing all that, and the change was gathering
momentum every day. In the meantime, nobody but the most
purblind nationalist could claim that India, as a whole, was a
modern country. Some of it was still in a period corresponding
to that of Peter the Great; some of it was Elizabethan; some of it
was unashamedly medieval; it was, in fact, a whole bunch of
historical anachronisms.

'*An attempt at "White House Simplicity*"' — so ran the last
paragraph — '*would be a piece of ludicrous affectation. The Hindus*

would laugh at it, the Muslims would despise it, the Princes would regard it as a form of lunacy.'

It was the reference to the Princes which caused the bitterest taunts and the wildest accusation. President Roosevelt, sitting in a plain wooden chair, was contrasted with Linlithgow, lolling on a throne surrounded by bejewelled satellites. What all these critics ignored was that the Princes *existed*, that they always had existed, and that the very fact of their existence was in itself sufficient justification for the size and splendour of the Viceregal *ménage*.

Let us make this point quite clear.

A number of Indian commentators write as though the Princes did *not* exist, or as if they were, at the most, a bunch of rich idlers, invented by the British for their own nefarious purposes.

This is a fabulous distortion of the facts. The Princes exist to the extent of ruling over nearly two-fifths of the entire territory of India and their subjects number no less than eighty millions. Moreover, their States, which number over five hundred, are sewn so firmly into the main fabric by the threads of history and of self-interest that any attempt to tear them out might cause the whole thing to fall apart. Some of these States, of course, are very small; they shine on India's quilt like tiny specks of gold; but others are nearly the size of France, governed by rulers with wide powers and lusty ambitions, who have not the faintest intention of retiring without a fight to the death. Many writers lightly assume that Gandhi is the sworn enemy of the Princes. If they turn to page 21 of *Gandhism; Nationalism; Socialism*, by M. N. Roy (published by Bengal Radical Club), they will find an account of an interview in which Gandhi declared his determination to defend the Princes and landlords *by all means* should ever any attempt be made to confiscate their property by violence.

Our critics speak as if *we* had invented these fabulous persons. They speak as though *we* had loaded them with their incredible jewels, stocked their harems, and caparisoned their elephants. We did nothing of the sort. We found all these things intact, functioning as they had functioned throughout the centuries; the Princely pantomime was already in full swing when the British broke into the Indian theatre.

Admittedly, we then proceeded to do a little discreet stage management, but it was always in the direction of making the theatre more of a people's theatre and less of a command performance. If one prince was overplaying his role and shouting down his neighbours, we cut his part. When the play became too obscene, as it sometimes did, we assumed the office of censor. To drop the theatrical metaphor, we kept the princes in order, laid down certain elementary principles of. justice and decency to which we obliged them to conform, required them to keep within their own boundaries and desist from aggression. With these limitations, they are still confirmed in their ancient privileges, still ruling over wide territories and teeming peoples, and in most cases, ruling pretty well.

Now if the critic tells us that the British Viceroy, who is the overlord of these glittering personages, would be more suitably housed in a small villa, we are obliged to suggest that he is talking through his hat. The prospect of the Nizam of Hyderabad, the richest man in the world, being ushered into a stuffy hall by a rumbling house-parlourmaid is really lacking in artistic fitness. It is also decidedly un-Indian.

However, this argument has already stretched to inordinate ·lengths. If the reader has not already been convinced, we must· agree to differ. To console him, before we turn out the light, we will point to to-morrow's engagement list. It bears on it the name of Doctor Ambedkar.

And Doctor Ambedkar, after all this pomp and circumstance, is likely to prove a very different cup of tea.

CHAPTER III

BELOW THE BOTTOM RUNG

'A MAN of about fifty. Waiting for me in a wicker chair on the veranda of his house. Bulky, dynamic. Very charming manners, but nervy, inclined to fiddle with his shoe-laces. Seemed to be on his guard, as though ready to parry taunts from all directions. Well, after all it's only to be expected . . .'

So runs an extract from my diary.

The man is Doctor Ambedkar. And in a moment we shall see why it is 'only to be expected'.

Ambedkar is labour member in the Government of India, and one of the six best brains in India. He is of the Cavour school of statesman — an implacable realist. When he speaks in public he is galvanic, creative, and almost embarrassingly to the point. To compare the average oration of a Congress politician with a speech by Doctor Ambedkar is like comparing a Hindu chant with a fusillade of pistol shots.

As a result, he is one of the best hated men in India.

And why is it 'only to be expected' . . . this nervousness, this suggestion that he would be ready to take offence?

Because Dr. Ambedkar, in the eyes of most of the 180 million caste Hindus, is 'untouchable'. A person to bring pollution if his Mayfair dinner-jacket should happen to brush against their dhotis. A creature from whose touch the extreme orthodox must fly as though he were a leper, a monster whose slightest contact compels them to precipitate themselves into the nearest bath-tub, to soap and pray, and pray and soap, and soap and pray, so that the filth of Dr. Ambedkar — (M.A. London) — the shame of Dr. Ambedkar — (high honours at Columbia University) — the plague and scourge of Dr. Ambedkar — (special distinction at Heidelberg) — should be washed for ever from their immaculate and immortal souls.

We are not talking of the past, but of the year 1944. These are not legends, fairy-tales, gipsy songs; they are news paragraphs, stop-press.

30

Untouchability — history's most flagrant example of man's inhumanity to man — is still deeply rooted in the Hindu social system; nearly all attempts to abolish it have met with failure. If a ten per cent improvement has occurred in the last fifty years, that is an optimistic estimate. A large number of people in England and America, deluded by Gandhi's propaganda, imagine that this disease — for what else can we call it? — is on the wane. They have read with approval the Mahatma's denunciations of it, they have seen photographs of him with his arm round the shoulders of the outcasts, and they know that he gave the title of 'Harijan'[1] to his own newspaper, which circulated among the high and mighty of the land. 'Surely', they say to themselves, 'such a powerful example, in these enlightened days, must be having some effect?' It is not. As for Gandhi being the untouchables' friend, let us listen to Dr. Ambedkar, who is their indisputed leader. He said to me:

'Gandhi is the greatest enemy the untouchables have ever had in India.'

A little knowledge of recent history is necessary in order to understand this accusation. But first let us refresh our memories with the theory of untouchability, and then illustrate that theory with a few facts.

II

As Macaulay's schoolboy would tell you, there are four main castes in the Hindu religion.

At the top come the Brahmins, hereditary holy persons, but without a church. The stormy and brilliant Nehru, whose autobiography was a best-seller on both sides of the Atlantic, is a Brahmin, and it is wise never to forget it. It weighs a great deal more heavily with him than the fact that he was educated at Harrow and Cambridge.

C. R. Rajagopalachari, ex-President of Congress, and the chief link between the Extremists and the British, is also a Brahmin. So is Pandit Malaviya, the leader of the extreme right wing of Hinduism. So are most of the Congress bigwigs.

---

[1] Harijan really means 'Child of God'. It has come to be associated with the untouchables. The Government of India's name for them is 'Scheduled Classes'.

The Brahmins might be said to play the same role in India's political life as the old Etonians in Britain. The main difference is that they have no organized labour to keep them in order. By and large, they are masters of all they survey — except when they turn round and take a look at the Muslims.[1]

The three other castes are the *Kshatriyas* or warriors, the *Vaisyas* or traders — (Gandhi is a *Vaisya*) — and the *Sudras*, or cultivators and menials.

Way off in the outer darkness, sunk deep in the mind, are the casteless ones, the untouchables, nearly 60 million of them.

This classification is drastically simplified. There are actually 2500 castes, all with their taboos, their social restrictions, and their almost incredible ingenuity in complicating the most simple process of life.

These castes split the Hindu fabric into a sort of crazy quilt, lacking all homogeneity, held together only by fear — fear of each other, fear of the Muslims, fear of British law. Over and over again it must be emphasized that these castes are a matter of modern, not ancient history.

A homely little instance may sometimes make a point more vivid than any amount of statistics; here is one. Not long ago I spilt a bottle of iodine on the floor of a flat where I was staying. I had nothing to wipe it up with, and I called for a servant to ask him if he would kindly get a rag and remove the stain. There were five servants in the flat and they had nothing to do; it seemed a reasonable request. It was not granted. One after another they came in, regarded the stain, and departed, with black looks. Losing my patience, I went to the kitchen, found a rag, and wiped the thing up myself. 'What is the matter with you all?' I demanded, when I handed back the rag. They explained that Dido, the sweeper, the untouchable, was out having his lunch, and only *he* could wipe up the stain. They would be degraded if they did it themselves, and he — Dido — would lose respect for them if he heard about it.

---

[1] The Brahmins, in spite of their lofty position, have not attracted much love to themselves in the long history of India. An ancient saying, still current, is 'If you meet a snake and a Brahmin, kill the Brahmin'. Perhaps this is due to the preposterous nature of their claims. For example, Manu, maker of laws, ruled that to accuse a Brahmin of a crime was sinful even if the Brahmin was guilty.

Heaven knows, this may sound a trivial instance, but when you multiply it by millions it ceases to be trivial; it becomes a major problem, not only for India but for the whole democratic world.

III

Very briefly, let us consider the life of the untouchables.

It is largely a matter of negatives.

They may not use the public wells, which means that they are condemned to drink any filthy liquid they can find.

Their children may not enter the schools; they must sit outside, whatever the weather, even in the monsoon.

They may not go near the bathing places. Hence, through no fault of their own, they are usually unutterably filthy.

The temples are closed to them. This is the unkindest cut of all, for if you take away their faith from a people so sunk in misery, you take away the only consolation they have. Admittedly, one or two dramatic gestures have been made in the past few years, by enlightened rulers and statesmen, who have thrown open temples to all comers. But what happens? As soon as the untouchables flock in, the orthodox flock out. The temple becomes an 'untouchable' temple, it is tainted, unholy, and as such it ceases to be an object of reverence even to the untouchables themselves.[1]

Among other restrictions, the barbers may not cut their hair, nor the washermen wash their clothes.

One thing they *can* do is to tend the earth closets and carry away the night soil from the villages. This they do in large wicker baskets, which they put on their heads. The baskets leak, and the untouchable is not a pretty sight when he, or she, has finished the job.

Still — say the Hindus — it is their own fault; they are paying for the sins of a previous incarnation; why should we have any

[1] The classic example of this tendency was afforded by the great temple at Madura, 300 miles south of Madras. Premier Rajagopalachari went so far as ordering a government official to lead a group of untouchables into the temple. The great majority of Brahmins have refused to set foot in it ever since.

pity for them? A convenient doctrine, if you happen to have been born in the right bedroom.

'Ah, this is very old stuff,' you may say.

'Of course it is,' we answer. 'And it is also very new. It is as old as the hills and as new as the morning dew. It is a long way B.C. and it is also A.D. 1944.'

Let us have a few more examples from personal experience. Slight though they are, they may help us to realize the bitter struggle which these 60 millions must make for the most elementary decencies, a struggle which is being carried on as you read these words.

IV

SCENE ONE. A bungalow on a small island lying a few miles off the west coast. We have just finished dining on the veranda and a British subaltern joins us for a drink. He has walked up the hill from the seashore, where he is in charge of a training camp for young Indian engineers. He looks tired and depressed.

'Had a trying day?'

'Pretty sticky.' He flings himself into a chair. 'Trouble with recruiting.'

'Aren't they coming in fast enough?'

'Oh — they're coming in all right. But I have to send 'em away again. ·Look over there.'

He jerks his thumb over his shoulder. We see two young Indians standing in the shadow of a eucalyptus tree, staring at the dust. They are of exceptional physique, and they are spick and span as though they were dressed for a party.

'See those chaps? Well, they're two of the best who've ever come my way, physically and mentally. Well above standard. They want to join my lot; I want to have them; and I can't.'

'Why on earth not?'

'Untouchable. Sweeper class.'

'But that's preposterous!'

'Of course it is. But it's India. My men would just down tools if I took 'em on.'

'But surely', I exclaimed, 'you've got some authority as their commanding officer?'

'No, I haven't. Not in a thing like that. Why, the very rumour of those chaps coming has caused a hell of a row all day — desertions, insolence, insubordination. I had to give in. I don't want to start another Indian Mutiny.'

He swallowed his drink, and sighed.

'Sounds silly, I know', he said, 'but the worst of it was that one of the chaps *cried*. Said I'd broken his heart. *Me!* It's pretty grim when a chap like that starts crying.' He laughed uneasily. 'Maybe I'm well shot of him — maybe he was a cissy. Oh, what the hell, anyway.'[1]

SCENE Two. A village in a remote part of the south-west. I have come to see a temple which is reputed to be of great beauty. The expedition is not a success; the temple is devoid of any architectural interest and is only notable for the astonishing obscenity of the Phallic scenes which are carved round its base. This has a curious affect on an American lady who is also going the rounds. Acting on the principle that evil, like beauty, is in the eye of the beholder, she decides to put on a bold front, and drags me round the building, prodding her umbrella at the most abandoned exhibitions and trying to treat them from a purely aesthetic point of view. We came to one scene where everybody was so upside down and inside out that it should have been labelled 'Sex in the Gymnasium'. She regarded it with a cold, unblinking stare. 'Definitely the Jain influence', she proclaimed, with a ring of challenge. I had never heard it called *that* before.

Having digested the obscenities, I was at a loose end. The lady took her leave as it was very hot, and she was obviously exhausted by her unwonted championship of the Religion of the Red Light. But I wanted to explore the village, so I left her sitting in the shade of the temple, silhouetted in lofty isolation against a background of ape-like ecstasies.

I came to a big mud hut. It was the village school. I peered

[1] This story could be multiplied *ad nauseam*. However, it is worth noting that the Army, once it has got hold of a man, is proving a powerful instrument in undermining the extreme caste system. Discipline, comradeship, and above all a common sense of danger shared, have worked wonders in the present war. When the boys come marching home we may look out for fireworks.

through the window. About a hundred little boys were squatting on the floor, gazing at a blackboard on which a young man was tracing letters in Canarese. They made the prettiest picture — the rows of dusky faces and the snow-white eyes turning from right to left, like marbles rolling on a dark cloth.

I drew back my head from the window and strolled round the corner of the building. And there, to my surprise, were twelve little boys, sitting on a bench, huddled together as though they were frightened of something.

'What are those little boys doing? Are they in disgrace or something?'

The young Hindu guide answered me. 'They are of the Scheduled Classes', he said curtly.

I stared at the little boys, who had huddled themselves closer together. They were thin and almost naked and none too clean, but they *were* little boys, after all. Each of them was 'somebody's bairn', as one might say, if one were sentimental and Scotch.

Perhaps one should have kicked up a row about it. Those kids were supposed to be allowed into the schools. They had passed all sorts of laws for their protection in this State. But what could one do? If one reported the matter it would only get the teacher into trouble, and it probably wasn't the teacher's fault. He looked a decent sort of chap even though he was half starved on his 25 rupees a month. It was more likely due to the parents of the children inside.

So I walked away and left the little outcasts to their fate, straining their ears towards the window, listening to the teacher's voice. Now and then one of them would scribble something in a tattered notebook.

Young India, getting education.

SCENE THREE. A dinner table in Peshawar. Dramatis personae, Pandit Malaviya and B——, one of the leaders of the opposition in the legislative council. The year is 1933, and Peshawar is full of bustle and excitement, for there is a great conference in full swing, which will settle the fate of the Hindu-Sikh minorities. The venerable old Pandit is being entertained by B——, and they are both anxious to please each other.

But the dinner party is not a success. Why? Because the Pandit cannot eat. Why? We shall see.

B—— had taken a great deal of trouble about this dinner. He knew that the Pandit was a vegetarian, and so he provided only fruit; moreover, he chose only such fruits as Nature had ensured from outside pollution, such as oranges and bananas. And he had been even more careful than that. *He had bought an entirely new dinner service*; for he was aware that if the Pandit were asked to eat off a plate which might once have had meat on it, the worst would happen. The Pandit would be horrified beyond measure; he would never feel clean again.

So there we are. Fresh fruit, covered with thick skins. New plates, never used before. Old gentleman, anxious to please host, staring at banana or whatever it is.

All to no avail.. He *cannot* eat the banana. Sometime, some-where, somehow, somebody might have touched something, and made it unclean. He dare not risk it. He is a brave old man but he is not as brave as all that. So the demands of courtesy must be set aside. The dinner, we repeat, was not a success.

This story has been told flippantly, because at first sight it falls into the category of farce. But is it entirely farcical? Malaviya, at the time, was leader of Congress. He was, and still is, one of the most powerful personalities in India. He is the sort of man who, if and when India gains independence, will help to represent his country at international conferences. To put it mildly, his extreme orthodoxy may tend to slow up the business of the day.

Supposing that we translate this situation into Western terms. Imagine a conference between Churchill, Roosevelt, Stalin and Chiang Kai-Shek on orthodox Hindu lines. What would happen?

Well — most of them would be popping in and out of the bath-room during the greater part of the proceedings. Churchill would sign a document with the same pen as Roosevelt and would rush to have a shower. Stalin would inadvertently drink a cup of tea handed him by Chiang Kai-Shek and hurry away to gargle. Roosevelt would constantly be calling for a flit spray, and if anybody ever got any business done it would be such a miracle that half the war debt would have to be sacrificed on the altar of Krishna.

Nevertheless, Malaviya, in spite of these foibles, is entitled to our respect. Extreme Hindu as he is, he has fought the battle of the untouchables, and admitted hundreds of them into the Hindu fold. That proves that his heart is very much in the right place, for only a deep love of his fellow-men could make him challenge the faith of his fathers. He starves himself for that faith, and yet he takes up the cudgels for those whom the faith has made pariahs. It would be ungenerous to deny that he comes out of this story pretty well.

v

We left Dr. Ambedkar, leader of the 60 million Untouchables, proclaiming that . . .

'Gandhi is the greatest enemy the Untouchables have ever had in India.'

This will come as a violent shock to most people. Gandhi has ceaselessly proclaimed his detestation of untouchability. He has untouchables in his ashram, he has adopted an untouchable child, and he has declared, 'I would rather that Hinduism die than untouchability live'. This often-quoted remark, by the way, does not really make sense. Untouchability is as integral a part of the Hindu faith as anti-semitism of the Nazi; begin by destroying untouchability and you will end by destroying all caste. And caste is the only cement which saves the incredibly complicated Hindu structure from collapse. None the less, Gandhi was probably sincere when he spoke.

So what did Ambedkar mean?

We can best explain it by a parallel. Take Ambedkar's remark, and for the word 'untouchables' substitute the word 'peace'. Now, imagine that a great champion of peace, like Lord Cecil, said, 'Gandhi is the greatest enemy of peace the world has ever had'. What would he mean, using these words of the most spectacular pacifist of modern times? He would mean that passive resistance — which is Gandhi's form of pacifism — could only lead to chaos and the eventual triumph of brute force; that to lie down and let people trample on you (which was Gandhi's recipe for dealing with the Japanese) is a temptation to the aggressor rather than an example to the aggressed; and that in order to have peace you must organize, you must be strong, and that you must be prepared to use force.

Mutatis mutandis, that is precisely what Ambedkar meant about the untouchables. He wanted them to be organized and he wanted them to be strong. He rightly considered that the best way of gaining his object was by granting them separate electorates; a solid block of 60 million would be in a position to dictate terms to its oppressors.

Gandhi fiercely opposed this scheme. 'Give the untouchables separate electorates', he cried, 'and you only perpetuate their status for all time.' It was a queer argument, and those who were not bemused by the Mahatma's charm considered it a phoney one. They suspected that Gandhi was a little afraid that 60 million untouchables might join up with the 100 million Muslims — (as they nearly did) — and challenge the dictatorship of the 180 million orthodox Hindus. When such irreverent criticisms were made to him, Gandhi resorted to his usual tactics; he began a fast unto death. (As if that altered the situation by a comma, or proved anything but his own obstinacy!) There was a frenzy of excitement, ending in a compromise on the seventh day of the fast. The untouchables still vote in the same constituencies as the caste Hindus, but a substantial number of seats are now reserved for them in the provincial legislatures. It is better than nothing, but it is not nearly so good as it would have been if Gandhi had not interfered.

That is what Dr. Ambedkar meant. And I think that he was right.

VI

What of the future?

It depends very largely on the British. If we knuckle under to Congress demands, the state of the untouchables will remain either stationary or deteriorate. And it cannot be too often emphasized that even if it remains stationary it will still be quite intolerable.

In spite of the much vaunted 'new approach', in spite of
Gandhi's soulful proclamations, how many untouchables have
managed to obtain university degrees? Five hundred! Five
hundred, in the whole history of Indian Education, in a country
with a population of nearly 400 million!

Congress, dominated by the Brahmins, has no intention of
changing this situation. It is highly significant that by far the
most sweeping measures to improve the lot of the untouchables
have been made in the States where the Congress writ does not
run. Mysore, for instance, could set an example to the whole of
India.[1]

If we give way to Congress, the untouchables might as well run
to the nearest village well and hurl themselves into it *en masse*. They
are forbidden to use it in life; they might as well use it in death.

Ambedkar said to me that the Cripps proposals 'would have
dealt a death blow to our interests'.

Some people challenge Ambedkar's right to leadership. They
would not do so if they had ever attended any of his meetings,
such as the great rally at Nagpur where 75,000 untouchables
acclaimed him with a fervour that even Gandhi might have
envied.

Besides, even if he had any competitors — which he has not —
his clear-cut, creative ideas demand the support of all men of
decency and sense. We will end this random survey by a few
sentences from my diary which throw light on those ideas.
Ambedkar said to me:

'The keynote of my policy is that we are *not* a sub-section of the
Hindus but a separate element in the national life.'

'Gandhi says to us "Trust us — trust the caste Hindus!" I reply,
"We will not trust you, for you are our hereditary enemies".'

'In every village there is a tiny minority of untouchables. I
want to gather those minorities together and make them into
majorities. This means a tremendous work of organization —
transferring populations, building new villages. But we can do it,
if only we are allowed.'

[1] The student who would like to know what *can* be done by a benevolent and
enlightened ruler should read *Harijan Uplift in Mysore*, published by the Government Press, Bangalore.

'We are as staunchly nationalist as any of the Congress. But we do not want the British to quit India till our rights are safe-guarded. If they do, our fate will be more terrible than the fate of any of the Oppressed peoples of Europe.'

Can any sane man doubt to whom we ought to give our sup-port? To Gandhi, the caste Hindu, who would fast unto death rather than grant these 60 million outcasts the right of uniting into an independent organization which might challenge him? Or to Ambedkar, who has himself risen from the depths, and fought his way through a ceaseless barrage of insult and superstition, to emerge triumphant as the champion of his people?

It is not always, in British history, that the path of honour is identical with the path of self-interest, but that is the situation in India to-day. There is only one path that we should tread, for our own sakes, and for the sake of the underdog. Let us hope that we tread it.

CHAPTER IV

THE STORMY NORTH

'HE can't be long now.'

·'I hope not.' The pain was rapidly becoming unendurable.

'He may be quite a good chap. These village doctors often are.'

A servant shuffled in with a hurricane lamp and set it on the table by the camp bed.

'Is that all the light they can manage?'

'Afraid so.'

'Supposing he has to operate?'

'Don't be morbid.'

'Well, *look* at the dammed thing!'

The damned thing was my foot. It was not a pretty sight. There was a purple ulcer on the heel which was suppurating badly, and the poison had spread up to the knee. If you put your finger in the flesh it left a mark as though you had pressed it into putty. And only a week ago they had discharged me from hospital as cured!

An author's aches and pains are the very last thing which — if he has any sense — he should offer for sale to the public; we have all quite enough of our own. However, this is such a personal record that it would be hardly possible to avoid all mention of this illness, for it was to last, on and off, for four months, involving me in several operations and a number of grotesque situations.

More important, it was to teach me much about the country and its people. Catherine Mayo, of *Mother India* fame, wrote at length about Indian hospitals, but she might have changed some of her views if she had seen as much of them as I did, from the inside. She had a number of wise things to say about the medical profession, but her remarks might have been even more penetrating if, like me, she has been carried upside down on a stretcher drenched with blood and ether into a Bombay ambulance through the middle of a religious procession whose followers appeared to regard one as a blood sacrifice.

We will try to keep out of the sick-room as far as possible in these pages, but we shall have to enter it occasionally, if only because it has much to teach us.

II

Certainly there is nothing of the sick-room about the scene which stretches before us as we are waiting for the doctor.

We are in a small rocky fortress on the North-West Frontier. Delhi (which we left two weeks ago, only to land straight into the Peshawar hospital) lies six hundred miles to the south, in the sweltering plains. Here it is cool; dusk is falling and a violet haze lies over the valley.

The view is melodramatic. Seventy miles to the west lie the wild outposts of Afghanistan. Due north, beyond a flat, monotonous plain, rises a range of jagged mountains, dust-coloured by day, indigo by night, layer upon layer, like a succession of 'flats' on the stage of a theatre. They are the first steps in the vast staircase that leads, via the Himalayas, to the roof of the world.

From far below echo the perpetual thunders of the Swat River, hurrying to join the giant Indus, whose valleys have rung to the march of the invader from times immemorial. Three hundred and twenty-seven years before the birth of Christ, had we been standing on the site of this fortress, we should have seen an army mustering in the valley below . . . an army that marched proudly, with the arrogance of countless conquests, plumed, helmeted, striking terror to the 'barbarian' — the army of Alexander the Great. But Alexander was not the first, nor by any means the last of the hungry hordes from the north, who have swept like bitter winds through the mountain corridors, to chill and blast the soft culture of the south. Till only yesterday — for what is a hundred years in the history of India? — those corridors yawned open, an eternal temptation to the invader.

But now, it is a different tale. Supposing that we tell some of that tale now? It will mean setting back the clock a few days, but we have plenty of time on our hands, for the doctor has a long way to ride, and the roads are rough.

III

I had come to the North-West Frontier for two reasons. Firstly, because it was, emotionally speaking, the most volcanic area in the whole of India. Even when the passions of the Frontier people were not bursting into actual eruption there were always sub-terranean mutterings and echoes of revolt. I wanted to know the reason why. Whose fault was it? Ours? Or was it a matter of temperament? Or of economics, or religion?

Secondly, they had told me in Delhi that the Frontier was quieter than it had been for twenty years, and again, it seemed profitable to inquire why. To whom should go the credit? Had we changed our ways or had they changed theirs? Were 'things' — meaning economic things — better? Was religious fanaticism on the wane?

It seemed reasonable to suppose that if one approached the most diseased part of the Indian body and carefully examined the local inflammation, one might arrive at a correct diagnosis of the sickness of the whole.

I began with the most obvious rendezvous of the sightseer — the Khyber Pass. We will make a brief trip up it together and perhaps we shall have learned something important by the time we return.

To visit the Khyber is to be forcibly reminded that the veneer of civilization, in those parts, is very thin. You can lunch in the country club at Peshawar, surrounded by pretty women in gay dresses, while a smart little orchestra plays pre-war jazz. An hour later you are far off in the mountains, in the world's grimmest country, jagged and treacherous. The road over which you are speeding is a thin ribbon of safety threaded through a blood-soaked fabric of danger and death. And before tea-time you are at the end of India, confronted by a gate that bars the road to Afghanistan.

The end of India, it must be admitted, is something of an anti-climax. A couple of corrugated iron sheds, a group of out-buildings — the customs and the passport offices — and then, a five-barred gate. When the gate is opened, a dog barks in a half-hearted way, and that is all. One feels that the gateway to so fabulous a country is worthy of something rather more imposing.

My guide up the Khyber was a young officer who had seen four years' service in the tribal area. From the very first moment, the Pass seemed strangely familiar, thanks to Kipling and Holly-wood. The famous signpost greeted us as though it were an old friend — the signpost that has been set up on the threshold of the pass for the benefit of the illiterate, with its picture of a motor car pointing to the high road on one side, and of a camel pointing to the camel-track on the other. No letters, just pictures . . . for of what avail would letters be, even to those who had learned to read? The Khyber is a babel of tongues; you would need a sign-post a mile high to transcribe them. That is a point that might be pondered, for a moment, by those who talk of the 'Unity of India' as though it were a law of nature.

I used to think that the one part of the world on which God had most surely set his curse was the basin of the Dead Sea, where the land is like the skin on a mummy's face and the air is heavy with a breath that seems to drift from the mouth of hell. But the curse of the Khyber is even more terrible. The Dead Sea is a place that God has forgotten, but the Khyber is a place that He has remembered and remembered with wrath. Surely these rocks were hurled down in anger by giant hands, the same that rent the trees and the grass from the hillside, leaving them so bare that even a few starved black goats can barely scratch a living out of them?

As we drive higher and higher, into deeper desolation, the only signs of civilization — if that is not too ironic a word — were to be seen in the preparations which the British had made, and were still making, for the Khyber's defence. The hills bristled with gun emplacements, the traps — and they were not traps for tanks only — were of a sort to give pause to even the most mobile mountain regiment. Nothing had been forgotten. As we turned a hair-pin bend we came to a sheer cliff in which there could be seen a series of doors. These led to an underground hospital, equipped with every modern gadget.

Yes — the Khyber looks ahead. You may ask — 'towards which enemy?' In these days, when international fraternity seems once again to be struggling into existence, such questions are obviously unprofitable.

Parching drought and raging flood,
Months of dust and days of mud,
Mixed monotony and blood . . .

So quoted my young guide. We had paused in the shelter of a ravine to gain a few moments' respite from the wind. It was like the Hall of the Demon King in an old-fashioned pantomime.

'The dust and the mud, yes . . . but why the blood?'

It seemed as good a place as any other to begin my inquiries into the causes of the Frontier's ceaseless unrest. 'Why all this bloodshed? Aren't the tribes ever going to stop fighting? If they aren't shooting at us they're shooting at each other, and usually both. If we can't stop them, would any other Power have a better chance? Could Gandhi do it?'

He chuckled. 'I see that there's no need to ask you if this is your first visit to these parts. D'you really want to know why these chaps are always scrapping? Well, there are two reasons.'

He paused, and lit a cigarette.

'The *second* reason', he said, 'is economic. But the first is a good deal more important. The first is Fun and Games.'

Fun and Games! One knew what he meant, of course. He was referring to the turbulent love of fighting for its own sake, the savage high spirits of a primitive people. None the less, the phrase came as something of a shock.

Fun and Games!

It fits none of the pigeon-holes in which the experts file their favourite Theories Concerning the Origins of Wars. It has no dignity, and obviously it would be impossible to compile any statistics about it, those beloved statistics which sound so convincing when they are published in White Papers to illustrate the aforesaid theories . . . the Economic Theory, the Population Theory, the Racial Theory, and heaven knows what else.

Any man who ventured to follow up these respectable titles by suggesting — 'And the Fun and Games Theory' — would sound like a little boy making rude remarks in class. Of course, if he dressed it up in long words, the experts might listen to him, because then he would call it 'The Psychological Theory' and it would have a long sub-section on the revolt of the ego imprisoned in the monotony of the machine age. However, 'Fun and Games' is shorter and, in fact, more to the point, particularly in the North-West Frontier. For the Frontiersman has never had any machine age to react against; the only machine which remotely concerns him is his rifle; and he glories in this, not for the beauty of its mechanism but because it is an enchanted rod which affords him the only means of self-expression which he knows. And men must express themselves, in one way or another, by pen, plough or pistol; otherwise they perish.

'May I have a month's leave, sir, to go and murder my cousin?'

Perhaps the question is not phrased quite so bluntly, but that is the gist of many earnest requests which are put to British officers by their Pathan troops in these parts.

'The word for "cousin" is the same as the word for "enemy" in the Pushtu dialect', said my friend. 'What's an officer to do when he gets asked that sort of question? Usually it's the best soldiers who have the bitterest feuds. Supposing I say, "No, you damned well can't have leave; you'll stay here and do an extra drill for having such naughty ideas" ... what happens? The man just deserts, taking his rifle with him. And that means another good man gone, and another sniper to worry about on dark evenings.'

'Don't the Pathans respect *any* sort of moral code?'

'Good Lord, yes ... though I suppose you'd call it a code of honour rather than a code of morals. It's best expressed in three words: *nanawatai*, *melmastia*, and *badragga* ... asylum, hospitality and safe-conduct. If a man breaks any part of that code, he's not a true Pathan. As for the women, their lives are probably the strictest and cleanest in the world. A Pathan can put his wife to death for adultery, and very frequently does.'

'But oughtn't we to stop that sort of thing?'

'Stop it?' He laughed, somewhat sardonically. 'Stop it? How? What with? A standing army of a million? A Gestapo of half a million? Is that what you suggest? If so, I can tell you who'd win. And it wouldn't be the army or the Gestapo.'

As he spoke, I remembered the faces of the four murderers who had been fellow-inmates of the hospital to which I was so shortly destined to return. (You may remember that we met them in the first pages of this book.) It was the night-nurse who first mentioned them and asked if I would like to make their acquaintance. 'They aren't going to be hanged', she said, 'so you needn't feel too badly about them.' I was wheeled into their ward the next morning. There they lay, with chains on their arms and legs, chatting to the guards who stood over them with fixed bayonets. They were all young men, and they were all 'good-looking' in both senses of the phrase; they had fine features and through those features there seemed to shine a fine spirit. And they were all there for honour or for love.

One had an uncle who had stolen from his friend while he was sheltering under his roof. What could one do with such a person but kill him? Another had a wife who had submitted to the embraces of a Hindu bird-fancier. How could such a snarer of doves be permitted to draw breath? The crimes of the other two were both crimes of sex perversion, though in these parts homo-sexual love is so prevalent that to describe it as perverse is almost pedantic. 'Whenever we have a murder in our regiment', said a hard-bitten old colonel to me, 'we always begin by looking for the boy.' It is the Pathan version of *cherchez la femme*.

And by the side of the faces of those four passionate youths I seemed to see other faces which had smiled or frowned or wept in those wards, and though there were some who were sick through no fault of their own, there were more who had been carried in riddled with bullets or slashed with knives — boys of nine who had grown old and scarred in blood feuds, striplings of twelve whose only means of answering a taunt was with the flash of a knife.

Stop it? You might as well try to stop the Indus from flowing to the sea. The best you can do is to keep these fierce human torrents within reasonable bounds.

And so it goes on, a never-ending struggle. 'Year in, year out, picquets must be set, patrols must be on the move, armed to the teeth ... scouts and militia, frontier constabulary and levies, *malik*, *khassadar*, and *badragga*.'[1]

---

[1] *North-West Frontier*, by J. M. Ewart (London Book Company, Peshawar).

IV

The trend of much modern history is to soft-pedal the power of personality, to attribute great world movements to economic causes rather than to the exertions of any individual. This trend can be carried to unwarranted extremes, till we are asked to believe that there would have been an Austerlitz without a Napoleon, or a Stalingrad without a Stalin. Obviously, no man, however great, can reverse the flow of the tide down which humanity is drifting, but he can enormously retard or accelerate its progress, blowing up dams of prejudice, cutting canals by which great human deserts are watered. It is both inaccurate and inartistic to belittle the Napoleons of history by regarding them merely as the embodiment of impersonal forces; they themselves can create those forces, the whirlwind which they unloose has its storm centre in their own hearts.

India teaches this lesson again and again. Gandhi, admittedly, is a typical Hindu, there are tens of millions of Gandhis in the bazaars and the temples and the paddy fields . . . with this little difference, that Gandhi happens to be, into the bargain, a creative artist.

The theory of 'Fun and Games', which we have just propounded, will be unacceptable to those who choose to drain the blood out of the human story and to write history as though they were compiling a ledger, for it explains facts in terms of temperament — not, admittedly, the temperament of an individual but of the mass personality of the people. But surely, this 'personality of the people' is also a fact? Surely it is as easy to chart, and as potent in its influence, as — let us say — the Straits of Dover? He would be strangely purblind who denied that the 'personality of the people' was, at least, a considerable factor in the Battle of Britain or the Fall of France.

When we come to the second question which we set ourselves, on this journey to the Frontier, we are once more confronted with the power of personality.

Why is the Province quieter than it has been for twenty years? My young friend had stated that one of the causes of the constant strife was economic. As we stood there we saw, far below in the

D

valley, the dust of camels and caravans moving in a long procession.

'Look down there', he said. 'There's wealth for you—bags of it, waiting to be seized in a single raid. In those caravans there'll be silks from Bokhara and Turkoman carpets and plenty of precious metal for the goldsmiths of Peshawar. There'll be men and women from every corner of Asia, from the border of China to Samarcand, Merv and Herat—Tajiks, Kabulis, Kisilbashes and Ghilzais, mixed up with Jews and Afridis and Uzbergs coming from Mecca.'

'And now look round you', he continued. 'What is there up here? Rocks and dust and thorn and scrub. No water. A handful of goats. And a hole in the rock for your home. Can you wonder that when they see a target like that the temptation's too much for a band of hungry men?'

'But you said that things were a bit better?'

'They are. Wages are higher, there's a better market for firewood, which is one of the few things they can sell in these parts. But it isn't only a question of simple economics; nothing ever is simple in India. It's a question of personality!

'Whose?'

'Sir George Cunningham, for one. He's the Governor — and he ... well, he's 'tops'. He goes everywhere, knows everyone, speaks several dialects perfectly, is completely fearless, never bothers about being shot at and has a rollicking sense of humour. But then, of course, you know all that. There are other people you ought to meet. For instance the Wali of Swat.'

'The one that Lear wrote a nonsense rhyme about? So he really does exist! What's he like?'

'Why not go and see?'

I went and saw.

v

'That's where Gunga-Din used to do his act.'

It was two days later and we were on our way through the Swat Valley. To me it all seemed very wild and strange, partly because I had been so often obliged to look at it upside down. By now I

was being transported on a stretcher, and the cliffs were precip-
itous.

However, at the moment we were in a comfortable car, spinning
along a well-metalled road, and it was possible to re-enact the
drama of Gunga-Din. Imagine a jagged cliff, its base lashed by a
yellow river, and across the river a rambling shell-pocked fortress.
This is the Fort of Chak-Darra, which had been invested by the
Lashkars. Gunga-Din was attached to the picquet which was
stationed on the heights of the cliff above and how any man, even
the hero of a Kipling ballad, could scramble down those heights
under shell-fire, was a mystery. Still, there it all was—the fort, the
river, the water-hole, and every now and then we passed replicas
of Gunga-Din, tramping down the road, magnificent types, with
fierce eyes and aquiline features. In my present condition I felt
that any personal encounter with these warriors would begin,
and end, with . . . 'You're a better man than I am, Gunga-Din.'

'Twenty-five years ago', said my companion, a British resident
officer of long experience, 'we shouldn't have been able to come
down this road without an armed guard. We'd have been ducking
our heads half the time. To-day, you could walk down these
roads, at any rate in daylight, with nothing more than an umbrella, without coming to any harm. Twenty-five years ago you'd
have seen nothing but misery and starvation. To-day — well,
look at 'em. And there are half a million in this State, solid,
united and prosperous. Why? Sheer personality. The old Wali's
a genius. He's an extraordinary mixture of Saint Francis and
Machiavelli. He began with a tremendous advantage, because he
was the grandson of the Akoond of Swat who was a great religious
figure. He's exploited that advantage to the utmost.'

'It all sounds rather irregular,' I suggested.

'Well, isn't this part of the country faintly irregular itself?'

The irony of his comment was justified. Nevertheless, I found
myself thinking how extremely difficult it would be to explain the
whys and wherefores of this situation to an audience of those
enlightened liberals at home who are so convinced that we have
only to march out of India for the whole country to blossom overnight with the benefits of representative democratic institutions.
Here was a land of ex-brigands, dominated by a religious genius,

surrounded by a sort of Balkan confederation of wild and hostile States who have been kept in comparative order only by the constant vigilance of a few British ... who, in their turn, were forced to adapt and modify the nature of their rule according to the nature of the tribesmen concerned. It was not quite so simple as it seemed at home, over the quiet firesides of Hampstead.

Consider, for example, the administration of the law. A people less wise in government than the British would have attempted to enforce the British legal code throughout the Wali's dominions. Obviously, in theory, we *should* have done so; if India is a nation, every member of that nation should be subject to the same law. However, the British, who are always at their best when they forget about theories and trust to their own sense of what is right and expedient, have left the laws precisely as they found them.

'And a good thing too', said my friend. 'The laws here are simply tribal customs. They're not codified, and the British have no say in them, but they fit the people like a glove. They're fanatically religious and when they take the oath in a criminal case you can bet your life that they'll tell the truth. I've known men accept a sentence of fourteen years' rigorous imprisonment rather than take a false oath. Except, of course, the Wazirs. They'd lie about anything.'

'There's another reason why the tribal custom is actually *better* than British law in these parts. That's because of the Mullahs ... the priests who are the real leaders. A mullah can give a man dispensation if he takes a false oath against the British government, but he can't give dispensation if he takes a false oath against the tribal custom: The liar must go to hell, and the mullah can't do anything about it.'

It might have been profitable to pursue the subject, but by now we were approaching the outskirts of the little town of Swat. I saw some neat buildings — a hospital, a school, a mosque, and then a pleasant country house which proved to be the palace. If it had not been for the soaring purple mountains that surrounded us, and the sheets of pink and white striped tulips, that grew wild in the meadows, we might have been in Sussex.

VI

'Enter the Wali ... Sensation ... flourish ... climax ... anti-climax!'

This note in my diary, which is an accurate description of the dramatic sequence of the first few minutes of our arrival, needs a little explanation.

'Enter the Wali ... Sensation' is a quick way of putting the fact that the old man bristled with personality to an extent that was almost frightening. Not that he was aggressive — far from it; he was more like a priest than a prince, with his white beard and his benevolent eye. It was simply that you felt the eye looked straight through you, when he shook your hand you winced with pain. He was a little man, he was short-sighted, he had no teeth, and he spoke no English, but he dominated us as effectively as if he had been Hitler addressing a meeting in the Munich beer hall.

We stood stock still at attention, under the penetrating gaze of this hypnotic old gentleman. That is the explanation of the word 'Flourish', for the band outside had suddenly burst into the strains of 'God Save The King'. I had remarked that band, with awe, as we drove through the palace gates; it was composed of very old men with fierce military moustaches dyed bright henna. Their instruments were five bagpipes, one cornet, and a big drum. With what type of music did these ancients propose to enchant us? We did not have to wait long to find out. It was 'God Save The King', which they had slightly amended by omitting half of the fourth and the last bars.

They played it through, and we were about to relax, and sigh, and assume the insipid smiles which usually accompany the rendering of the national anthem on unexpected occasions when suddenly the band was off again and we rapidly resumed our positions at attention. Once more they omitted half the fourth and the last bars. A roll of the drum was added at the conclusion ... and now, surely we could relax? Polite smiles began to wreathe our faces ... but no, here it was *again*. Really, this was too much. I was standing on one leg, propped against a chair, and was doubtful if I should be able to maintain this position much longer. Perhaps the Wali noticed my predicament, because

at the end of the third rendering he looked through the wall —
at least, that was how it seemed, as though his piercing eye pene-
trated the brick-wall — and the band lapsed into silence.

And now, anti-climax.

For it transpired that the Wali only ate four times a week, and
this was one of his days off. After a few conventional expressions
of hospitality he took his departure, and we went into lunch with
his sons and his chief minister.

The rest of the day, for me, was a slow crescendo of pain. We
were driven miles over the country, shown bridges, water-works,
hospitals — they all seemed blurred and indefinite. It spoke well
for Swat that in spite of the mist through which I saw it I carried
away a strong feeling of order and sanity and happiness.

So back we are where we began, waiting for the doctor, on the
little fort that crouches among the dark mountains.

My first Indian doctor . . here he comes! Do you see those three
swinging lights, coming up the hill? They are the burning
braziers in which he is going to sterilize his instruments. The
lights come closer and closer, and as their bearers step on to the
terrace I feel that they have walked straight out of an early work
by Leoncavallo—'I Zingari', for choice; they are the complete
brigands of any small Italian operatic company. But there is
nothing in the least brigand-like or operatic about the young
Indian doctor. He is swift and skilful, with a delicate touch that
would make him a fortune in Harley Street. He does what he
can, and informs me that if I wish to remain a biped I must
return to hospital early in the morning.

Whither we will now proceed.   .

CHAPTER V

LESSONS IN BED

THE first thing I learnt in my first Indian hospital was that there is only one trained nurse to every 65,000 Indians.

On a basis of population this figure corresponds, roughly, with 200 nurses for the whole Dominion of Canada. Or if that is too far away, with two nurses for a town the size of Brighton.

The next thing I learnt was that in the City of Peshawar alone there were 60,000 cases of tuberculosis. The type-setter has not made a misprint, the noughts are as they should be, the figure is sixty thousand. So that if we allotted only one nurse to every *ten* of these unfortunates, *we would need to employ the entire nursing community* of *India in the city of Peshawar alone.* And not so vast a city, at that.

These figures used to dance through my brain at night, as I lay watching the shadows on the ceiling. One for every 65,000 . . . 65,000 crying for one . . . 'Nurse! Nurse!'. It was gruesome, and in a strange way, humiliating. If 65,000 were in need of one, what right had a patient like myself to the almost exclusive attentions of two? It seemed shameful to be lying in bed under a bell which would summon a nurse who was needed by 65,000 people in pain.

Pain. 'Every philosophy', I thought, in those lone nights under the flickering shadows, 'ought to start by defining its attitude to the word "pain"'. Pain was the ultimate judge; the acid test. Wilde was right when he wrote that 'at the birth of a child and a star there is pain'.

Pain should be the daily and nightly preoccupation of the politician; it lies at the beginning and end of every road; it is the pain of the soldier that we should remember when we are balancing the scales of war and peace, and the pain of the hungry when we are making our budgets. Yet the trend of politics is more and more impersonal. We wax so passionate about systems of book-keeping that we forget that behind the figures there are faces. It

is a long step from Wilberforce to Keynes, from Dickens to
Beveridge.

Especially is this true about India. There is more sheer pain
to the square mile in India than in any part of the world, but the
thought of it seems to keep very few people awake at night.
Perhaps this apparent callousness is due in some measure to the
Hindu doctrine of Karma. If you believe that a child in pain is
merely paying for its wickedness in a previous incarnation, why
should you pity it? Pity plays a very small part in Hindu
philosophy.

Time and again I used to draw people's attention in India to
pain in some form or another; it may have been only to ask why
a child was crying in the street or it may have been to indicate
some widespread social abuse. They were seldom interested
objectively; their reactions were not direct; pain, to them, was
merely something which must be fitted into the political pattern.
In whatever shape it appeared it must, somehow or other, be
made the responsibility of the British Raj. 'When we get independence', they said, 'all these things will cease.' I was tempted to
suggest that even in 'free' countries men still have toothache.

II

Consider the two shocking examples with which we began this
chapter — the shortage of nurses and the scourge of tuberculosis.

A Congress propagandist, of course, would blame the British
for both these deplorable facts. He would say, 'You have been
here for 150 years; what have you done about it?'

Well — what could we, what can we do about it?

In India nursing is still regarded as a dishonourable profession
by the vast majority of Indian women. They would degrade
themselves by tending the sick and wounded. The prejudices of
Victorian England, which Florence Nightingale had to fight,
are mere whims and fancies compared with the hide-bound rules
of caste and custom which govern Hindu womanhood. India is
still in the days of Mrs. Gamp.

That is why so large a proportion of the tiny corps of nurses is composed of Anglo-Indian girls, most of whom are Christians. The humiliations which these girls often have to suffer are past belief, particularly when they go on private cases. One girl, of high culture and intelligence, told me that she was expected to eat with the sweepers, and that after bathing her patient with antiseptic the patient always insisted on bathing again in order to wash off the 'pollution' of her touch.

Whose fault is it that there are only 65,000 nurses in India? The fault of the British women? There are not even 65,000 British women in India, let alone nurses, and there never have been.

And those 60,000 cases of tuberculosis?

Well, at least 50 per cent of them are due to an institution over which the British have absolutely no control — Purdah. If you walk through the streets of Peshawar you will never see a female face. The few women you meet are covered from head to foot; two narrow slits for the eyes and a tiny hole for the mouth — that is all the fresh air they ever get.

'If anybody had tried to invent a costume that was quite ideal for the incubation of microbes', said the doctor in my ward, 'he could not have done better than Purdah. We fight it year in and year out, but we can't fight it too openly for fear of offending the religious susceptibilities of the people.'

Religion — always religion, fighting progress, darkening the windows of the surgery, playing fantastic pranks with the bottles in the dispensary. As the days went by I began to feel that I was in a sort of crazy monastery, rather than a modern hospital.

'There's trouble in one of the wards in the next wing,' said my nurse one Monday morning. 'A girl with acute appendicitis. She ought to be operated on at once. But she won't have it done till Wednesday.'

'Why not?'

'Because to-morrow is not an "auspicious day". By Wednesday she'll probably be dead.'

· 'More trouble', she said, another morning.

'What's the matter this time?'

'A little boy's just arrived with eighteen relations who insist on sleeping by his bed.'

'Eighteen?'

'Yes. Parents, grand-parents, aunts, uncles, brothers, sisters, cousins, to say nothing of three babies howling their heads off. And he has to have absolute quiet.'

'Why don't you get rid of them?'

'We can't. If we asked even one of them to go they'd take the boy away, and he'd be dead before the morning. The poor little chap will probably die anyway, with all that uproar.'

How is it suggested that we should tackle problems like that? We did not invent the Hindu joint-family system, and if we were suspected of attempting to undermine it, the heavens would fall. Families of twenty or more living under one roof are common in India. 'This is the agnatic unit which Hindu law constantly seeks to uphold, the father, mother, son and grandson, together with the corresponding womenfolk, joint in food, worship, and estate.'[1] And joint, it must be added, in expeditions to hospital.

When I was well enough to be wheeled about in a chair I used to explore the quarters of the other patients. Many of the rooms were miniature Bedlams. Every inch of floor space was occupied by some member of the family, from aged crones to screaming babies. In one corner of the room somebody would be cooking rice, in another somebody else would be washing a saree. In the centre lay the poor patient, weary, distracted, breathing a rich assortment of germs. It seemed somewhat ironic when the nurse came in, pushed her way through the crowd, and dipped her thermometer in antiseptic before putting it in the patient's mouth.

III

People were dropping in to see me. Muslims, Hindus, Sikhs ... but now I look back on it, never an 'Indian'.

The Muslims are in a great majority in the North-West Frontier. For the first time I began to realize something of the intensity of communal feeling. Up till now it had seemed an academic problem, something that one had read about in books; it suddenly

---

[1] *India*, by T. A. Raman (Oxford University Press).

became very real as Muslim after Muslim bent over my bed, breathing fire and slaughter against the hated Hindu.

'Hinduism is filth!' That is what a famous Muslim had said to me in Delhi. 'Hinduism is filth!' He had quoted numerous instances to prove the point that it was 'a social disease'. He had waxed particularly fierce against a fellow member of the assembly, Mr. Krishamachari, who, he alleged, declared that 'Gandhi is more than a god to us Hindus'. He said that it was impossible for an Englishman to understand how deeply this remark had offended the Muslims.

Although he was a prominent member of the assembly, and a person of considerable responsibility, I had imagined at the time that such bitterness was exceptional, that it was probably a personal eccentricity. I began to see that it was not.

These Muslims seemed passionately anxious to impress upon me their profound difference from the Hindus, because, so they said, 'You can reach the ear of the public, and the public never hears the Muslim case. We are poor, we can't afford to spend millions on propaganda'.

One of the first men who came to see me was the venerable Malik Khuda Baksh, advocate-general and leader of the opposition in the Legislative Council from 1932 to 1937 (the name 'Baksh', by the way, has the beautiful meaning 'Bestowed by God').

'Never forget', he warned me, 'that Muslim and Hindu are different *cultures*, not merely different religions. That is the point.' His face lit up with a gentle smile. 'God is everywhere', he said. 'A tree does not deny its shade to a man who does not believe in Him.'

He was not pro-Pakistan, he did not believe in the political unity of Islam, but he insisted that the Muslims were a different *people*. He was particularly eloquent about the language question. 'The Hindus are trying to supplant our Urdu by their Hindustani', he said. Again he smiled, this time not so gently. 'But Urdu is tough. Do you know what the word Urdu means? It means "army"! And it is an army that will never be conquered by Hindustani.'

Another distinguished visitor, of very different convictions, was

Dr. Khan Sahib. He was Premier of the Congress Ministry which took office in 1937, but his greatest claim to fame is that his brother is Abdul Ghaffar Khan, better known as the 'Frontier Gandhi'. The exploits of this brother are remarkable. He is physically gigantic, he is a Muslim, and a fighter; but he fell so completely under Gandhi's spell that he became a devotee of non-violence, and imposed his convictions on his followers, the Red Shirts. This organization, as its name implies, has many Fascist tendencies.

The Frontier Gandhi was in prison when his brother came to see me, and I felt a little embarrassed in consequence. But Dr. Khan Sahib was courtesy itself. However, when he began to talk, he seemed at once to lose himself in a welter of conflicting ideologies. At one moment he was praising Gandhi's anti-industrialization programme, explaining the doctrine of non-violence as a practical policy in the modern world, and poo-pooing the suggestion that Hindu-Muslim differences could not be entirely eliminated as soon as the British quitted India. And then he talked for another hour, praising Nehru's industrialization programme, bemoaning the fact that India was not properly armed, telling me numerous stories that showed up Hindu-Muslim differences in the most glaring light, and ending with a suggestion that the cure for India's ills was Bolshevism.

When he rose to go I was obliged to tell him that I had not the faintest idea what he wanted or what he really thought. 'Never mind', he said, with a charming smile, 'we will agree to differ.' But even that was impossible; you cannot 'differ' with a smokescreen, you can only get lost in it.

After he had gone, one of the doctors who had been treating me, came in to see me. 'Hullo', he said, 'your temperature's up. Whose fault is that?' I told him that Doctor Khan Sahib, though a delightful person, had been somewhat fatiguing.

'Particularly about the communal business', I added. 'He suggested at one moment that we encouraged it and then in the next breath he told me stories which proved that we did nothing of the sort.'

'And I'll tell you another,' said the doctor. 'As soon as Dr. Khan Sahib became Premier there were serious riots in Peshawar.

On the first evening six people were killed, and dozens were seriously injured. Things looked very ugly indeed. Who did Dr. Khan Sahib send for to treat the casualties? A British doctor! Why? I can only conclude because he trusted them more than the Hindu or Muslim doctors. A wounded Muslim would feel that a Hindu doctor wanted to get his knife into him in more ways than one, and vice versa. But they trusted the Englishman because he didn't care a damn what their religion was.'

Which shows that Dr. Khan Sahib can think clearly in a crisis. If only he would not talk so much he might be an able leader. However, it is only fair to admit that my own physical condition at the time may have made me over-impatient with his subtleties, which are so dear to all Congress apologists.

IV

The stream of visitors continued. Most of them, naturally, were Muslims, nearly all of them were fanatically anti-Hindu. Their hatred was not political, and it appeared to have very little economic motive; it was more like a deep-rooted instinct.

The majority of them were pro-Pakistan, though they were not very clear as to what Pakistan was. When I suggested that the Muslims would suffer economically if India were split in two, they said . . . 'What does it matter whether we're rich or poor? That's *our* business.' When they were asked how they would defend their frontiers, they laughed. 'The southern frontier, that is to say, the *Hindu* frontier', they said, 'we should treat with contempt. The northern frontier would be an Imperial responsibility.'

They lost no opportunity to impress on me the decadence of Hindu philosophy. One man told me of Lakhshmi Devi, the Hindu goddess of Wealth, and of the ceremony where once a year the rupee is worshipped. Another, who came from Kashmir, told me that one of his friends had been transported for life because he had accidentally killed a cow (which of course is the supreme symbol of sanctity to the Hindu). 'A few years ago', he said, 'the penalty would have been death.' They inveighed against innumerable Hindu customs, from the habit of drinking cow's urine to the indifference with which they allow their children to play among the phallic obscenities of the temples.

The climax came one afternoon when a rising young barrister and politician, whose name I will not mention for fear of damaging his career, began to abuse everything Hindu with such violence and in such ringing tones that I had to request him to desist.

'All right', he said, 'I'll stop. But if I do, will you read something that I'm going to send to you — just one page out of a book?'

'Which book?'

'*More Tramps Abroad*, by Mark Twain.'

'What on earth has Mark Twain got to do with Hinduism?'

'You'll see. By the way, you're going to Benares, aren't you?'

'I hope so.'

'Well, the passage I want you to read is about Benares, which is the Hindu Holy of Holies. It concerns the belief that Hindus who die on the wrong side of the Ganges are reincarnated in the form of a . . . But wait and read it for yourself.'

The book arrived that night. It was almost the only Mark Twain I had never read, and the first few sentences had his authentic tang — dry, crisp, sunny, like a frosty morning. But first let us read the passage about Hinduism.

Here it is. As you study it, remember that it was the considered opinion of a very great American, a man who loved his neighbour, and feared God.

'*In Benares they tell you that if a pilgrim should ever cross to the other side of the Ganges and get caught out and die there he would at once come to life again in the form of an ass. Think of that, after all this trouble and expense. You see, the Hindu has a childish and unreasoning aversion to being turned into an ass. It is hard to tell why. One could properly expect an ass to have an aversion to being turned into a Hindu. He would lose dignity by it, self-respect, and nine-tenths of his intelligence. But the Hindu who changed into an ass would not lose anything at all . . . unless, of course, you count his religion. And he would gain much. He would gain release from his slavery to two million gods and twenty million priests, fakirs, holy mendicants and other sacred bacilli; he would escape the Hindu hell; he would also escape the Hindu heaven. These are the advantages which the Hindu ought to consider; and then — he'd go over and die on the other side.'*

It was strange that the yellowing pages of an old American classic should have set me wondering if, here at last, was the key to modern India. Mark Twain, one would have thought, was somewhat dated. But that passage was not dated, it was still white-hot; and in spite of its apparent persiflage it seared the soul. The urbane old humorist, for once in a way, had dropped the mask, and the face he revealed was stern and terrible.

'He would escape the Hindu hell; he would escape the Hindu heaven.'
What was the Hindu hell? What was the Hindu heaven?

Those were the questions I set myself, in the weeks of pain that lay ahead. You will find the answer in Part Two.

PART TWO

CHAPTER I

SEARCHLIGHT ON HINDUISM

BY WAY OF FOREWORD

THIS chapter must so inevitably cause offence that a few words of introduction seem called for.

It is a criticism of the Hindu religion, or rather, the groups of religions, philosophies and cultures which to-day parade themselves under the wide banners of Hinduism. So much,. it would be ridiculous to deny. But it most certainly is *not* an attack on the Indian character or the Indian peoples.

There is no colour prejudice in this book; psychologically, spiritually, and socially I am colour blind. There seem to me to be no heights to which the Indian peoples might not rise, and by heights I mean heights of character and virtue, in the good old Latin sense, as well as heights of intellect. India might have her Wilberforces, her Florence Nightingales, her Father Damiens as well as her Tagores and her Jagadish Boses. The fact that she is so singularly weak in the type of selfless characters who brighten the pages of Western history is not due to any flaw in the Indian character; it is due to the deadening influence of Hinduism. Hinduism as it *is*, not as it *might* be. It might be, or rather, have been, anything; the original source was crystal clear and sprang from high hills of the spirit. But the centuries have filled it with mud and sediment till to-day it is a gigantic sluggish stream, wandering through low and unhealthy valleys.

Of the many fine, truthful, unselfish Indians I met, hardly one was a sincere Hindu. Almost all had shaken themselves free from the influence of the drug . . . for drug it is. This was in no way the result of British influence for most of them — though kindly disposed to individual Britons — were intensely nationalist. Nor was it the result of any tendency towards Christianity; having rejected one religion they were in no hurry to adopt another. It was simply that they were men of intrinsic virtue, men to whom God — as He sometimes does — had given grace by nature.

64

It is because of my friendship for such men that this chapter has been so peculiarly painful to write. It may, and probably will, be construed as an attack on a people. In reality, it is an explanation of them. If it prompts any Indian to retort with an exposure of the faults of the modern Christian, so much the better. We could do with the lesson.

A book about India which is not a religious book is not a book about India at all.[1]

This sweeping statement will come as a shock to those whose opinions about the country have been influenced by the younger generation of Indian intellectuals, who shine so brightly on Western lecture platforms. These young men make no embarrassing display of their convictions; their conversation is flavoured with an amiable agnosticism; and though they do not deny India's claim to 'spiritual leadership' — (for that is admirable propaganda, particularly in the women's clubs of Chicago) — they poo-poo the legend of India's 'religiosity'. All this, they suggest, is a thing of the past; the mists have lifted, the incense has drifted away, and next door to the temple they are going to build a municipal swimming bath.

For themselves they are, quite possibly, speaking the truth. Many of the cub reporters who dog the footsteps of visiting authors have no religion at all, and are at pains to emphasize the fact. If you ask them why, in this case, they offer such an unquestioning allegiance to Mr. Gandhi, who has so often and so publicly prostrated himself in worship of the Sacred Cow, they regard you as a tactless person. Which of course you are, for you

---

[1] The reader should understand that in this part of the book the word 'India' refers to *Hindu* India. Hindus make up the bulk of India's population. There are 240 million of them as opposed to 100 million Muslims and a mere 40 million of other religions. And though the creed of the Hindu differs from the creed of the Muslims as sharply as night from day, Hinduism has a curious quality of colouring every other creed with which it comes in contact. A good parallel would be that of a Muslim temple in the middle of a Hindu jungle. Little by little the jungle encroaches, the vines twist round the chaste columns, the courts of Allah are choked with weeds; only by the utmost vigilance can the guardians of the temple preserve it. That is what has actually happened in some parts of India, where the clean, simple lines of the Muslim creed have been blurred and perverted by centuries of Hindu influence.

E

have drawn attention to a very deep fissure in India's political pattern, the fact that Young India wants to march to the factory while the Leader insists on dragging them to church.

But *how many* of these young agnostics are there in the sub-continent? 340 million Indians are illiterate, and can therefore be discounted. Of the tiny proportion of the literate it is safe to suggest that only those who live in the big cities, in constant contact with Western influences, have thrown off the faith of their fathers. At the most generous estimate this gives us only a very few thousand who can claim to be iconoclasts in any sense in which we understand the word. The rest — the 'teeming millions' — remain bowed at the feet of the idols.

Let India speak for herself. Here is the diagnosis of one of her most distinguished scholars, Professor D. P. Mukerji, of Lucknow University:

'*Examinees begin their answers, clerks and shop-keepers begin their work, with an invocation to their favourite deities at the top of their books. A good division at the examination, a rapid promotion in service, and a smart deal in the Bazaar or the Stock Exchange can all be secured by God's grace administered through a religious preceptor. No leader so openly waits for divine inspiration as Mr. Gandhi, nor is so admired for it, none so constantly mixes politics with religion even in his most millennial moments ... No social scientist in India has got a chance against the scientists of transcendental knowledge, no non-theological school of metaphysics ever had or ever can have any considerable prestige.*'[1]

This is a very old subject but it is also a very new one. Of the hundreds of writers who have called attention to India's 'religiosity' I do not recall a single one who has faced up to its implications in the modern world — who has shown how, in this year 1944, religious fanaticism in sweeping its way into the surgeries, turning the handles of the movie cameras, directing the wheels of industry. Hinduism in its most extreme and aggressive form is a living and turbulent force. Its voice rises above the roar of the factories and the workshops, it dominates the assemblies of politicians and students.

[1] *Modern Indian Culture*, A Sociological Study, by D. P. Mukerji ('India Publishers', Allahabad, 1943).

It is very important that the world should recognize this fact and realize its implications. The following pages represent an endeavour to help at least a few people to do so.

It will be best if we divide our argument into three main parts.

Firstly, we must gain a clear impression of what Hinduism really is.

Secondly, we must illustrate the extent to which it is a living and aggressive force in the India of 1944.·

Thirdly, we must try to assess the probable reactions which will ensue from the impact of this force on the modern world, which is shrinking so rapidly.

II

What is 'Hinduism'?

I am writing this in the hills far away from dictionaries and religious textbooks, but they would not be of much assistance even if they were by my side. Hinduism is almost indefinable, because it is a hotchpotch of almost every fear, dream, and delusion which has ever drifted through the tangled shadowy jungle of man's brains.

Hinduism has no church. It has no Pope. It has no Bible. True, it has a mass of ancient texts, songs and legends, which might be said to take the place of a Bible. But there is no ultimate authority to establish the truth of this formidable collection of antiquities. You can believe one and reject the other, as you choose.[1]

---

[1] The only approach to a Hindu Bible is the *Bhagavat Gita*, a work of great spiritual beauty, which can be ignored by no student of the inner life. According to legend it was spoken by Krishna on the battlefield of Kurukshetra; its true authorship is lost in the mists of history. There were possibly several contributors. Its main teaching, which is at once the strength and weakness of Hinduism, is that true knowledge is to be found only within the Self. Browning expressed this view in *Paracelsus*:

> 'Truth lies within ourselves; it takes no rise
> From outward things, whate'er you may believe.
> There is an inmost centre in us all
> Where Truth abides in fullness; and to know
> Rather consists in opening out a way
> Whence the imprisoned splendour may escape,
> Than in effecting entry for a light
> Supposed to be without.'

That is the message of the *Gita*; and for the saint, for the man of natural spiritual inclinations, it is easy to read. For the ordinary sinner it is full of dangers; it denies

The only thing which you *must* believe, with all your heart and soul, is the law of caste. You must believe that sixty million of your fellow men are 'untouchable'. You must believe that you are polluted if you eat certain foods and damned if you drink with certain people.. Caste is the sheet anchor of the Hindu ship, which might otherwise have dashed itself to pieces on the rocks of sterner and more solid faiths. It seems hardly necessary to observe that it is the precise negation of democracy, for which the Hindus clamour so loudly.

No Church, no Pope, no Bible. But most important of all, no *History*.

Hinduism is the only great world religion which has absolutely no historical basis whatsoever. There are many historians who deny the divinity of Christ, but only a very few have ventured to suggest that He did not at least *exist*. There is an equally imposing array of historical evidence for the existence of Mahomet and, to a lesser degree, of Buddha.

But the Hindu pantheon is stocked only with the creatures of dream and delusion; we shall search in vain for the figure of a prophet who taught in the simple shape of man.[1] Here, lurking in the shadows, is Ganesh, with his elephant's head and his mouse's chariot; and here is Krishna, playing his flute with five arms — or is it seven? Here is the dreadful face of Shiva the destroyer, and the strange and twisted bodies of Indra and Varuna, the gods of rain and water. Such are the Hindu gods. It is no concern of ours to discuss them as objects of worship. However, it *is* our concern to point out that they have no historical authority, because this complete lack of factual background is the reason for Hinduism's intangibility, fluidity, and elusiveness.

---

[1] We shall search in vain, that is to say, for any historical personage responsible for giving permanent shape to the original body of doctrine, or even for any figure —(such as St. Paul)—who interpreted the divine revelation. Needless to say, there have been innumerable seers and commentators, but these, by the very nature of Hinduism, are independent spiritual explorers, each ploughing a lone furrow.

---

the need for Grace and casts him most tragically on his own pitiful resources. At best it lends to morbid introspection, at worst to gross indulgence; the average man is not a casket of 'imprisoned splendour' but of base and selfish instincts. Nevertheless, the *Gita*, if read in the right spirit, cannot fail to be a source of permanent inspiration. The best translation is Annie Besant's. Of the many commentaries, the most impressive I have read is *The Yoga of the Bhagavat Gita*, by Sri Krishna Prem (Watkins, Charing Cross Road, London, W.C.2).

III

'Negatives — nothing but negatives. Tell us what Hinduism *is*, not what it is *not*.'

The reader would be justified in making such an interruption. But Hinduism is like a temple in a jungle; there is a mass of spiritual undergrowth to hack away before any clear outlines can be revealed.

And now we have to face the greatest negative of all. It will involve a considerable diversion, but it is a vital diversion if we are to gain a true impression of India's religious landscape.

Hinduism is not Christianity.

At which the reader might feel entitled to make an even sharper expostulation. 'Obviously it isn't', he might say. 'Everybody knows that.'

But everybody does *not* know it. There are millions of amiable, loose-thinking men and women in the West who glibly accept the idea of the 'Universality of Religion', who choose to regard all religions as merely different aspects of the same Great Truth. Romain Rolland, for instance, spent the greater part of his life trying to propagate this theme. To these people, Hinduism and Christianity are merely 'rays of light that sparkle from the facets of a single diamond'; or they are 'drops from the same clear water of the Universal Ocean'. There is an almost inexhaustible stock of cheap metaphors at the disposal of the 'Universal Religionists'.

It is a comforting doctrine. Warm and cosy and soothing to the anxious spirit. There is only one drawback to it. Namely, that, in order to believe it, you must be completely ignorant of history and theology; you must understand nothing of the life of Christ on the one hand, and you must not take even a peep into the Hindu pantheon on the other. For those who are prepared to shut their eyes and keep them shut, the doctrine of the 'Universal Religion' is most helpful.

To mention only one of its advantages, it entirely eliminates any awkward feelings of being 'different' from the Indians. Nice people don't like to feel 'different'; they are embarrassed by the thought that they may be 'superior'; and if Christianity and

Hinduism are only two ways of saying the same thing, if there is really nothing much to choose between them . . . well, there we are! God, Hindu or Christian, is in His Heaven — (Universal Variety) — and all's right with the world . . . so let us not worry about these awkward questions, but all go in to have lunch at Ye Mystic Vegetarian Taverne, run by that charming old theosophist lady who gives such wonderful lectures about Gandhi's resemblance to Christ.

However, there are some people who are not prepared to keep their eyes shut, and it is for them that I am writing. And even these will not be required to open their eyes very wide. One would have thought that two simple symbols would have been enough to raise somewhat serious doubts in the minds of those who prattle about the 'Universality' of religion.

Let us consider these two symbols.

The symbol of Christianity is the figure of our Lord on the cross — the figure of a perfect Man, who, even if we deny him divinity, has given the world its most beautiful legend and its most exalted code of conduct.

The symbol of Hinduism — or rather, one of the most widely revered of its many symbols — is the figure of Ganesh, half man and half elephant.

Let us have a 'close-up' of Ganesh.

I shall never forget my first visit to a Ganesh temple. It was in Bangalore. We drove to a sacred hill at twilight. The Indian twilight is an eerie thing — the last rays of the sun have a theatrical quality, like spotlights slanting dramatically from a gigantic lamp, while swiftly the draperies of the dusk are drawn across the sky. The sun shone on a tiny building of crumbling brick, and inside this building the monster squatted, awaiting us. He was carved from a single hulk of black, shining stone, and his trunk and his misshapen limbs were contorted like angry serpents. The forgotten sculptor who had evoked this creature from the rock, so many centuries ago, was a genius, but he was — I felt — an evil genius, a man possessed. For this Ganesh was imbued with a malevolent life; in the fading light his limbs seemed to twitch, as though impelled by ancient lusts. He could escape if he wanted; a flick of that sinuous trunk, a gesture of those twisted arms, and the walls would crumble, and he would walk abroad in the darkness.

Christ on His cross, giving to the world a last, shining phrase — 'Forgive them for they know not what they do' — Ganesh in his cave, twisting his trunk, riding in a chariot driven by a mouse. Can any but a fanatic seriously contest that these two symbols are worthy of equal honour in the 'Hall of Universal Religion'?

'But they are only symbols', you may tell me, 'and as such they are of no consequence. The same sun shines on both of them; it is God's sun and that is all that matters.'

Such talk is nonsense, and very poisonous nonsense too. The symbols are of the utmost consequence. If you doubt it, listen to one of India's foremost Hindus, C. Rajagopalachari, ex-President of Congress and one of Gandhi's closest friends. This is what he thinks of Ganesh the elephant god:[1]

'People of the West might not find beauty in Ganesh and might say that the figure was funny and that at best it was a mascot. But to the Hindus Ganesh represents the sense of universal unity . . . beauty and ugliness are combined to make one ineffable beauty in Him. He has the body of a fat man and the head of an elephant, with a mouse as His vehicle. He is fond of good eating but He is not stupid as a Westerner might suggest. We are a curious people; let us continue to be curious, that is my prayer.'

It is a strange thing when a man must apologize for his God; one hardly finds it necessary to apologize for Christ. It is an even stranger thing when, having apologized, he continues to worship. Yet that is exactly what Rajagopalachari does in the above speech. Yes, the Hindus are indeed 'a curious people'.

IV

We are still dealing with negatives. We are still showing what Hinduism is not, rather than what it is. But this seems to be the quickest method of clearing away the spiritual undergrowth, so that

[1] Report of a speech delivered to a gathering of the Maharashtra Mandal, quoted in *The Hindu* for September 8th, 1943.

the walls of the Hindu temple may be shown in their true outlines.

We have compared the two symbols of Christ and Ganesh. The comparison was dramatic, but it may be claimed that it was merely a literary conjuring trick, a verbal sleight of hand, proving nothing. The critic may suggest that it would be just as easy to play the trick the other way round, to point to some cheap tawdry image of Christ, pink and white and tinselled (such as one sees in the back streets of Naples), and compare it with some noble statue from the great temple at Conjeveram. We will let the critic make his point. It is not of great importance, for we were not really concerned with idols but with ideals. And now that the time has come to examine those ideals, we shall find ourselves · on such firm ground that no critic will be able to dislodge us.

'By their fruits shall ye judge them', said Christ. We will obey this injunction. We will put the fruits of Christianity and Hinduism side by side. This will be no mere clash of symbols, it will be a clash of systems, a war of two worlds — two worlds that can never meet.

We can introduce (and summarize) our argument with a striking generalization that ought to be written over the entrance of every Christian legislature.

'*Little by little, Christianity creeps into the statute book.*'

It was, I believe, Lord Morley who wrote this. Whoever may have been its author, the generalization is illuminating; it precisely describes the trend of modern legislation in civilized countries, which is 'progressive' in exact ratio to the extent to which it embraces Christianity.

We will match it with a generalization of our own.

'*Little by little, Hinduism creeps* OUT OF *the statute book.*'

That is an unchallengeable description of the trend of modern legislation in India. It is 'progressive' in exact ratio to the extent to which it *rejects* Hinduism.

This contrast is so significant, its implications are of such grave consequence, that the casual reader is asked to ponder the two generalizations for a moment, and to clothe them with substance from his own experience. He will not find such difficulty in doing so, even if he only chooses his examples from comparatively recent history.

Every British and American advance in the last century, every step towards the light, has been a step towards applied Christianity. Christ gathered the children unto him, saying 'of such are the kingdom of heaven'. The Factory Acts dragged them out of hell. Christ taught that all men are brothers; the abolition of the slave trade was at least an attempt to realize His ideal. Christ told us to care for the sick and the aged; and in conformity with His wishes — even though we may not openly acknowledge them — we have a host of free hospitals and an intricate system of pensions.

Christ told us, too, that those who take to the sword shall perish by the sword. Bitterly has the world learnt the truth of His words. But at least we have *tried* to obey Him; we have wrestled with the devil and built strong fortresses to keep him out. The name of one of those fortresses was Geneva. It crumbled and fell. But even its ruins are glorious; they are ruins in which Christ could walk without shame or grief.

Men *cannot* advance, except towards Christ. He is at the end of *every* road that leads uphill, towards the light.

Compare our record, brief and casual though it may be, with the record of Hinduism.

If ever there was a man-made act which would have gained the sanction of Christ, it was the Child Marriage Restraint Act, to penalize infant marriages, which came into force in April 1930.[1] This act was a clear-cut example of Christianity conquering Hinduism. It came into being largely because of the international uproar created by *Mother India*, whose author, of course, was a Christian. And it was fought, tooth and nail, by the orthodox Hindus, in the name of Hinduism itself.

The religious fervour with which so monstrous a custom as child-marriage was defended by the Hindus in their fight against the Child Marriage Act will come as a revelation to the average Westerner. He is inclined to suppose, loosely, that its abolition was due to the triumph of the most venerable elements in Hindu life. Precisely the opposite is the case; it was due to the *defeat* of those elements. For instance, at mass meetings throughout the country, this sort of resolution was passed:

[1] Better known as the Sarda Act, from its sponsor, Divan Bahadur Harbilas Sarda.

'This meeting of the citizens of Alivartirungare records its emphatic protest against the Child Marriage Bill, *as it strikes at the very foundations of the Shastraic principles guiding the Hindu society*, and regrets the unwarranted interference of legislatures in a matter *purely affecting the life of the Hindus.*'

The citizens of Alivartirungare were quite right; the Bill *did* strike at the roots of their religion. One would like to ask those who try to mix Christianity and Hinduism in a general hotch-potch of 'The Universal Religion' what they have to say about *that*. It is as though a nineteenth-century legislator were to protest against a Bill abolishing witch-burning on the grounds that this was a custom that had the divine authority of the words of Christ.

'But all these evil things were a long time ago', the critic may answer, 'and anyway, they are now a thing of the past.' The critic would be utterly wrong. These evil things were *not* a long time ago; the Sarda Act was only passed in the last decade. As for their being a thing of the past, a mass of authorities could be quoted to show that they are nothing of the sort. Thus, a distinguished friend of India, Sir Edward Blunt, asserts: 'Reformers who have attacked the marriage customs have nearly always been defeated by the orthodox majority . . . *the Sarda Act has proved well-nigh ineffective.*'[1]

I myself have stood in the Monkey Temple at Benares while streams of little girls, who could not have been more than twelve years old, were dragged towards the idols to implore the 'blessings' of fertility. Their faces were stamped with the memory of terrible things, and their bodies cringed, as though in shame, because they had not yet fulfilled the divine duty of maternity. I have seen those same little girls in the Kali Temple at Calcutta, cutting off locks of their long black hair and twisting them round the branches of a sacred cactus, while the Brahmin priest mumbled a string of prayers to hasten the advent of pregnancy.

A thing of the past?

But even if it were a thing of the past in practice, which it is not, it is very much a thing of the present in theory. The sacred texts,

[1] *Social Service in India*, edited by Sir Edward Blunt (H.M. Stationery Office, 1938).

the immemorial traditions, the ancient books of Brahmin ceremony — these stand firm against all comers. Any such thing as a
Hindu 'Reformation' is quite unthinkable; once you had finished
reforming Hinduism you would find that there was nothing left to
reform.

And yet, let us thankfully admit it, things are a *little* better —
say ten per cent. The darkness *is* lifting — ever so slightly.

v

'*Little by little Hinduism creeps* OUT OF *the statute book.*'

Suttee,[1] Thugee,[2] infanticide, enforced widowhood — these
were all part and parcel of the Hindu religion; they were all abol-
ished, at least on paper, by the Christian British, and their
abolition was fiercely contested by the Hindus in the name of
their religion — that religion which, we are asked to believe,
springs from the same source as Christianity.

It was the same with the devadasis, the temple prostitutes who
were dedicated from childhood to minister to the pilgrims and
the priests. There are not so many of those prostitutes as there
were, and they have been driven out of the big cities, particularly
since the war, which has flooded India with American soldiers.
It would not be very good propaganda for Congress if young men
from Milwaukee wrote home describing the orgies of pure and
unadulterated Hinduism; it would not fit in at all with the
picture of a great 'spiritual' nation which was only prevented from
giving the world the inspiration of her 'spirituality' by the
'chains' of the British.

However, there are still plenty of devadasis to be found; you
have only to go a little way off the beaten track, as I went, in the
south, to see them sitting at dusk in the doorways of the little
houses that are grouped around the temple area.[3] Their hair is

---

[1] The Hindu religious custom of burning widows alive.
[2] The 'Thugs' were professional religious assassins, who strangled their victims
by the hundreds. They worshipped Kali, the Hindu goddess of destruction, and
invariably gave a share of their spoils to her.
[3] The most flagrant examples of the devadasi cult in modern India are probably
to be found in the temples of Srirangaum—(near Trinchinopoli)—and Tirupati.

threaded with sweet-smelling blossoms of frangipani, their nails are painted scarlet. The pilgrims pass by, dusty of foot, hot of eye, clutching a handful of annas in a twisted rag. They pause before the girl of their choice . . . often she is a mere child. There is a muttered conversation, the girl smiles and rises, the pilgrim follows her in, the door is shut. And the gods are pleased and the priest gets a rake-off.

Such little cameos of India's 'spirituality' might not be well received in Milwaukee.

But even if all this is denied, as of course it will be, by Hindu apologists, they cannot deny the printed evidence of their own most eminent protagonists. Among the many rejoinders to *Mother India* was *Father India*, by C. S. Ranga Iyer. It contains so many breath-taking examples of the convolutions of the Hindu mind that nobody should be allowed to write about India till he has read it. This is what Mr. Ranga Iyer says about devadasis on page 51 of his book:

'The idea of allowing the young girls of the prostitute class to grow up in the atmosphere of the temples is to instil into them some religion, some fear of God, so that when they come of age they may not indulge in promiscuity. *The prostitutes of India are, therefore, one of the most god-fearing and loyal class of mistresses known to that unfortunate profession.*'

V I

So what is Hinduism?

The plain fact of the matter is that no answer can be given to this question. It is everything . . . and it is nothing.

All that we can say for certain is that in its very early origins it was a mystical way of life, of exceptional difficulty and extreme abstraction, which was celebrated and immortalized in a few great works of art such as the *Gita* and the *Upanishads*. Owing to the fact that it possessed no historical authority and no church this 'religion' — which, in any case, would be totally beyond the achievement or even the comprehension of any large body of men — became perverted beyond all recognition; it borrowed here, there and everywhere, it accumulated to itself a mass of purely human superstitions, deifying instinct, sanctifying convenience, and giving divine authority to human passion, till it found itself saddled with several thousand 'gods', some of them of the most disreputable character, 'gods' of greed and 'gods' of lust.

As the old Abbé Dubois wrote, a hundred and fifty years ago:

'*The Hindus originally possessed a conception, imperfect though it was, of the true God; but this knowledge grew more and more dim, until at last it became extinguished in the darkness of error, of ignorance and of corruption. Confounding the Creator with His creatures, they set up gods who were merely myths and monstrosities, and to them they addressed their prayers and directed their worship, both of which were as false as the attributes which they assigned to these divinities. And as a matter of course, the taint of corruption which characterizes all the religious institutions of the Hindus has duly left its mark on their social morality. How, indeed, could virtue prevail in a country where all the vices of mankind are justified by those of their gods?*'

Those are hard words, but they cannot be gainsaid. There may be many who suggest that Christianity is equally mythical; they are entitled to that belief; but they can hardly suggest that it is equally monstrous. Christian children are not taught to prostrate themselves at phallic symbols, they do not worship in the shadow of fantastic obscenities which no Hindu has ever dreamed of veiling. Christian children are not taught to hate and despise their brethren, to shrink from their very shadow.

The symbols still stand, in this year of 1944; the untouchables still grovel, in this year of 1944; Hinduism is still going strong in this year of 1944. That is the point, and that is why it is urgently necessary for the rest of the world to face it, however startling its implications. If Hinduism were a dying creed, we could afford to ignore its practical effects. But it is as full of savage life as the jungle from which it so largely emanated.

This has not been a pleasant chapter to write. That it will be resented by the Hindus is obvious; that it will be deplored by the British is inevitable. It has been our time-honoured policy not to interfere with the religious susceptibilities of the peoples over whom we have authority. This policy has not caused us many pangs, for the simple reason that religion, to the average

British public servant or soldier, is a matter best left to parsons, who are well advised not to make too obvious a parade of their peculiar ideas.

Those of us, however, who think that the most important thing that ever happened to the world was the birth of Christ, and believe that Christianity is not only true but wholly *modern*, cannot very well keep it out of our discussion of modern problems. It is the only standard we accept, and if it makes other standards look shoddy, we cannot help it. We want to clear the air, to let in the light, even if it shines, with merciless clarity, on our miserable selves.

BY WAY OF POSTSCRIPT

Once again let us emphasize what this chapter is, and what it is not. It *is* an attack on a system, it is *not* an attack on a people. The necessity of insisting on this distinction is emphasized by a remark made to me by a Muslim friend who has just read these pages. He said, 'Do you wish to imply that there are no good Hindus?' The answer, of course, is an emphatic negative. There are 'good' Mormons, there are 'good' atheists, and in every walk of Indian life there are 'good' Hindus, men and women who are pure of heart and kindly in spirit. But they are 'good' in spite of their religion rather than because of it.

For the last time, these are our two main points.

A. Pure Hinduism, as expounded in the *Gita*, is an intensely difficult and exceptional state to attain, involving complete concentration on the Self with the ultimate object of uniting the Self with the Absolute. As a social force it may therefore be almost entirely discounted.

B. Everyday Hinduism, as preached and practised by millions, has inevitably degenerated because it has no historical authority and no body of doctrine. Such a degeneration of the Christian, Muslim or Buddhist religions, however decadent their exponents might become, is almost unthinkable. There are certain things that the Christians, Muslims and Buddhists *must* believe. The Hindu, on the contrary, can believe almost anything he likes, with the result that his religion has become a hotch-potch of the baser passions, sanctified by the Brahmin caste, and personified by crowds of 'gods' and 'goddesses' who are as hideous as the instincts which created them. One day a psycho-analyst should study the deities of the Hindu pantheon. He would find in it, crystallized into the shape of men or monsters, representations of almost every vice known to man.

This is the force that drives one-fifth of the human race. It is therefore a fact of urgent and continuous significance to the world.

CHAPTER II

PAUSE FOR BREATH

OUR wanderings in the Hindu jungle have thrown out of gear all our attempts to keep to any sort of chronological order.

Where were we? In hospital in Peshawar. And where are we now? In Bombay. Much water has flowed down the Ganges in the meantime, and we are wiser though a good deal weaker. An author's aches and pains, as we previously observed, should not be regarded as marketable commodities. So we will content ourselves by saying that two major operations, in the height of the Indian monsoon, do not exactly set a man up.

One other 'aside' . . . the opinions set forth in the last chapter were not formed till many months after the time of which we are now writing; they were the result of study and observation all over India, from the ashrams of Pondicherry to the temples of Benares. In Bombay, where we now find ourselves, my ideas were still vague and fluid; I knew practically nothing, and rejoiced in the fact. His ignorance, to a man of inquiring mind, should be a constant stimulation and delight; it has the same quality of excitement as an uncharted map. He can say to himself . . . 'here are seas of philosophy that I have never sailed and mountains of doubt that I have never climbed'. So he reasons, and exults at the thought of the vast cerebral territories which are still waiting to be explored.

I wanted to see everything and do everything. At the moment all I could do was to walk very slowly round a small table for a minute or so in the afternoon, holding on to the edge, and adding a few extra steps every day. Aches and pains again! But at least this enforced solitude made me unusually sensitive to certain aspects of Indian life which can only be appreciated by those who lie, week after week, on a sick-bed.

And so, while we are waiting to get stronger, let us watch, and listen, and see what we can learn. Here are some extracts from my diary of the period; even if they serve no other purpose they may help to re-create the atmosphere of the place and the period.

I I

SOUNDS

'My life goes by to a chorus of the strangest sounds; that is all there is to measure it by, except the visits of the nurse and the doctor. The calls of the street vendors are enchanting; the prettiest comes from the ice-cream man, who has two strips of metal, tuned to C Sharp and F, on which he tinkles away at the street corner. The most melancholy comes from the seller of sweet cakes; he has a long phrase of about ten bars in six-eight time. It rises to a quarter tone, which he hits dead in the middle, and dies down to a deep moan on a totally unexpected note. On first hearing him I thought that this call was an improvisation, and that the quarter-tones and unexpected sharps and flats were a mistake. But no — the phrase is always exactly the same; and it is so complicated that it would tax the ingenuity even of Elizabeth Schumann to sing it.

'The weirdest call is appropriately reserved for the weirdest profession; it comes from the *pinjara walla,* who is the "fluffer" of cotton mattresses (he also engages to rid the mattresses of bugs). He has a crude instrument with one string tuned to a very deep note, and when he twangs it the reverberation echoes far and wide. As a sound it is quite unique; if those two great orchestral innovators, Wagner and Tschaikowsky, had known of it, they would certainly have used it. It is very like the voice of doom.

'The crows, of course, are ubiquitous and eternal. Nobody else seems to notice them; they drive me nearly mad. Yet one cannot repress a sneaking admiration for their outrageous pertness. A crow in a queue is unthinkable; he would caw and peck and push his way through all comers.

'They begin at dawn with thick guttural squawks just outside my window. When I sit up in bed and clap my hands, they merely squawk back—"go to hell!" When I get better they shall have balls of paper thrown at them. Then they may condescend to flop over to the branches of the nearest coconut tree and squawk from there.'

PARSEE CUSTOMS

I am staying with some charming Parsees, friends of A——, who have kindly taken pity on me, though if they had known how long all this was going to last, with the Press and the rumours and the reporters and the nurses, they might well have thought twice before issuing the invitation.

As the stretcher was carried into the flat I noticed something very pleasing and curious. On each side of the doorway there were little patterns of flowers, traced in chalk on the polished floor. At first sight you would say that somebody had dropped a wreath of daisies. I asked what they were for. They said that this was a Parsee custom of great antiquity. In the old days they used to scatter the chalk, which is faintly antiseptic, at the entrance to their dwellings, partly for hygienic purposes and partly to discourage evil spirits.

Every day the chalk is dusted up, and the design is changed. It is made by pouring the chalk into delicately perforated tins; you tap the tin on the floor, and there you are! There seems to be an endless variety of designs; one day it will be a fish, the next day a feather, or a fruit. One of the prettiest is a group of magic letters, which A—— says is a sort of Persian incantation to help sick persons. The Ayah is going to try this one every day, to see if it does any good.

MONSOON

The monsoon has begun. Pure Lyceum melodrama. If Somerset Maugham had been sitting in the stalls watching a rehearsal of *Rain* and if the producer had turned on the tap so violently and put so much indigo in the lights he would have stopped the rehearsal and told the producer — quite rightly — that such extravagances would make people laugh.

The monsoon is ham; there is really no other word for it. The clouds pile up like the clouds in ancient *Punch* cartoons when Britannia is standing alone on a storm-lashed rock waving a trident in one hand and the scales of justice in the other (the caption normally accompanying this old-time favourite is 'Watchman, what of the night?').

After the clouds have gone on piling till the suspense is really intolerable, the Drop comes. The single, portentously significant Drop. The Drop with a capital D ... the Drop that is the 'harbinger' (no other word must be used) of the gracious torrents, the life-giving floods, the babbling brooks and all the rest of it, including the bank balances of the fat Hindu grain merchants who have been gambling on a good harvest.

I love rain, but this rain goes too far; it is sadistic. Not only from stormy skies does it hurl itself but from clear blue heavens, turning streets into rivers, and human beings into ants under a watering-can.

SERVANTS

I simply cannot get used to the number of servants in the flat. There is Lionel the butler, and his assistant, Jackie the cook, and *his* assistant, Ramah the house-boy, Ayah the maid, and my own bearer Hussein. Seven, for a small flat with three bedrooms — the sort of place which in England would be kept in perfect order by one old charwoman working three hours a day.

The servants sleep in the strangest places. Anybody who comes in late at night has to step over three of them, curled up in the lobby. Jackie sleeps on the kitchen table, and the Ayah sometimes retires into the linen-basket. One day Ramah did not appear in the morning. He had been given up for lost when, just before lunch, A—— noticed a small foot protruding from under the sofa. The foot belonged to Ramah, who was fast asleep. How he managed to crawl into so small a space is a mystery.

Yesterday we had a typical example of the way in which religious superstition dominates the average young Indian. For some reason or other, the kitchen boy came into my room. His leg was covered with dreadful sores. When the doctor arrived that night I said, 'You really ought to do something about that boy's leg'.

'I've been trying to get him to go to hospital for weeks,' he replied. 'But he won't go.'

'Why not?'

'Because he got the original sore by falling off a pipal tree. As you know, a pipal tree is sacred, and he ought not to have climbed up it at all. So he thinks that he fell off because the gods are angry with him, and that it would be wicked to try to avoid his punishment.'

Hussein, my own bearer, ought to have been introduced long ago. He has been with me everywhere, and carried me in his arms on many occasions when I could not walk. He is a strapping Pathan, over six foot, with a variety of costumes which strike awe into the eye of the beholder. He first endeared himself to me by a remark he made when I asked him the profession of his previous employer.

'He very good sahib,' he said. 'He lieutenant in army and navy.'

He is very jealous of my friends. For instance there is a charming young Chinese girl staying here, who sometimes comes in to sit and talk. Hussein glares at her as if she were poison, and bitterly resents my asking for her company. 'Is Miss Wong in?' I inquire innocently. 'Yes sahib', he retorts. 'That China memsahib, she is in. She is always in. She is never going out, not that China memsahib.'

Every morning, when he comes in to draw the blinds, he looks at me and shakes his head. 'Lot of trouble, sahib, you have in India. Lot of trouble.' Then he adds, 'But God, He will be coming down one day.'

I pay Hussein far too much — so very much too much that if any English people ask what he gets I tell them half, and even then, they explode. This over-payment is due to weakness rather than generosity, on my part. Or is it? Weakness in one sense, yes, because I simply have not the face to ask servants to go out and buy flowers which cost as much as a whole week of their salary. But perhaps I may also claim to be animated by more altruistic motives. The average wage for a bearer in the city is 35 rupees a month, which is just about 13 shillings a week. On this he has to feed himself and his family, send money to his relations, amuse himself, and 'save'. When I suggest to other employers that he must find life somewhat difficult, they snort and say, 'These people can live on the smell of an oil rag'. Maybe they can, but I do not like to be surrounded by people living on the smell of oil rags. To put it at its lowest, it makes me feel socially embarrassed.

Last night a friend of A—— inadvertently discovered the awful truth about Hussein's wages and bounced into the room to de-

liver a long and — I thought — extremely officious lecture on
·'spoiling the market'. I got very shaky and hot and said that if I
was spoiling the market I was delighted to hear it, and that the
sooner such markets were spoiled the better. The nurse broke up
the argument by coming in with a thermometer, which registered
101 degrees of righteous indignation.

LOUIS BROMFIELD

A young Indian student arrived, and said that he hoped that if
ever I wrote a book about India it would not contain quite so many
elementary mistakes as Louis Bromfield's. He reeled off a number
of instances, of which I can recall only two. Apparently, in *Night
in Bombay* the hero sails into the harbour and sees the Elephanta
Caves to the east and Juhu to the west. This would only be possible
if he had a high-powered telescope. And in the film of *The
Rains Came* the Maharajah wore a turban that would only be
worn by the lowest sweeper class, while the Maharani went about
bare-footed, which is as unthinkable as Mrs. Roosevelt addressing
the Daughters of the American Revolution in pyjamas.

CHAPTER III

GENTLEMEN OF THE PRESS

WE have paused long enough; it is time that we resumed our explorations.

In the meanwhile, through doing nothing at all but lie in bed, I had become front page news. One morning A—— came in with the papers, saying:

'They've got you in bigger type than the Russian offensive. You may be offensive but you can't be as offensive as all that.'

He threw a bundle of papers and magazines on to the bed. They all told the same story in screaming headlines. BEVERLEY NICHOLS MYSTERY DEEPENS — NICHOLS STILL SILENT, etc. Leading articles commented ponderously on my 'mission'; gossip paragraphs abounded with hints as to my whereabouts; there were columns of impassioned correspondence, two cartoons and a number of photographs.

Normally such publicity would be flattering; to-day it was embarrassing. My idea had been to go round India quietly, as an independent investigator. And now the Hindu press was already clamouring for answers to all sorts of highly controversial qu' *tions which it would have been improper for me to attempt to answer.

'Even Stafford Cripps didn't get it much worse than you're getting it,' said A——. 'Look at this.'

'This' was a large photograph of a young man lying in bed with a bandaged foot. Underneath was a cunningly worded caption suggesting that it was a portrait of myself. The title was 'My Foot'. The paper was one which had been clamouring for a photograph for several days.

'What are you going to do about it?' asked A——.

'Nothing.'

'I think you'll change your mind after reading them.'

I did. The campaign had assumed such proportions that some sort of action had to be taken. It was no longer suggested, but openly stated, that I was an agent of the British Government, that my opinions reflected official policy, and even that I had some sort of power to 'negotiate' . . . though with whom the negotiations were to take place, and what we were to negotiate about, was not stated.

And so, a few days later, I dragged myself out of bed, was carried down the stairs, and driven in an ambulance to meet the gentlemen of the Indian press.[1]

I I

'Indian Journalists Run Amok — Beverley Nichols Courts Bitter Experience.'[2]

That was the general way in which the press described the affair. It was somewhat of an understatement.

I hobbled into a room that was packed from floor to ceiling with journalists, most of them young and all of them, so it seemed, in a state of hysteria. They crowded round the table, twining round my knees, and breathing down my neck. I was almost the only white person present apart from the Chairman, by name Mr. Horniman. For many years he has been the editor of a violently anti-British evening paper called *The Bombay Sentinel*, and every evening he regales the city with a column on the front page entitled 'Twilight Twitters'. The title is apt. The 'twilight' is an apposite description of the writer's mentality, the 'twitters' is a just comment on his style.

Needless to say, his column is a huge success.

It may be gathered that I did not take to Mr. Horniman. That is quite true. It is equally evident that he did not take to me. For weeks after the meeting, he filled his paper with gibes, lampoons and insults. No sneer was too cheap, no rumour too fantastic, for *The Bombay Sentinel*. The most sensational canard which his paper produced was its assertion, on the front page, that I had been

[1] That is to say, of the *Hindu* Indian press. The Hindus have nearly all the money and therefore make nearly all the noise. By comparison, the 100 million Muslims are very inadequately represented. Their chief organ is *Dawn*, and though it is in no way pro-British, it treats its opponents with consistent courtesy. Doubtless there are Extremist Muslim papers, but compared with the shrieking sheets of the Hindus, the Muslim press is sober, sane, and above all, straight.

[2] *Kaiser-I-Hind*, May 5th, 1943.

selected by the British Government as the next Viceroy of India. For safety's sake, however, he denied the rumour. 'Nichols refused it point-blank' he assured his readers. 'He was too appalled by the complexity of the task.'[1]

This meeting was typical of many which I subsequently addressed, for from the first moment it was evident that nobody had any intention of listening. I still did not feel competent to talk about India, and so I began to talk about England instead — about the average Englishman and Englishwoman, whom I called 'Mr. and Mrs. Smith'. What were they thinking? How had they changed? What would be their attitude to world affairs after the war? I was reasonably qualified to answer these questions; they were of wide and obvious importance; and they had a direct application to the Indian problem.

After a few minutes it became impossible to continue. Screams, shrieks and yells rent the air. 'Question ... question!' they shouted, one after the other, till half the members of the audience were standing up, while the other half were trying to pull them down. In the meantime sheaves of papers containing written questions were thrown on to the desk.

My carefully nursed temperature began to leap up inside, as though somebody had plunged a thermometer into a cup of tea. I was face to face with hatred — mass hatred. Here was the slogan 'Quit India' come to life. These were the men who went out in the darkness and chalked things up on walls. Here, in spirit if not in practice, was the vanguard of the ignoble army of saboteurs. Here was Hindu nationalism naked and unadorned. And — to use a vulgar phrase — it didn't strip well.

The Chairman tried to quell the riot. For another few minutes I struggled on. It was useless. There was murder in those men's eyes. Fee, fo, fum, they smelt the blood of an Englishman. It was a startling revelation, to one who had come, like myself, with the idea of an informal chat over a glass of beer.

'Why don't you get out and let us try the Japanese for a change?'
'Why don't you hang Churchill?'
'What is the difference between Britain and Germany?'
Those were three questions of which I took note.

[1] *Bombay Sentinel*, May 5th, 1943.

They seemed almost as bitter against America as against Britain.

'Why don't U.S. officers let their coloured soldiers into their clubs?' At least six people asked that.

'How dare Roosevelt sign the Atlantic Charter when negroes are not given equal rights in America?'

'Has Britain signed a pledge with Roosevelt to murder negroes as the British are murdering Indians?'

For over an hour the bedlam continued. I will make no further comment on it. That is best left to the Indian journalists themselves, of whom there were apparently a few decent specimens in the room, though they certainly made no effort to interfere at the time. In the *Times of India* on the following day one of them was kind enough to say 'We can only admire the amazing tolerance and good humour with which Nichols faced the terrific barrage'. The *Indian Annalist* observed editorially, 'We only hope that Nichols will not judge India by this disgusting treatment at the hands of half-baked journalists seeking yellow press notoriety.' The *Sunday Standard* stated, 'If this is the reception we propose to accord to visitors who have, incidentally, given no possible cause for offence, we cannot expect to be treated seriously by world public opinion'.

Unfortunately, world public opinion *does* treat the Indian press seriously. We will therefore pause to examine it.

III

The first thing which strikes the professional journalist about the average Indian newspaper is the astonishing smallness of its circulation. At home, he is accustomed to thinking in terms of millions, or at least of hundreds of thousands; out here — in a country where everything else is on so vast a scale — he has to think in terms of two or three thousand, sometimes even two or three hundred.

Needless to say, this observation is not intended as a reflection on the quality of the newspapers themselves. Merit is often in inverse ratio to circulation, and a weekly review with a sale of a few thousands may move greater forces than a whole chain of popular newspapers.

However, the fact that Indian newspapers sell in such tiny quantities carries with it certain important implications. Firstly, it means that journalists do not earn a living wage, or anything like it. Whereas in England a successful journalist can compete on at least equal terms with the members of any other profession, in India, even if he rises to the top of the tree, he will still be a poor man. Indian journalists are very near the hunger line.

This means that very few of the best brains of India's youth are attracted by the profession. It is recruited from duds ... the 'failed B.A.s', the black sheep of the family. To be interviewed in India, by all but a few star reporters, is extremely fatiguing; one has to spell most words over three syllables and any reference to personalities of world importance is met with a blank stare.

There is another very grave consequence of this low rate of pay, it tends inevitably to corruption. In a later chapter I have quoted a remark made by one of the chief directors of Film Publicity for all India, himself an Indian. He said: 'Film criticism in India is either bribery or blackmail.' He might have applied his censure to any other form of criticism.

As a result there are practically no independent leaders of public opinion. Admittedly, in the West we are too inclined to let our newspapers do our thinking for us, but at least those newspapers provide a platform for a number of observers who are above corruption (for example, the cartoons of Low, in the *London Evening Standard*, are often in direct conflict with Beaverbrook's policy; and Dorothy Thompson's international outlook, in the early part of the war, must frequently have given severe headaches to her editorial board). But in India, nobody can ever ask, 'What has Dorothy Thompson written? What does Walter Lippman say? Has J. B. Priestley expressed any opinion?' For in India there are no persons even vaguely corresponding to these. There are no national oracles, outside the ranks of the politicians; there are not even any national jesters. And it goes without saying that there are no national critics of art or the theatre for the very simple reason that there is no art to study[1] and no theatre to

---

[1] See a later chapter entitled, 'In Search of an Artist'.

attend. India is a gigantic series of negatives, and this melancholy fact is faithfully reflected in her press.

The greatest negative of all is that, with the exception of the solid mass of the Muslims, there is no public opinion; there is only a heterogeneous mass of public opinions, which is a very different thing. In a country which is a nation you can 'feel the public pulse' — at least, in times of crisis; it beats rhythmically; it can be measured and assessed. In India, the 'public pulse' is incalculable, it is a series of conflicting flutters. Here is an extract from a Government of India White Book which will illustrate the baffling diversity of Indian political opinion, when compared with the simple Tory, Liberal and Labour groups of Britain.[1]

NEWSPAPERS	CIRCULA-TION	GENERAL REMARKS
Bombay Chronicle	18,000	Exponent of official Congress Policy.
Bharat	5,000	Very conservative. Pro Hindu Maha-sabha (Right wing of Hindu Party).
Bombay Sentinel	9,000	Strongly Communist, anti-British and uniformly critical of official Congress policy.
Independent India	3,000	Highly critical of present Congress policy. Pleads for India's partici-pation in war. Communist leanings.
Janata	3,000	Advocates the cause of Untouchables.
Janmabhumi	16,000	A strong advocate of the cause of Indian States' subjects.
Kom Sevak	3,000	Deals with matters pertaining to the Parsees. Moderate.
Muslim Gujarati	3,000	Highly communal. Pro-Muslim League.
Prabhat	6,500	Follows the Kesari School. Moderate.
Rozana-e-Khilafat	4,000	Champion of Muslim communal rights. A strong critic of Congress. Advocates extremest political view.

Where, precisely, do we find the 'Voice of India' in this little batch? If that is regarded as an unfair question, remember that

[1] Guide to Prominent Newspapers and Periodicals in English and Indian Languages published in British India and the Indian States.'

several of these are prominent and influential papers. There are nearly *four thousand* others, with an average circulation of less than one thousand. These sheets, semi-illiterate and always wildly contradictory, are seriously quoted by Congress propagandists as the opinion of the Indian people.[1]

IV

These are harsh remarks but they are the result of bitter experience. Any man with a wide knowledge of the world's Press will probably agree that in no part of Europe, the Empire, or the Americas has he encountered anything even vaguely comparable with the corruption and dishonesty of Hindu journalism.

Lying is carried to a fine art; there is the lie direct and the lie indirect, the lie of commission and of omission, the lie of suggestion, imputation, and insinuation. Here is an example. When I was ill I cabled back to England an article which was intended as a sincere tribute to the Indian doctors who were attending me. In this article there was also high praise of the skill and devotion of Hindu nurses . . . although it was pointed out that the lamentable shortage of nurses was unfortunately due to the low estimation of the profession by the mass of Indian women. The conclusion of the article was:

'*There is a great future for Indian medicine, provided that it is allowed to develop freely, not only by the British but by the Indians themselves.*'

The article was cabled back to India. But it was not spicy

[1] It is significant that the two largest circulations in India both belong to newspapers in the English language, the *Times of India* and the *Calcutta Statesman*; each have roughly 70,000 readers. The *Times* has no business interests behind it; it actually pays its own way. Other famous papers in English are the *Madras Mail*, the *Civil and Military Gazette* of Lahore and the *Pioneer*. The latter, which is published in Lucknow, still has a faint atmosphere of romance hovering over its pages, for it was Kipling's paper, and in the old days it sold all over India at the very large sum of a rupee per copy It was a Tory of Tories, and though it refused to march with the times it was astonishingly well informed, with its own special correspondents all over Europe. It had an aristocratic contempt for modern innovations; until 1926 all the type was set by hand—300 pairs of hands! It was always late with the news, and did not condescend to start printing till 11 a.m. Since those grand old days it has gone through many vicissitudes and to-day it gives the impression of a seedy old gentleman pathetically trying to adjust himself to an age he does not understand.

enough for Indian journalism, and so it was 'edited'. 'Just one word was cut out from the above passage . . . the word 'only'. If you read the sentence with this omission you will notice that the entire sense is altered. After editing, the article created the usual uproar in the Hindu press.

That sort of thing happened over and over again, till in the end, when it was impossible to escape from reporters, I used to greet them with the following words:

'You do not want to listen to anything I have to say; if you did listen, you would not understand it; if you should understand it, you would misreport it. You are here for only two reasons, either to make me tell lies or to tell lies yourselves.'

'You have a low opinion of us,' they would observe, after this outburst.

'The lowest. Have a drink.'

We usually left it at that. Oddly enough, occasionally got the truth across, to the astonishment concerned.

v

One last word on this sordid subject.

This hotchpotch of rumour, prejudice, and is forms the Indian Hindu press — the infantile para journalism — is allowed, by the British Government, a freedom of expression which would be singular in time of peace and is staggering in time of war.

For a few annas, at the time of writing, I could go round the corner and purchase enough anti-British, anti-American, and anti-war propaganda to keep Dr. Goebbels supplied for weeks.

Every ignoble motive, every type of squalid intrigue, is attributed to Churchill and Roosevelt. The Viceroy is insulted with a bitterness and a vulgarity worthy of Streicher at his worst. One day a young Hindu editor — who must have been strangely misinformed about my personal opinions — hustled into the room with a large cartoon which he proceeded to unfold on the bed. It showed a picture of Lord Linlithgow, stark naked, grovelling on the ground before Mr. Jinnah and licking his toes (this was a comment on a guarded reference which the Viceroy had made, in one of his speeches, to the rightful aspirations of the Muslims).

'What do you think of it?' asked the young editor.

I could only reply that I thought it was very ugly.

'Yes — but the *idea*?'

I excused myself by saying that anything quite so ugly as that did not give me any ideas.

'Anyway, I'm going to put it in.'

'I'm sure you are. The Indian press is free.'

At which he burst into gales of laughter. The Indian press free! Oh — that was a good one . . . that was rich . . . he must tell his friends!

Well — what was he laughing about? If the newspapers and magazines, lying on the bookstalls outside my window, had been able to speak, they might well have asked that question. Look at them! 'Quit India', by Gandhi. 'Uncle Sham' . . . An Exposure by an Indian, of the decadence of the U.S.A. Endless pamphlets and articles against Britain, against the war effort, against the Muslims, against everything and everybody that is non-Hindu, libelling, lying, snarling, spitting. All sold freely, casually, in the open market.

Naturally, in a war to the death, the censor's scissors have sometimes snapped. Naturally, in a country stiff with enemy saboteurs, the police have, on a few occasions, confiscated or suppressed material that was comparatively innocuous.

The stark and vital fact remains — and I challenge any Hindu to deny it — that throughout the course of this war the vast bulk of the Hindu press has been singing a Hymn of Hate aimed at the British Raj, day in and day out, in a thousand voices. However loud this Hymn of Hate has swelled, however false its tones and however harmful its echoes, the British have seldom succumbed to the temptation to suppress it. The Hymn goes on, with the enemy standing at the gates.

If that is not at least a measure of freedom, it is a very fair imitation.

CHAPTER IV

HINDU HOLLYWOOD

LET us go to the pictures, and see an Indian film.

It was the first thing I did, when I was well enough to hobble about again, and it would seem that no other Englishman has ever had such a wild idea before.

'What are Indian films like?' one used to ask.

'Good heavens, how should I know?'

'But haven't you ever seen one?'

'*Seen* one? An *Indian* film? Really!'

Blank amazement greeted the suggestion that it might be interesting to see an Indian picture. And yet, the films are a living mirror of a nation's life; even if one did not understand everything that the mirror showed, it would surely repay a few hours of study.

I was particularly anxious to visit the studios themselves, and after a little wire-pulling obtained permission to witness the shooting of a big historical picture which was being made within a reasonable distance of Bombay. Let us make the trip together.

II

The film star sat cross-legged on the floor of the studio, occasionally dipping her spoon into a bowl of freshly sliced mangoes, iced and glistening and golden. With a gesture of her pretty hand she beckoned to a coolie to move the fan nearer to her; and as he did so its breeze stirred her hair — her own fabulous hair, which rippled far below her waist in an enchanting cascade.

It was overpoweringly hot, and as something seemed to have gone wrong with the mike I decided to go outside for a breather. To reach the door one had to step over about a dozen nearly naked coolies, who had seized the opportunity to lie down and sleep in the dust. It wasn't at all like Hollywood in that studio.

It was even less like Hollywood outside.

Imagine a group of shabby Edwardian houses, built of white

95

stucco, clustering near the main road of a Bombay suburb. Down the road passed an endless stream of the rumbling bullock-carts which form the eternal background of the Indian pageant. The coconut palms were noisy with big black crows and the burning skies echoed with the perpetual 'ghee-wee' of kites. At the entrance gate stood an attendant in a mauve and white pugree, lost in dreams, under a tangled mass of morning glory.

Then I turned round, and saw a gaunt building of steel and concrete, painted in staring letters 'Stage Number Four. No Smoking'. The impact of East and West was startling.

In the corner of the yard was a very beautiful tree, with a gnarled trunk the colour of old ivory, and thickly-clustering glossy leaves that Cézanne would have loved, leaves that seemed to drip green paint into the shadows below. My friend pointed to it.

'I'm going to paint that tree,' he said.

'You'd better hurry up. The director said they were enlarging the studios, and they'll be cutting it down.'

'They'll never cut that tree down. Its a pipal, and a pipal is sacred; if they cut it down they might as well blow up the studio; nobody would work here any more.'

So this was the pipal — the same tree which Ramah had climbed when he hurt his leg! Well, it was certainly a lovely thing. And if India has to be cluttered up with sacred objects it is just as well that some of those objects should be trees; it is a pity that there are not a few sacred trees in England. Nevertheless, when you come to know India better, you begin to feel that at times the sacredness of the pipal is somewhat overdone. It spreads its shade far and wide, in the mountains and the valleys and the cities of the plains, and sometimes it spreads it in the most awkward places. Bang in the middle of narrow streets; just over the one spot where a builder wants to put a septic tank; right outside the windows of a room where it is vital to have light. To make a very bad pun, local Government in India is largely government of the pipal, by the pipal, for the pipal.

We walked over and stood in the shade of the tree. It was cool and pleasant here, and it seemed a good place to collect a few statistics from my friend, who was one of the most knowledgeable men in the business.

'How big is the film industry in India?'

'Pretty big, and getting bigger every day. For instance, there are over a hundred production companies. Their chief centres are Bombay, Calcutta, Poona, and Madras, and between them they employ about 80,000 people.'

'What about the movie theatres?'

'Well of course they vary tremendously, from air-conditioned palaces like the Metro in Bombay to bug-ridden barns with wooden benches in the smaller cities. Even so, there are over 1600 buildings capable of showing talkies.'

'What about the villages?'

'The vans go out to them. Little travelling talkies — about 500 of them. They usually show one long religious picture, and a Government "short". Some of the shorts are pretty good; they give elemental lessons in sanitation, first aid, rotation of crops, etc.'

'And the stars — what about them? What sort of money do they earn? And what sort of people *are* they?'

'Let's go back to the studio and see for ourselves.'

III

On the 'set' things were beginning to move. The lady with the fabulous hair had finished her mangoes, and was standing in the entrance of the village hut which formed the centre of the scene. The director, who even in the most heated moments never removed his Gandhi cap, was giving her a few final instructions. By her side was an elderly, bearded actor, who was playing the role of a wandering fakir.

The scene showed a spirited argument between the star, who was supposed to be the village belle, and the fakir. The dialogue went on for what seemed an interminable time, and was eventually broken up by the entrance of the girl's husband, which was the cue to cut.

'O.K. Lights.'

'Lights ... lights!' echoed a dozen Indian voices in varying accents.

The lights came on; the noise of the whisperers was hushed; the make-up man dashed across with a final dab of powder for the

G

star's nose. Make-up men in India have an exhausting job, trying to keep the stars' faces dry at ninety in the shade.

Dead silence. The old, old feeling of agonizing tension. Business. Action.

The star appeared, the dialogue began, everything appeared to be going well. And then, without any warning the actors dried up.

There was an awful pause.

'Cut!'

The producer hurried forward.

'Dim lights!'

The lights went out.

The producer began to rehearse the actors once again.

. Now there would be no point in narrating this incident, which is common in all film studios, were it not for the fact that it happened again a few minutes later — and again and again, in all *eight* times. The lights went on, the lights went out, the make-up man dashed backwards and forwards, but aways it ended in the middle with the producer shouting 'cut'. And the curious thing was that he shouted it with the utmost good humour and the stars, instead of looking peeved or embarrassed, merely smiled.

'Does this always happen?'

'Pretty often. It isn't because they've got bad memories but because they try to do too much. For instance, this girl's only half-way through starring in another picture for another company. She'll be acting in *that* to-morrow. No wonder she gets her lines mixed!'

'But why do the producers allow it?'

'They can't help it. Indian film stars are the most independent people in the world.'

Other people's money is always interesting. Here are some financial facts about India's Hollywood. For one film a star may get as high a fee as 75,000 rupees, which is about $25,000. If she does three of these a year, which is quite possible, she is actually better off than if she were in Hollywood, because Indian income tax (even when the collector manages to extract it, which is seldom) is a fleabite compared to the British or the American.

This fortune she cherishes with remarkable diligence. No big cars, no grand houses, and not even a hint of a gigolo. Bombay's

Beverley Hills is a quiet suburb which does not boast a single swimming pool. No tourists even go to see it, no photographers ever pry their way over the garden walls. When the star walks out to her taxi in the morning, nobody turns his head. There is no demand for 'personal appearances' in India.

Maybe she lives so quietly because her career is so short. Its end is as sudden as its beginning. Strange as it will sound to the Western director, an Indian girl may be starred in a full-length role within a few days of her first screen-test, and neither she nor anybody else sees anything odd in it. She twinkles brightly for a very few years — three is considered quite a long life — and then, suddenly, she disappears. The public have had enough of her. Why, nobody seems to know. She may be prettier, she may be a better actress; it makes no difference. Out she goes.

Compared with the wages of the stars, the wages of the rest of the personnel are modest, and of the writers, pitiable. For the complete scenario and dialogue of a full-length film an author considers himself lucky to receive two hundred rupees, which is about sixty dollars. That is one reason why Indian films are marking time. But there are others, as we shall see. We can best illustrate them 'on the set'.

IV

It was late in the afternoon when we returned to the studio.

A love scene was in progress. At least, it appeared to be a love scene, but somehow it never seemed to get going.

The village maiden was making sheep's eyes at a young man with a swelling chest. If ever a girl was saying 'Come on' she was saying it, and if ever a chest were swelling because its owner was activated by 'Coming on' instincts, this was the chest in question.

But nothing happened, nothing, that is to say, in the nature of a clinch. The eyes shouted 'come on' in even louder accents, the chest swelled to bursting point (till, in sympathy, one found oneself puffing out like a pouter pigeon), fingers were twined, necks were arched, eyelashes fluttered like the wings of moths — but no clinch.

'This can't go on,' I found myself muttering. 'But really, *no*.

All this titillation. Something will snap, burst, come undone.'
And *sotto voce* I said to my friend:

'When *is* he going to kiss that girl?'

'Kiss her?' he echoes in astonishment.

'Yes, kiss her. When?'

'Never.'

'But why not?'

'They never do.'

'What — those two? Is there anything the matter with them?'

'No. Not only those two. Nobody.'

'Nobody kisses?'

'Nobody, never. Not on the Indian screen.'

I took a last hasty look at the swelling chest. It was — as the French say about steaks — *au point*. Something was about to burst. This was past endurance. I grabbed my friend's arms and we went in search of a fresh limejuice.

While drinking it I learnt the astonishing history of The Kiss on the Indian Screen. Astonishing because it is a history that has not yet begun to be written.

The kiss is taboo.

Only once, ten years ago, in a gipsy film called 'Zarinah' did an iconoclastic director allow a male star to press his lips against those of a female star. He did not press them very hard and he did not press them very long, but he pressed them quite long enough to cause a major explosion. It may not be true that large numbers of people immediately jumped from high buildings, to propitiate the Gods, but it is true that there were angry scenes in the theatres, meetings of protest all over the country, and an almost unanimous outcry from the critics.

'Disgusting Western degradation! Keep the Indian screen clean!' So ran the headlines.

'Zarinah' was India's first film kiss — and her last.

Which is another reason why Indian films continue to mark time.[1]

[1] The Abbé Dubois, writing at the end of the eighteenth century, is as up to date as ever even if we apply his remarks to the movies. 'What we call love-making is utterly unknown among the Hindus', he writes. 'Although they see no harm in the most outrageous and licentious excesses, there is no country in the world where greater attention is paid to outward propriety. The playful sallies, jokes, and compliments in which our youths are so profuse would be looked upon as insults by any Hindu lady, even the *least* chaste, that is, if they were offered her *in public*.'

V

But the real reason for the stagnation of India's Hollywood (which is almost entirely dominated by Hindu capital) is the same as the reason for the stagnation of everything else — religion.

The great majority of Indian pictures deal, in one form or another, with religious or mythological subjects. The camera is permanently focused on the remote past. The screen is literally a shadow screen across which there flits an endless procession of saintly ghosts, whispering the stories of ancient superstitions.

And all this in a land which hums with stories! In modern India, plots grow on every tree; the very air is thick with drama; but none of the drama gets into the studio.

Now and then, it is true, an advanced producer will attempt what he calls a modern 'social'. Since most of the script-writers are unable to think up any new ideas for themselves these 'socials' are pinched almost in their entirety from old American successes. They lift situations which were originally devised for somebody like Lucille Ball, wearing pyjamas against a background of sky-scrapers, and they hand them to dove-eyed young women in flowing draperies, capering through miles of mango groves. The result is, to put it mildly, unhappy. Sophisticated back-chat doesn't ring true in a saree, particularly when the temple bells are ringing in the distance.

Yet what a treasure trove is waiting for the producer and the script-writer — to say nothing of the star!

Here are one or two examples. First, the theme of 'untouch-ability'.

Why not take a boy who has been born an 'untouchable', trans-port him to the free air of Britain or America, and let him make good, as thousands have made good before him. (Oh yes, I know all about the colour-bar. But the colour-bar is a minor irritation compared with the major slavery of untouchability.) Make him rich and famous ... and bring him back to his native village.

What a theme it would have been for Arnold Bennett! He is not allowed to draw a cup of water from the village pump? Very well — he builds his own reservoir. He is so degraded that the lowest washerwoman will not touch his clothes? Then he builds

his own laundry. His children are forbidden to go near the village
school? He builds a school of his own and staffs it with the finest
teachers in the world.

If only some courageous producer would make a picture worthy
of this subject's tragic possibilities — and damn the box office!

Another subject which cries out for dramatic treatment is the
institution of 'purdah' — the Muslim tradition which compels a
man's wife to cover her entire body in a thick veil for the whole
of her life, so that no other man may ever see her. It is not for me
to criticize this custom — we may well leave that to the Muslims
themselves, whose more advanced members attack it bitterly and
consistently. They describe it as cruel, morbid, unnatural, unhealthy, crippling to the body and torturing to the mind. They
call it an evil relic of the dark ages of women.

What a theme for a film — for a hundred films — the rending of
the veil, the struggle to the sunlight!

But in order to make the most of these dramatic riches you must
have a producer who is something of an iconoclast; he needs bite
and speed and punch, he must have the spirit of attack.

There are such producers in India, but they can be counted on
the fingers of one hand. Among them must be mentioned Sohrab
Modi, who recently showed me his film 'Sikander', which deals
with the Indian invasion of Alexander the Great. This is a
virile picture, with pace and flair, well up to the standard of
that old masterpiece 'The Birth of a Nation'. Another highly
intelligent producer is J. B. H. Wadia, who made history with
'The Court Dancer', India's first motion picture with English
dialogue. However, even 'The Court Dancer' cannot be called an
unqualified success. It has some poetical photography; but to
Western eyes its popular star Sadhona Bose is regrettably heavy
on her feet, and its English dialogue is startlingly jejune. For
instance, on numerous occasions, the only verbal come-back to a
dramatic statement is the bald interjection 'Oh!' The effect of
this is unintentionally comic. 'Darling, they are coming to kill
you,' says the hero, or words to that effect. 'Oh!' replies Miss
Bose. It is not an inspiring monosyllable, delivered in bulk.

Yet both Modi and Wadia have touches of genius; both are
determined to devote their lives to lifting Indian films out of the

slough of despond into which they have sunk. Their task will be a stern one. The attitude of most of their contemporaries, even when they attempt to face up to the ancient tragedies with which their country is beset, is one of weary resignation. For example:

> *A Hindu Maiden had a Muslim brother! And in their*
> *Holy Friendship was embodied a Nation's sigh!*

So runs the advertisement of an important film called 'Bhalai', which is a big box-office success. Need one say more? It is a theme that calls for blistering satire, and all it gets is a sigh. It is all very well to advertise a star like Ramola as 'The It girl of the Indian Screen', or to ape the jargon of Hollywood in the publicity of Winayak's 'My Child' ('A skyful of stars! An eyeful of spectacle!! A soulful of sentiment!!!) In spite of this veneer of modernity, the religious element creeps in almost invariably, and needless to say, it is coloured by the personal religious prejudices of the producers — most of whom are Hindus.

As a result there is practically no honest film criticism in India. With a very few honourable exceptions, the critic's pen is twisted according to his caste, his creed, or his political convictions.

Let me hasten to add that these statements are fully substantiated by Indians themselves.

'*Film criticism in India is either a matter of blackmail or of bribery.*'

It was one of the chief publicists of Indian films who said that; I omit his name to spare him embarrassment.

'There is *no* honest film criticism to be found in the whole of India. There is *no* newspaper or magazine which cannot be influenced. *Nobody* attaches any value to film reviews.'

It was a Hungarian, F. Berko, who said that (he did not say it in India, of course, but in an American movie magazine).

'The world's low' — 'a collection of journalistic sewer-rats' — 'clowns with dirty fingers'. These are only a few of the epithets which Indians have coined for their own brothers of the critical profession.

VI

This is a gloomy picture, but it is not an ungenerous one, and though it is painted by an Englishman it is not as dark as that which is painted by some Indians themselves, who seem to have lost all hope of advancement.

I myself *have* hope, very great hope, and in spite of all that has gone before I believe the Indian screen may have a brilliant future. Why?

There are many reasons. Three will suffice.

The first may sound trivial but is actually important. Until recently all Indian films were of quite intolerable length; fifteen thousand feet was nothing out of the common. The audience demanded it. So intent were they on getting their money's worth that they would sit in silence through a whole list of credits, unmoved by the names of the stars, the authors, the directors, only to burst into wild applause when the length of the film was flashed across the screen. 15,487 feet. Whoopee! That meant the film *must* be good!

The war has put a stop to these inordinate *longueurs*; owing to shortage of celluloid Government has issued an order that no film may be more than 11,000 feet. And though the audience chafes, and mutters that this is yet another example of the brutality of the British Raj, the producer — and the intelligent filmgoer — heaves a sigh of relief.

That is a negative reason for hope; it shows that Indian films can get into step with modern ideas, even if it takes a war to bring this miracle about.

The other two reasons are more positive. The first concerns the Indian actors themselves. They form the true riches of the Indian screen. They have a born sense of drama; it is as natural for them to act as for thrushes to sing. We mentioned above that a girl may be given a star role a few days after her first screen test, and that nobody sees anything odd in it. Well, there *isn't* anything odd in it. She *is* a star and — though it sounds incredible — she has very little to learn.

Unlike his Western prototype, the Indian producer has to be constantly curbing his actors and actresses; their features are so mobile, their gestures so eloquent, and their emotional equipment so rich and spontaneous that his task is to damp the flame rather than to add fuel to it.

Moreover, the country abounds in magnificent types. There is no finer male specimen in the world than the Pathan. In the streets of the big cities you will see droves of lovely girls, with the huge eyes, the small chins, the delicate noses and the frail but firm figures which are the dream of the casting director. As for the eccentric types — the fanatics, the clowns, the wizards, the grotesque — India has them by the millions.

And the other reason why Indian films may one day flash brilliantly across the world's screen? I have already indicated it. It is hidden deep in the eyes of Mother India herself; it is written in every wrinkle of her ancient face. Mother India is the world's greatest story-teller; her legends are inexhaustible, and every league of her sun-scarred territory has a tale to tell, of blood or of passion or of sacred fire. And now that at last Mother India is awakening, to all this store of ancient history will be added the thrill of history in the making; the air will be strident with the echo of snapping chains and rending veils. It is for Mother India herself to walk out of her ancient prison, which is so largely of her own making, to breathe the fresh air and think the free thoughts of the new world, and then, to translate them into terms of art.

Can she do so?

I think the answer is 'yes'.

CHAPTER V

• IN SEARCH OF AN ARTIST

It is at this point that the book really begins.

It begins now, after months of hospitals and stretchers and getting out of bed and going back again. I was at last able to stand on my own feet. And a man sees as much with his feet as with his eyes.

Let us sum up our progress to date. For a brief space we have watched the pageant from the steps of the Viceregal throne. We have met a few celebrities. We have had a glimpse of the wild North-West Frontier. We have seen the inside of an Indian hospital. Many voices have echoed round our bedside, and they have set us studying the heart of India's problem, the Hindu religion, which has taken us back into the misty beginnings of history. At the other end of the scale we have learned something of the Indian press and the Indian films.

It is not a very impressive array of material, though it is more than some authors have considered sufficient for a book on India. However, at last we shall be able to add to it, in good measure.

We have a great deal to do and a great deal to see, and it is difficult to know where to start. If we were principally interested in politics, the obvious person to interview would be Gandhi, but Gandhi happened to be locked up. Whether he was rightly or wrongly locked up is a matter which we shall eventually be obliged to consider; in the meantime it need not greatly concern us. For though we are extremely interested in politics we are even more interested in people — and the question is, how do we get to know the people? Is there any short cut to an understanding of the national psychology? Where can we find mass emotion condensed, mass aspiration crystallized into significant form?

Obviously, in art. The modern Indian artists and the modern Indian architects are the men to guide us to the people, to show us the patterns in which they are grouping themselves, the high lights and low lights of their thought. The accent, of course, is on the word modern. The temples, the mosques, the monuments of antiquity, these can come later. After all, they are part of everybody's cultural heritage. A thousand photographs have given a foretaste of the Taj; we have all seen reproductions of the Ajanta frescoes; the museums of the world are well stocked with Hindu sculpture, Moghul miniatures, and the line drawings of the Rajputs. To see these things will be a joy, but it will be a familiar joy, like listening to an artist whom one has already heard on the gramophone.

The search is for fresh woods and pastures new.

II

It is unfortunate that we are obliged to begin our quest in Bombay, because this is a city of such unexampled architectural depravity that even a cursory glance at it is enough to send the sensitive visitor home on the next boat.

From the Gateway of India (which, by the way, is a sort of obese edition of the Marble Arch, cunningly placed so as to appear permanently out of drawing) to the slums round the cotton mills, it is one long agony.

Why did Aldous Huxley describe Bombay as being architecturally 'one of the most appalling cities of either hemisphere?' Why 'one of'? Surely he cannot have encountered anything worse? In Bombay, the cult of hideousness rises to the pitch of fanaticism. One walks the city through a succession of horrors in concrete and plaster, saying to oneself, 'This can't go on — look at this—no, look at *that* — it *must* stop soon'. But it doesn't. There is always something worse round the corner.

A walk through Bombay, for any person of even moderate sensibility, is a sort of aesthetic blitz. The architecture is not merely hideous, it is fiercely aggressive; the public buildings are like the evil creatures of a nightmare, crouching to spring. They are silhouetted against a background of shoddy tenements, that have sprung up in a rash all along the sea-shore.

This revolting city, in which there is hardly a building which could be charitably described as third-rate, is a disgrace to the British Empire. It puts us on a level with the Huns. And the strange thing about it is that nobody, apart from Mr. Huxley, appears to mind it in the least. For instance, in the centre of the

city are a number of municipal buildings which strongly resemble
a group of neolithic monsters having a fight. They are not only
monstrous but mongrel to the point of obscenity; in a single façade
you can find Gothic, Saracenic, Tudor, Hindu, late rococo and a
dash of Louis Seize. Sir Edwin Arnold, contemplating this gruesome display, observed that they were 'all very remarkable
structures' upon which he had looked 'with admiring eyes'. And
that great journalist G. W. Steevens thought Bombay had 'the
richest and stateliest buildings in India, challenging comparison
with almost any city in the world'. He added that 'the Briton feels
that he is a greater man for his first sight of Bombay'.

It made *me* feel that the sooner the British quit India, the better.

However, this was hardly a fair way of looking at it. A nation
gets the architecture it deserves. The vast majority of Bombay's
inhabitants are Indians. It is they who run the municipality, with
practically no outside interference; it is they who provide the
capital necessary to build these fiendish things, whether they are
private residences or business houses. Nobody — British or otherwise—dictates to an Indian millionaire when he puts up a block
of flats that is an affront to God and man.

It is what the Indians *like*. No . . . that is wrong. They neither
like nor dislike. They are indifferent. And it seems to be impossible to shake them out of their indifference.

I once tried to do so at a mass meeting at the Taj Mahal Hotel.
I stood up before an audience which included the majority of
Bombay's intelligentsia and insulted their city in the most uncompromising terms for nearly twenty minutes. The abuse was
laid on with a trowel. To make it more stinging, it was extremely
personal. I mentioned name after name, suggesting that the
residence of one famous millionaire resembled a 'malformed
wedding cake' and that the house of another was 'a gilded mouse
trap'. Any self-respecting horse, I hinted, would refuse to pass
these places, but would prefer to rush violently into the sea. I
even advocated sabotage, claiming that any member of the
audience who chose to blow up these things would be conferring
a real benefit on suffering humanity.

These remarks, one would have thought, were reasonably
succinct. It would be difficult to interpret them as compliments;

unless one lapsed into the language of the bargee it would be hard to express oneself more forcibly.

What happened? Bland smiles — amiable little smirks. No red faces, no angry interjections, nothing at all like that. Judging from the reaction — or lack of it — you would think that the audience had just been told how prettily the roses were growing round their doors.

On the following day I bought the newspapers, expecting splash headlines. After all, the journalists ought to know a good story when they met one. Here was a person — me — whom they had made the Oracle of the Hour, for reasons best known to themselves. The oracle had spoken — nay, had roared, hissed, spat in their faces. And the roaring, hissing and spitting had been about something which concerned them all, their own houses, their own streets, their own places of business.

But not one newspaper considered it worthy of a single paragraph. Oh, yes — the splash headlines were there, all right; the mild little political platitudes, in which the rest of the speech had consisted, were set in type which challenged the assault on Kharkov. But the one interesting thing, the one *creative* thing (for I had followed the attack by a detailed plan for the creation of an Indian Ministry of Fine Arts) was completely ignored.

Nobody cared.

This apathy blankets all India like a fog. If you were to tell Indian millionaires to their faces that their palaces should be blown up or turned into zoos for the more loathesome form of diseased reptiles, they would only smile blandly. They would not *hear*. They explode at the most innocent political generalization. But they merely smile when you tell them that they are the first of the Philistines.

It is apt to be fatiguing in the long run.

III

We now come up against a blank wall.

The blank wall is Art in Bombay.

If you turn to the official guide book of Bombay — a closely printed volume of 122 pages — you will find no reference to art in any shape or form.

If you ask the average European where you can see some pictures he will, firstly, direct you to the nearest cinema, and then with a hearty laugh, to the red light district.

If you apply to the Indian intelligentsia they will say 'Ah! Mr. A has several pictures by Mr. B in his house. He will be delighted to show them to you. His house is only 200 miles away, and soon he will ask you to tea.'

If you proceed to make inquiries about Mr. B's pictures you will find that nobody else has ever heard of them.

Then, by chance, you run into some fellow eccentric who likes looking at modern pictures. You bombard him with questions, to which the invariable reply is a weary negative.

'But there must be *some* collections?'

'There aren't.'

'There must be *some* studios — personalities — private stuff?'

'None.'

'There must be *some* critics — magazines — study circles?'

'No.'

Seeing your insistence, however, he will make one admission. 'There *is* the Bombay Art Society.'

Having exhausted so many expletives in describing the architecture of Bombay we will not weary the reader by describing the products of Bombay's Art Society; it is sufficient to state that in no other country in the world would they be given wall space. However, as we swiftly draw a veil over these depressing daubs we observe that they fall, roughly into two classes.

The first, and by far the largest class, consists in a series of slavish imitations of the Ajanta frescoes[1] and the Moghul[2] and Rajput schools.[3]

[1] The Ajanta caves were carved from the solid rock of a mountainside in Hyderabad State. Their original purpose was to house Buddhist monks. Begun in about 200 B.C. the frescoes which adorn their walls reached their highest pitch of perfection in the fifth century. They are incomparably the richest artistic inheritance in India, and it is interesting to note that if it had not been for the British they would probably have been lost for ever. After centuries of neglect, in which they nearly perished, some British soldiers stumbled on them in the year 1819, cleared out the tribesmen who were using them as cattle-sheds, and reported their existence to the British authorities, who were just in time to save them from destruction.

[2] A.D. 1550 to 1800. Coinciding with the period of the Moghul dynasty. Principally notable for its portraits in miniature.

[3] A.D. 1550 to 1900. Essentially Hindu in expression. Emanating from two large areas of Northern India, Rajputana and the Punjab Himalaya.

The second class consists in an equally slavish imitation of the French impressionists up to Renoir.

We need not concern ourselves at all with the second class.

But we *must* concern ourselves with the first, for we shall meet it all over India. Time and again we shall find the artists of young India staring fixedly into the past. For them the sun never rises, it only shines as a distant gleam in the gold of the Ajanta draperies. This is a very significant fact; there is food for thought in the spectacle of these young dreamers. They are, of course, fiercely nationalist; they are always shouting 'forward', and they are always looking back.

There is something to be learnt from this phenomenon. We shall best learn it by leaving Bombay and taking the train to Hyderabad.¹

IV

We have chosen Hyderabad because of all the states in India it is the one where we might most reasonably expect the young artist to get a square deal.

It is as large as France; it is 'progressive'; it is very prosperous. Its ruler, the Nizam, is notoriously the richest man alive. The value of his jewellery alone has been estimated at £300,000,000. His personal holding of gold bullion is so enormous that if he were to invest it he would cause an economic earthquake throughout the world. He is reputedly 'enlightened', and though a constitutional monarch he has great personal power.

Moreover, around the sun of His Exalted Highness revolves a positive constellation of minor social planets; palaces in Hyderabad city are as common as tobacco kiosks in Paris; and as if this were not enough, there is a considerable intelligentsia, whose members flutter in and out of the salon of the sparkling Mrs. Naidu, ex-President of Congress, and one of Gandhi's closest friends.

¹ The only possible exception to this survey is the J. J. School of Art, Bombay. However, everything good in it happens to be British. Its principal, Charles Gerrard, is himself a distinguished artist, and occasionally hypnotizes his pupils into following his lead. Doris Gerrard, his wife, is a sculptress of genius, completely wasted in India.

Surely, the young artist might feel justified in saying to himself: 'If paradise on earth there be, it is here, it is here, it is here!'

We will now enter this paradise.

My search for modern art in Hyderabad began on the day of my arrival. The lines it followed were so typical that they will be described very briefly for the last time. They will then serve, with equal accuracy, for Madras, Mysore, Calcutta, Lahore, etc. etc.

'I would like to see some modern India art.'

'Ah yes, you must see the Ajanta caves.'

Interlude during which it is explained that I would like to see something a little later than the fifth century. Painful pause. Then . . .

'You have seen the mosque of Mecca Masjed?'

Getting warmer. The foundation of this exquisite building was laid in 1023. But still, not quite warm enough.

We proceed through a long list of mosques and temples, advancing at the rate of about a century a minute. By persistent reiteration of the word 'modern' we reach the beginning of the nineteenth century, and there we stop.

'But I want to see the work of some Indian artist who is *alive*.'

'Alive?' they echo, 'Alive?'

And then at last they register — sometimes. They *do* know of one Indian artist who is alive — just one. It is always the 'greatest Indian artist' and it is always a different man. In Bengal it is Tagore, in Delhi it is Jamini Roy, in Madras it is Choudhuri.

Here, in Hyderabad, it was Chugtai.

'We have a very fine collection of paintings by Chugtai,' they said.

I had heard of Chugtai, though I had seen no reproductions of his work. However, at the moment, the quality of his work seemed less important than the singular fact that he was not dead.

'You are *sure* that he is alive?'

'Oh yes, he is quite alive,' said the first guide.

'Much alive,' agreed the second.

The aliveness of Mr. Chugtai being firmly established, we set out to see his paintings. They were, as far as I could gather, the *only* modern paintings that were hanging in the city of Hyderabad at all.

V

Hanging? Did I say hanging?

The word was premature.

For now, a very curious thing happened, which must be recorded even though it may sound trivial.

When I arrived at the gallery, and explained my business to the Curator — a charming old man — he led the way down long corridors and up winding stairs, past hundreds of faded, ancient miniatures, until at last we arrived at a back passage near the gentlemen's lavatory. And here, stacked against the wall and covered with dust, were quantities of pictures by the aforesaid Mr. Chugtai — who, you will remember, was so notably alive.

'But why . . .' I began, and then stopped, for the half-formed question might have sounded impertinent. Why, I wanted to ask, was Mr. Chugtai sitting covered with dust outside the gentlemen's lavatory? He appeared to be the one and only modern painter whose work was recognized by the artistic authorities of Hyderabad; at any rate he was the one and only painter who had been brought to my attention. Why this invidious position?

'We have not anywhere to hang his pictures,' said the Curator, with a note of apology.

'But surely there must be *somewhere*?'

'No; there is nowhere. It is a pity, because we think he is India's best modern painter.'

'How long have they been here?'

'For several years.'

'And do you mean to tell me that there is not a single room in the whole of Hyderabad city which contains a wall on which you can hang all these works by somebody whom you describe as India's best modern painter?'

Evidently not. It was incredible, but it was true.

Marvelling at this strange state of affairs, I began to examine the pictures. And then, there came a painful shock. For however alive Mr. Chugtai might be in the flesh it was only too glaringly apparent that the life he celebrated was — judged by Western standards — a wan and anaemic abstraction. It may be claimed that Western standards are inadmissible in assessing such work, in

H

which case, of course, any attempt at comparative aesthetic criticism is futile. However, if we do admit them, Chugtai's work, in spite of his considerable technical equipment, seemed to me to tell the same old story, the tragic story that India tells in a thousand voices: the artist had his back to the sunlight and was staring into the darkness of the past. He was conjuring up visions of ancient legends, desperately trying to recapture on his canvas a gleam or two of the glory that had so long faded. But the visions were as the shadows of waxworks, and the glory persistently evaded him.

In his disciples, who are numerous, these tendencies are woefully exaggerated. Chugtai owes much to Beardsley, and his copyists fill their drawings with Beardsley's twice-removed; he owes even more to sixteenth-century Chinese art, and again, his copyists make their canvases sprout with bamboos. But whereas the Chinese made their bamboos sing in the wind, the students only make them rustle in the dust. Here, there and everywhere is the influence of the Ajanta caves, with this difference, that the Ajanta artists, in those caves, have seen a great light and captured it, while their modern disciples have only groped pitifully in the darkness, and stumbled over a broken lamp.

I felt profoundly depressed, and as soon as possible I took leave of the kindly old Curator, and refreshed my eyes with the sweet and vivid colours of some early illuminated manuscripts of the Persian School, thankful to step back into the living past, out of the dead present.

In spite of all this, I still think that the works of Mr. Chugtai are worthy of a more elevated site than that which has been accorded to them, outside the door of the gentlemen's lavatory. At least he knows what he wants to say and is technically capable of saying it. The hosts of little Chugtais who follow in his footsteps can claim no such merit.

VI

'For heaven's sake stop grousing and find *something* pleasant to say!'
So the reader might exclaim, and I could not agree with him more fervently.

But how? What? Where? It is not as easy as you might imagine.

Listen to an Indian opinion for a change. In *The Cultural Heritage of India* the distinguished scholar, Dr. Coomarswamy, observes:

'*It may be said without fear of contradiction that our present poverty, quantitative and qualitative, in works of art, in competent artists, and effective connoisseurship is unique in the history of the world.*'[1]

It would be difficult to make a much more sweeping charge than *that*! And we could fill these pages with fragments equally damning, from the pens of Indians themselves.

However, we will push on. The next port of call was Mysore. There was nothing to be found there except an art school where the Curator had been for so many years at Ajanta that the very curves of his body suggested that he was part of a fresco himself. The work of his students was correspondingly derivative.

After passing through a number of smaller towns, and finding nothing, always nothing, we eventually arrive at Madras, the third largest city in India, immensely rich, a great seaport, vibrating with life.

The usual questions were made, the usual answers given. Nobody, Indian or British, had ever heard of any artists in Madras. ('Nobody' does not mean merely the bell-boy and the taxi-driver, but the most distinguished citizens.) They did not think that there was such a thing as an art gallery ... though, they added brightly, there was quite a good photographer not far from the Connemara Hotel.

In spite of these assurances, I persevered. It became a sort of obsession. This state of affairs seemed altogether too grotesque. There *must* be something . ... somewhere.

There was.

There was Mr. Choudhuri's art school.

It revealed itself by accident. I was driving through the city one day when we passed an old building which, for a change, was not markedly hideous. This was such a pleasant surprise that it seemed a good idea to get out and look at it. There was a little

[1] *The Cultural Heritage of India*, Coomarswamy. Vol. iii, p. 510.

garden stretching round the house, and a flight of steps leading to
something that resembled a studio. Was it possible that an artist
might possibly be lurking within?

It was. I walked up the steps, knocked on a door and found
myself in a lecture room where an art class was in progress. As
nobody seemed to mind my being there, I stayed and watched.

Over the productions of the students, we will draw the customary
veil; our sensibilities have already been sufficiently strained. But
when the students had departed I had a long talk with Choudhuri, and saw some of his work. It is not calculated to set the
Ganges on fire, but at least it is alive. Choudhuri has something
to say on canvas, and is technically competent to say it.

But what he said in words was more interesting than what he
said in paint. It was precisely what I have been saying throughout
this chapter. India was an artistic desert. There was not even a
polite pretence that art was of any importance. Artists might play
a small part in commerce — though, of course, the photographer
was regarded as a higher type of being. Otherwise, the artist was
on the level with the untouchable.[1]

VII

We will cut short this weary quest. Although it lasted for months
and was pursued all over India, it produced only one artist of any
consequence, by name Jamini Roy.

I saw my first Roy at Mrs. Naidu's in Hyderabad, and later
discovered considerable collections in Calcutta, Lahore, and other
places. After the sickly, smoky efforts of his contemporaries his
pictures have the effect of high explosives. He has several distinct
and highly stylized techniques (his early work had strong affinities
with Van Gogh) but the perennial source of his inspiration is the
folk art of Bengal, which is strong and gay and masculine.

He is an interesting person. Finding himself stifled by the deadly
atmosphere of commercial Calcutta, he cut short a career which

[1] Gandhi is probably typical of the modern Hindu's complete insensibility to art;
it simply does not enter his scheme of things. He might say about it what G. K.
Chesterton once said about music . . . 'I understand it so little that it does not even
annoy me!'

had every promise of success and fled to a remote village, where he proceeded to remodel his life, and his art, anew. This is how he set about it:

'The first thing he did was to change his palette. He left the European colours he had been employing for those that are found in nature and are used by the villagers. For the yellow ochre he adopted the holy *mati* and for bright yellow, *harital*. The Indian red he obtained from *geri mati*, blue from indigo, white from *kak khori* and white clay, black from burnt coconut shells and soot at the bottom of cooking vessels.'[1]

In any other country Roy's art would have attracted numerous disciples. He would have founded a 'school'. That he has not done so in India is presumably due to the fact that he is completely free from either religious or political prejudices; there is nothing in his painting to tell you whether he is a Hindu or a Muslim or a Christian; he simply looks life in the face and paints it. That is something which is quite beyond the comprehension of his contemporaries, to whom art must always be the handmaiden of politics which, in its turn, is the handmaiden of religion.

There was only one other 'art centre' of any importance in India which I might have visited. It was called Shantiniketan, and this chapter would not be complete without a word about it.

Shantiniketan means 'The Abode of Peace', and it lies high up in the hills near Darjeeling. It was founded some forty years ago by Rabindranath Tagore, who had an idea of turning it into a university. The university never materialized, but his brother, Abanindranath Tagore, developed it as an art school, and such it is to-day.

It has a great reputation throughout India. So, for that matter, has anything even vaguely connected with Rabindranath Tagore. Of course, if you are among those who think that Tagore was one of the world's greatest geniuses, to be spoken of in the same breath as Milton or Goethe, you will wish to go to Shantiniketan. If, however, you are of my opinion, and think that he was merely a charming minor poet, who owed more than he cared to admit to Yeats, you will probably stay away.

[1] From *Prefaces*, by Shahid Suhrawardy, Professor of Fine Arts at Calcutta University.

And you will *certainly* stay away if your main object is to see modern Indian art. I do not propose to waste any more expletives on the paintings of Abanindranath and his disciples. It is enough to say that they tell the old, old story which we have heard *ad nauseam* throughout our quest . . . they stare back into the past, feebly retracing the patterns of Ajanta. Here is the best that can be said about them by one of their most generous apologists, Percy Brown, A.R.A., Curator of the Victoria Memorial Hall, Calcutta, in his book *Indian Painting*.

'They have sought out the old historic painting of the past, the frescoes of Ajanta and Sigiriya, the religious banners of Tibet, and the miniatures of the Mughal and Rajput schools, and on these the new movement has been founded . . . The earnestness of these artists is undoubtedly a great asset, but whether this is a sufficiently stable basis on which to build up a national revival remains to be seen. . . .'

. It certainly does!

VIII

This chapter has been so exclusively in the minor key that it seems to call for a *coda* on a less depressing note. This can perhaps best be provided by a quotation from a lecture I recently delivered on 'India and the Arts' at the inaugural meeting in Bombay of the Society for the Propagation of Education and Culture. Owing to the fact that my fellow speaker was Professor Hill, President of the Royal Society, the meeting received more publicity than it might otherwise have done, and the unexpectedly favourable reaction to my ideas throughout India indicates that they may have had some value.

After attempting to define the word 'art' in its widest interpretation, by suggesting that it was 'a method by which man tries to bring some sort of order into the apparent chaos of the universe, to make a pattern out of the stars that seem to have been scattered so carelessly on the floor of heaven', and after suggesting that art was a more direct method of creating this 'order' than either science or religion, because it was sufficient unto itself, and neither

offered nor demanded any explanations . . . I chose the obvious
example of Rembrandt as an artist whose genius was so powerful
that it lit up the most drab and homely objects with a glow of
beauty and moulded them into forms of permanent significance.
(The reader is asked to pardon this chicken-food; he must remember that I was speaking in Bombay, where art, to the upper classes,
means ordering the Mona Lisa on your Christmas cards instead
of the customary robin in the snow).

In particular Rembrandt's butcher's shop seemed worth drawing to their attention, if only because a butcher's shop, to a Hindu
artist, is an indecent and sacrilegious object. I said:

'Take a crude piece of life like a butcher's shop in some poor
part of the city, with its hunks of meat, its patches of blood, and
the flies buzzing round it. The scientist, passing that shop, thinks
only how unhygienic it is, and how foolish men are to waste their
money on a diet so deficient in vitamins. The priest, passing that
shop, is reminded only of the cruelty of the slaughter, and the
passion of men's appetites. But when Rembrandt passed a shop
like that, 300 years ago, he paused, and his eyes lit up, and he
rejoiced, for he saw something quite different. He saw a pattern
of life, and it was a beautiful pattern, rich in colour and subtle in
design. And he sat down and painted it so that we, to-day, can
look through his eyes on to that butcher's shop, and feel, in doing
so, that we are looking through one of the many windows by which
men catch a glimpse of heaven.'

This, I suggested, summed up in a simple example, was what
was wrong with modern Indian art — the artists were not looking
at the butcher's shop (it is an interesting sidelight on the standards of Indian art criticism that several newspapers promptly
construed this as an attack upon vegetarianism!).

My final plea, which is really the only excuse for reprinting
these extracts, was as follows:

'It is up to the young artists to dip their brushes into the vivid
cauldron of Indian colour and to transfer it to their canvases. For
instance, I would like to see a young modern paint a religious
procession without even considering whether it was Hindu or
Muslim or Sikh or whatever it might be, but simply seeing it as
though it were a ballet, a feast of colour, the pink and gold of the

idol, and the purple flowers that are scattered before it, the streaks
of vermilion that are smeared on the foreheads of the worshippers,
and all the kaleidoscopic colours of the crowds that throng the
streets. I want to see somebody paint the monsoon, in all its
incredible drama, when the sky is like a giant curtain in a theatre,
just as the lights are sinking and the play is about to begin. Above
all, I want to see the young Indian artist paint the tragedy of
India, because it is only when a nation's tragedy is transfigured by
the means of art that it is seen in its proper proportions, that it
ceases to be merely a source of bitterness and frustration, and becomes an inspiration, a driving force towards better things. To
take an extreme example, the recent famine in Bengal was most
emphatically a subject which should have inspired the young
artists of India — it was a subject worthy of a Hogarth or a Goya —
it offered them an opportunity to create works which would have
aroused the world's pity and the world's shame. I do not say that
in any spirit of callousness, because I myself spent many days among
those forsaken people, and no man with half a heart could speak
lightly of such an experience. It is not from any idle desire to
make copy out of the misfortunes of others that I make this
suggestion, nor most certainly, because I believe in art for art's
sake. I do not. I believe in art for life's sake, art for India's sake,
and it is for the sake of India that I entreat the artists to come
down from their ivory towers, to step out into the open, into the
arena of modern life. They *can* do it. They *have* done it. And
always, when they have done it, it has been tremendously worth
while.

'Up till now I have been speaking to you, largely, of a record of
depressing failure. Let me reverse the pictures, for a change, and
give you an example of resounding success. One of the most
beautiful and important modern buildings that I have ever seen,
not only in India, but in any part of the world, is the Osmania
University at Hyderabad. As an example of the genius of the
modern architect it would be difficult to surpass, either in Europe
or in America. And why is this work so triumphant? Not because
the architect was inspired by the ideal of art for art's sake — which,
in India, means art for Ajanta's sake — it was because the architect was inspired by *life*. He looked at India and he saw that it

was torn by the communal problem. And instead of avoiding that problem, burying himself in his studio and ignoring it, he faced up to it, he said to himself, "Very well, there is the Hindu, and there is the Muslim, and I do not suggest, even on paper, that they are one and the same, because they are not. But I do suggest that they both have beauty, I do suggest that I can use both those types of beauty, and I'm damned well going to bring them together."

'And he damned well did bring them together. He brought them together in a superb unity, balancing a façade of Hindu pillars with a delicate Muslim arch, enriching a Muslim window with a border of Hindu decoration. It is as though the geniuses of the two cultures, each so separate, each so personal, each so highly characteristic, suddenly realized that in spite of those differences they spring from a common source, whose name was beauty.'

It was only some weeks after paying my tribute to this solitary example of 'Indian' architectural prowess that I discovered that the greater part of the original scheme and design of Osmania was the work of a *Belgian*, Monsieur Jasper!

CHAPTER VI

MUSICAL INTERLUDE

THE ideal travel book should be full of sounds. The dialogues should be set against the hum of traffic or the surge of seas. In the shades of the palaces there should be countless echoes — the echoes of footsteps in the corridors and rain on the roof. But most writers of travel books seem to be deaf; they enamel their skies to perfection but rob them of the birdsong; they trace most delicately the façade of a temple but forget the barrel organ which is bawling at the gates.

Though this is not a travel book it is a book in which we do a good deal of travelling, and in order that it should come to life we must now take note of the fact that throughout our wanderings we have been accompanied by a perpetual undercurrent of strange sounds. They have drifted in through the window when the peons were singing over a fire of wood and dung; they have rung out in the streets as a religious procession has wailed along in the wake of a pink and gold idol; they have burst from the radio like a sudden calamity; and sometimes, in the evening, as we walked through a village, there has been the sound of flutes from the paddy fields.

In other words, we have travelled to music. And since all art— in Walter Pater's over-quoted opinion — 'tends to the condition of music', it is high time that we cocked an ear and went out into the highways and by-ways in an endeavour to understand what this music is saying. Our quest may lead us to some strange places and some curious conclusions, but when it is over it is possible that we shall have learned several things about India which might otherwise have remained obscure.

II

The first act is laid in exalted circles. Since Indian music, to most Europeans, in not only quite incomprehensible but actively

repulsive, we must be quite sure that we hear the best.[1] We therefore enter a rich car, driven by a giant in white and apricot, and
sweep through the gates of a great white palace.

This palace is the residence of His Highness the Maharajah of X,
who has kindly arranged that his private orchestra shall give us a
command performance of Indian music for our especial benefit.

The Maharajah is an intensely musical young man. It is sym-
bolical of him that though his drawing-room is crowded with
photographs of royalty, his Steinway concert grand, in the corner
of the room, remains naked and immaculate. Everywhere else, on
tables, chairs, and bureaux, photographs abound in massive silver
frames, and from these frames the royalties seem to glare at one
another with mutual distrust, till you would think the air was full
of whispers ('My crown is bigger than yours' . . . 'you stole those
pearls from my aunt' . . . 'your ermine tails are coming off'). But
the Steinway remains sacred, inviolate.

When the Maharajah first granted an audience, he had not been
talking for ten minutes before it was clear that what he did not
know about music was not worth knowing. Not only had he an
encyclopaedic grasp of the classics but he revealed a remarkable
acquaintance with the *curiosa* of music . . . faded arias from Bellini,
obscure fragments of Couperin; at the same time his appreciation
of modern music was eager and sincere. He was even aware of the
existence of Benjamin Britten, Michael Tippett and Alan Raws-
thorne, which is more than can be said for the majority of the
British public.

There seemed to be only one gap in this formidable critical
equipment; he refused to discuss Indian music. When he heard
that I could not understand it, he merely smiled.

'Surely one *ought* to understand it,' I insisted. 'It oughn't to be
completely meaningless to Western minds? Or ought it?'

Still he smiled.

A last attempt. 'Does your Highness think . . .?' But whatever
His Highness did or did not think, he was evidently not disposed to
discuss it. He waved his hand and changed the subject.

---

[1] Europeans are by no means the only persons who feel this way. The Emperor
Aurangzeb once exclaimed, from the depths of his soul· 'Let Indian music be buried
so deep that neither voice nor echo shall issue from the grave.'

· The mystery remained as deep as ever. It was a most tantalizing business, as though one were straining after an echo from over the Eastern hills, that faded into silence just before its meaning was disclosed.

III

A few days after the audience with the Maharajah, a card arrived from the Palace announcing that a special performance of representative Indian music would be given that night for my benefit.

We will attend this concert without further delay.

It is held in a small room adjoining the royal apartments. The audience consists of the Lord Chamberlain, the Master of Ceremonies, the Private Secretary, and an unknown Personage who, judging by the size of the diamond on his finger, must be something very grand indeed.

Before us, squatting on their haunches, are the thirteen members of the orchestra, looking very attractive in their snow-white uniforms.

A word must be said about the composition of this orchestra. For though the basis of music, as of all arts, is rhythm, the means by which this rhythm is enunciated is through various types of sound which — in Western music — are beautiful *in themselves*. The trill of a flute is sweet even though it is saying nothing in particular; it has the pleasing quality of bird song. Tauber singing a simple scale, the rich beat of a well-tuned drum, the G string of a Stradivarius, the common cord of C on a Steinway . . . these are *in themselves* agreeable to the ear. They are not, of course, music, but to the Westerner, at least, they are the appropriate components of music, as opposed, let us say, to the screech of a tram car or the squawk of a crow.

These observations are elementary, but they are also necessary, for they immediately bring us face to face with one of the most startling differences between Indian and European music . . . *the actual quality of the sound with which the Indian makes his music is of altogether minor importance*. For instance, there is no such thing in India as 'a beautiful voice' as we know it; Caruso would receive no better marks than the nearest rag and bone merchant. For this reason, there are no Indian singing teachers, as we understand them, and no schools of voice production; the few Indian singers who have obtained wide reputations have won them for reasons which are only remotely connected with the vocal cords — their looks, their personality, their repertoire, their publicity — and, of course, their reputation for holiness.[1]

This is a simple but fundamental point, and until we have grasped it, Indian music will be meaningless. The fact that I have not grasped it will become apparent in the following description of the instruments of the Maharajah's orchestra. It was written immediately after returning from the concert. To-day I might be inclined to modify or, at least, to annotate it. We will let it stand, if only because it conveys fairly vividly the first impact of Indian music on a mind trained in the traditions of the West.

Here, then, are the Maharajah's Court Musicians.

5 Veenas. This is a sort of off-colour guitar. As a decoration it is charming, elaborately inlaid with silver, resting on a green lac-quered base. Played at a distance, in a high wind, it might soothe the savage breast, but it is hardly a thing to leave in the vicinity of nervous persons.

2 Thumbooris. This is a Veena that stands up instead of sitting down.

2 Mrudangams. This faintly resembles a drum.

1 Tabala. This is really another Mrudangam; it faintly resembles two drums, one sharp and one flat.

1 Flute. Of the Sicilian variety, sweet and plaintive, but quite inaudible when played within a hundred yards of the afore-said tongue-twisters.

2 Violins. At least, they looked like violins. However, they were both fitted with trumpets. And there was one other significant difference . . . the strings were of wire instead of catgut.

---

[1] This point is brought out very clearly in *The Music of India*, by Herbert Popley, B.A. (Oxford University Press). It quotes an illuminating comment by no less a person than Tagore, in the *Adyar Bulletin*, Madras. Tagore, discussing the singing of an Indian lady who had been trained in Europe, said: 'In India, any finesse in singing is regarded with contempt; no trouble is taken to make either voice or manner attractive. Singers are not ashamed if their top notes are cracked, their bass notes unnatural, their gestures violent. They take it to be their sole function to display their mastery over the forms and formalities of classic traditions.'

It was the tact of the gentleman with the diamond ring that averted a terrible gaff about these violins.

'You were wondering about the strings?' He spoke very softly.

'Yes, Why . . .?'

He held up his hand. 'Our religious traditions' . . . and his voice sank to a whisper, 'do not permit us to use catgut.'

So that was it! The same old story, which has had a thousand variations in Indian history, from the grease on the cartridges of the 1857 mutineers to the latest depredations of the sacred cows in the nearest bazaar. It all seemed strangely remote from pure music.

These instruments which now confront us are, broadly speaking, the *only* instruments ever available to Indian musicians. You can see pictures of exactly the same sort of thing in early sixteenth-century Moghul miniatures. They are, presumably, the best of their kind. They do not suggest themselves as appropriate for the expression of any very subtle or delicate emotions.

A programme was handed round. The first item read:

Hindustani Bhorgahi-Milanaba. Asavari Trilala. Thyagaraja.

The 'trilala' part sounded promising. Who would play it? A hasty glance at the orchestra revealed that there were signs of great emotion on the part of the first Thumboori player. He was a very ancient gentleman, who looked as if he ought to have been in bed hours ago. Perhaps he was going to do the trilala? He was certainly going to do *something*, for he was clearing his throat, and biting his nails and slithering on his behind in a manner quite frightening to behold.

A gentle voice broke the silence. It was the Lord Chamberlain. 'They may proceed?'

'If you please.'

He gave a signal.

Instantly, Bedlam was let loose. So shattering was the onslaught of sheer noise in the tiny room that for a few moments it was impossible to discern where it was all coming from; one could only clutch at the arms of the chair, blinking, and trying to locate the storm-centre of this cyclone of discord. Gradually, as the ear became attuned to the hullabaloo, it was evident that the main source of the trouble arose in the throat of the Ancient. He *was*

Trilala. *Tout ce qu'il y a de plus Trilala.* And he was emitting all the sounds of the slaughter house, with incredible gusto and abandon.

I stared at him with a horror that was difficult to conceal; how could so withered a creature produce so many farmyard noises at the same time? There was the sound of slaughtered pigs, of neighing horses, and gobbling turkeys, all cascading simultaneously from his lizard throat. He accompanied this cacophony with ceaseless shakings of the head and hunchings of the shoulders, and all the time his fingers plucked angrily at the strings, as though he were trying to tear them from their sockets.

The pandemonium ceased as abruptly as it had started. The Ancient, panting, regarded us with a malevolent eye. The Chamberlain turned and said:

'You find it interesting?'

'Indeed, yes.'

He nodded approvingly. 'It is a piece by Thyagaraja, one of our most celebrated composers.'

'Is he . . . is he dead?' I tried not to sound too hopeful.

'He died a hundred years ago.'

That was something.

Evidently further questions were expected. 'Has the piece any special significance?'

'Of course,' replied the Chamberlain. It is a prayer to the god Rama. Nearly all Thyagaraja's pieces are prayers to the god Rama. This one says 'O Rama listen to me, come closer to me O Rama!'

One could not help thinking that if Rama had come any closer to the Ancient he would have incurred so grave an injury to his eardrums that all future prayers would have been addressed to him in vain.

IV

The concert proceeded, and we burst straight into the ravishments of item 2, which proved to be a form of artillery bombardment entitled: *Sri Raghavendra, Gowlipuntha Adithala, Vainkapravina (Mr. Venkatagiriyappa).*

Once again the sounds of the slaughter house were much

evidence, but this time they came from the Tabala player whose voice, if possible, was even more raucous than that of the Ancient, but was mercifully somewhat less powerful.

Meanwhile, the violins were scraping away on the note of A . . . nothing but A, A, A, in a maddening monotone, as though they had forgotten themselves and turned into bagpipes. Whatever the singer did — and there wasn't much that he didn't — the violins kept on A. There was a terrible temptation to shout 'Come off it! Come unstuck—try A sharp, A flat, B, C, anything!' However, after a few moments it did not matter so much, for the drums came in and throbbed with such ferocity that they threatened to drown everything else.

On and on went the drums and the violins and the cattle noises; a glance at the clock showed that it was nearly a quarter of an hour since the devil had entered into the throat of the Tabala player, and judging from the look on his face it would be a very long time before he would be dispossessed.

Something must be done, and done quickly, or there would be a scene; I should howl or go berserk; and then there would be international complications, royal dungeons and all manner of unpleasantness.

Fortunately, at that moment, I had an idea. But before we mention what it was the reader must pardon yet another diversion. If he is bored by the discussion of aesthetic theory he can skip the section that follows.

First, a word in self-defence.

My irritation at the surrounding uproar was not merely a nervous reaction to the sheer blast of noise, nor was it in any way the result of complacency or superiority. Very much to the contrary.

It was due to a disagreeable suspicion that the root of all the trouble was not in the music but in myself.

It seemed impossible to believe that the music could be as frightful as it seemed; it was against all sense. Surely four hundred million Indians couldn't *all* be wrong? After all, several Western critics — not very many, not especially eminent, but at least worthy of a hearing—had written with sympathy of Indian music.[1] Besides—and this weighed more heavily—the Indian *people*, the peasants, the street-hawkers, the riff-raff in the bazaars, were obviously of a musical bent. They were always chanting and humming to themselves. If this was the sort of thing they liked, there must be something in it.

I *must* be wrong.

After this gesture of humility, I feel entitled to claim to be as well equipped as the average journalist for the expression of reasonable opinions on music. It has always been my first love; I was fairly advanced in counterpoint before my copy books had been discarded, and could read a full score at a time when newspapers were still beyond me.

I wish that it were possible to avoid this constant use of the first person singular. But the matter is so personal that there seems no other manner of approach. Perhaps the reader will take it not as a sign of egotism, but as a necessity of technique.

Where were we? Oh, yes ... being wrong about Indian music, trying to admit that the fault was in ourselves.

It was at this point that the aforesaid idea was born. There were some sheets of manuscript paper in my pocket, which I always carry in order to jot down any stray tune that may be floating in the air. Why not attempt to write down some of the uproar? It would be an extremely difficult task, but there seemed no alternative. And it *might* succeed; what made nonsense to the ear might make sense to the eye.

So now there occurred a very exhausting scene of slithering about on the floor, squatting among the players, taking notes. At one moment I was trying to fix the rhythm of the drum; at another,

---

[1] One of them, Pierre Loti, had written with positive ecstasy. In the fifth chapter of his diary, *L'Inde*, there is a long purple passage describing an evening of Indian music. However, Loti is obviously more excited by the musicians themselves than by the sound they are making; most of his swooning prose concerns 'the rose-scented garments of the players' ... 'the wonderful eyes of the young drummer boy'... 'the thin nervous fingers of the punkah walla' When he attempts to describe the music itself the best he can do is to call it 'a sort of wail ... an intense and passionate moan'. Which does not really get us much farther.

chasing the slippery line of a melody which was as elusive as an eel. It was hot, dusty work, and the Lord Chamberlain did not look as though he approved of it at all.

At the end of half an hour, a halt was called in order to study the notes on the manuscript paper. There was silence, excepting for the panting of the musicians, so that it was possible for the first time to get a clear idea of what had been going on. And — according to the manuscript — what had been going on was sheer chaos; it was like the gibberings of a lunatic. The rhythms were jumbled in hopeless confusion; as for the melodic lines, if a blind man had dotted the paper at random the result would have been equally enlightening.

With one exception. The Ancient, who was sustaining the chief role, had been roaring away throughout the entire piece; and from the manuscript it appeared that there had been a certain method in his madness. His melodic lines had something of the same shape — it was a very ugly shape, but at least something which could be dignified by the term of 'form'.

If we could isolate the Ancient? Detach him from the throb of the drums and the wail of the Thumbooris, so that he was revealed in all his naked horror? It would be alarming, but it might result in a revelation.

The request was made. 'Would this gentleman be so very kind' as to sing for us again?'

The Ancient's eyes glittered, he opened his mouth in savage anticipation.

'Only a few bars,' I interposed hastily. 'The opening phrases of the piece which has just finished.'

The Chamberlain nodded; the Ancient gulped and began. It was now possible to transcribe the notes with some degree of accuracy. It was a wandering, indeterminate wail in a ragged five-eight time.

I held up my hand; the Ancient reluctantly trailed off into silence.

'Now, if it would not be too much trouble, could he sing that again?'

'The same song?'

'If you please.'

'Exactly the same? You would not prefer something else?'

'No, I want him to repeat it *exactly* as he has just sung it.'

The request was communicated to the Ancient. He nodded; he began again. And now — note this well! — there were very wide variations in the performance. True, it was mostly in five-eight time, but there were three bars of two-four interposed for no conceivable reason. In addition, half-way through the phrase there was an elaborate cadenza which had not even been suggested on the first variation.

Once more I held up my hand; once more there was silence.

'That was exactly the same as the first time?' I inquired.

'*Exactly* the same. Did you not hear it?'

Oh yes, I had heard it. And I had heard something else besides. I had heard the secret of Indian music.

VI

The reader who is bored by aesthetic theory must start skipping again, though I wish he would try to grin and bear it, and read on. There is no reason why the critic of the arts should not be as exciting as the writer of detective stories. If you are on the track of an artistic crime the clues are as subtle, and the villains as contemptible — while the heroine is Beauty immaculate.

The best detective story that Edgar Allan Poe ever wrote was a literary essay. It was called 'The Rationale of Verse'; it described how he came to write 'The Raven'; and the manner in which he tracked down that awesome bird to its ultimate immortal perch was breathlessly exciting, even though his only instruments were dactyls and spondees, rhymes, and refrains.

So let us consider our little discovery as a clue in a mystery. The second version of the Ancient's song was quite different from the first, yet he claimed that it was exactly the same. Where does the discrepancy lead us?

It leads us, as we suggested above, straight to the heart of the secret. And that secret lies in the word *improvisation*. The Ancient was not singing a definite role, he was not interpreting a theme which had sung itself into the head of a composer and been fixed at the time; he was warbling at random. So were all the others. *The executants were themselves the composers.*

In case this sounds confusing, let us illustrate it with the simplest of parallels. It was precisely as though a group of actors had been taught the general theme of Hamlet, assigned their roles, given a few leading lines and then ordered to get on with the job. The result is easily imagined. Hamlet would dilate somewhat in this manner . . .

HAMLET To be or not to be, that is the question . . . that is the question . . . to be, to be, to be? Not to be? Not to be? Not to be?

(*Enter* OPHELIA)

OPHELIA Here are pansies, they're for thoughts, pansies, pansies, they're for thoughts . . .

HAMLET Whether, ah, whether 'tis nobler in the mind, the mind, the mind, to suffer.

OPHELIA Pansies, pansies, pansies . . .

We need not pursue the indignity. It is enough if the point is plain . . . Indian music is improvisation. And as such it is difficult to see how it can be judged as a serious art.[1]

Consider some of the extraordinary facts which are revealed to us as we delve deeper into this mystery.

There is no such thing as a piece of Indian music — a piece, that is to say, which can be taken up and rendered by any artist in any part of the country at any time. You cannot go into a shop and say 'I want X which was composed by Y', for the simple reason that Indian music is not printed; on the few occasions when it is set down at all it is written in various forms of local hieroglyphics which would be meaningless to any but the orchestra concerned. The best you can do is to go to some individual musician and learn one or two traditional themes (which are usually so primitive and threadbare that they hardly deserve to be called 'Themes'), and

---

[1] There are one or two important exceptions to this rule, notably in ballet music, where the precise movements of the dancers demand a similar precision from the orchestra. In ballet Indian music *is* fixed. But since ballet music represents barely one per cent of India's output, its existence cannot be regarded as invalidating our general argument.

when you have learnt them you can improvise to your heart's content. But even then, you cannot write them down for general consumption.

The implications of this basic fact are staggering. Who is the Indian Mozart? There is no such person. Who . . . to make it easier . . . is the Indian Strauss? You will search in vain.[1]

Occasionally, if you are lucky, you may hear the name of some 'composer', and for a brief moment you are persuaded that at last you are on the track of a real person, a flesh and blood artist whose work can be collected and assessed. In nine cases out of ten you will find that this 'composer' is only a sort of god in disguise, a mythical creature piping forlornly through the mists of antiquity. But now and then there seems to be some faint historical evidence for his existence.

You pursue your inquiries. This is what invariably happens . . .

'Is X still alive?'

'Oh no, he died a long time ago. Many, many years ago.'

'*Where* did he live?'

'Oh . . . in the south. Among the mountains. Beautiful mountains.'

'What did he write?'

'Songs . . . many songs.'

'Could I buy any copies of them?'

'. . . they are not written down.'

'. . . mes of the songs?'

'. . . o names.'

'. . . hey about?'

'Oh, many beautiful things. They sing of love and God and the beautiful sunshine.'

'I see. And who sings them?'

'Many people. In the villages and on the mountains.'

And that is as near as you will ever get to establishing the identity of any Indian composer. As material for an article in the

[1] It may be suggested that it is unfair to judge Indian music by the standards of Europe. Very well, judge it by the standards of a race which is considered inferior to the Indian — the negro. There is nothing in Indian music to compare in richness and virility with the negro spirituals. These have been shaped by time into forms of beauty and permanence; they will move men's hearts in a thousand years. But time has done nothing to Indian music; it has remained fluid, shapeless, and erratic.

Dictionary of National Biography it is, to say the least of it, somewhat sketchy.[1]

Now if you consider this question in a wider sense — the anonymity of Indian music, its fluidity and general vagueness — you will realize that it has more than a merely artistic significance; it is of real importance to the student of the Indian mentality, and of the political situation as it is affected by this mentality. For instance, owing to the lack of a common musical script, Indian music, like the Indian language, has remained entirely local. A Bengali song provokes ridicule in Madras; a Madrasi song is incomprehensible in Cochin; and both would be meaningless on the North-West Frontier. If the soldiers of India ever want to *march in step they will have to march in silence; if they try to sing, their feet will be caught in a tangle of warring rhythms.*

But these are matters for the student of national psychology; it is the purely musical argument which most interests me; and so the reader will perhaps pardon a few more paragraphs, of theory, before we revert to more mundane affairs.

VII

To sum up, our contention is that Indian music ~~cannot be~~ regarded as a serious art because:

(*a*) Indian music is almost entirely a matter of imp~~rovisati~~on.

(*b*) Art is not, never has been, and never can be, a ~~matter~~ of improvisation.

[1] The foregoing contentions will certainly be contested by apologists for Indian music. Fortunately there are a number of outspoken Indian critics who can be quoted in support of them, for instance Professor Prasad Mukerji of Lucknow University In his latest book *Modern Indian Culture* he boldly states:

'Indian music makes no distinction between composition and execution. Of composers in the European sense, i.e. as a class of artists whose function is not execution, *we have had none.*'

He makes a very illuminating disclosure, in this book, regarding the average cultured Indian's attitude to music as an art. It was recently proposed to incorporate a college of music in Lucknow University. There was an immediate outcry against this suggestion, for three reasons. 'It was claimed (1) that it would drag down the academic level, (2) it was not worthy of study because it was not a science, (3) *it would lower the social prestige of teachers and students alike, because music is associated in Lucknow with bad women!*'

There are practically no exceptions to this quite elemental rule, but as our case is so strong, let us be generous enough to admit them. Assuming that oratory is an art, let us grant that great occasions may sometimes provoke eloquence which is worthy of permanent record. Lincoln's Gettysburg speech is the classic example ... though even in this case he made rough notes on an envelope before delivering it. Again, legend has it that some of Chopin's music was improvised at a first sitting, in the exquisite shapes in which it was eventually crystallized for posterity. But after all, it *was* crystallized. If Chopin had sat down at the piano and run over the keys for the benefit of George Sand; and if when he had finished, that formidable lady had said 'Delicious — you really must play that again some time'; and if, after this compliment, he had left the piano, and there had been silence, broken only by the sound of soft embraces ... the music would have been lost, it would have melted away like the snow on the roofs of Paris. Perhaps Chopin did improvise, most composers do; but when his fingers strayed into some enchanting pattern of melody there was, thank heavens, an end of George Sand, an end of love, an end of everything — everything except sheets of manuscript, and bundles of sharpened pencils, and — most important of all — a well-worn piece of india-rubber.

This fundamental principle applies to all art. You cannot 'improvise' a statue; you cannot 'improvise' a fresco; you cannot even 'improvise' the lightest fragment of lyric poetry. Study the manuscript of Milton's *L'Allegro* ... so exquisitely named, for the title is like moonlit thistledown, and the whole work is spun of moonbeams. What does that manuscript tell us? That Milton flung himself into a chair at midnight, flicked a silvered quill, and transcribed his magic into an easy flowing hand? On the contrary. Very much on the contrary. The manuscript tells us that he got up early in the morning, and scraped and scratched, and chopped and changed, and frowned and faltered. The manuscript is like a battleground, strewn with slaughtered adjectives and strangled verbs. Only through a thunder-smoke of erasions and a barrage of blots did he eventually win through to victory. The victory was complete; the poem was perfect. But only God — and the students of the British Museum — realize the agonies he endured to attain it.

No, it will not do. Indian music has yet to suffer the pangs of birth, the pangs which are the inevitable accompaniment of all artistic creation. It must come down to earth, out of the everywhere into here. It must boldly proclaim itself on paper, in black and white. Till then it will remain like the roaring of the Ancient, a tale told by an idiot, full of . . .

But this book is already too full of familiar quotations.

CHAPTER VII

MUMBO-JUMBO

WE will now come down to earth.

The second part of our journey is nearly completed. It has been largely a journey through a desert. And yet . . . if we had paused to notice them . . . our attention would have been diverted by a number of strange growths which have sprung up in the waste places. These growths are the products of Hindu Nationalism. They have always been indigenous to the Indian soil, but only since the sun of independence has risen over the horizon have they lifted themselves out of the dust, waxed and prospered, and proclaimed their true shape and quality. They are of the utmost interest to the student of world affairs, for they bear no sort of resemblance to the social flora of any other country. Let us pause to examine them, beginning with what is perhaps the strangest growth of all — by name Ayurveda.

If the average British or American citizen were told that syphilis could be cured by drinking a cup of tea, he would be sceptical; modern civic education has taught him that venereal disease is not quite so simple as a cold in the head. He knows that syphilis, at least in its first two stages, is curable, but only after many months of skilled and specialized treatment by intravenous and intramuscular injections.

If he were told that this same cup of tea would cure tuberculosis, his scepticism would probably change into anger. He is aware that medical science is making wonderful progress; but this would not be an example of progress, it would be a piece of witchcraft. And when the same cup of tea was proffered to him as a specific for indigestion, and, as if that were not enough, for brain-fever, malaria, gonorrhoea, heart-failure, and bronchitis — *inter alia* — he would be inclined to throw back the cup of tea, rather violently, into the face of its inventor. For he feels that persons making such claims, even though they may themselves believe them, are among the enemies of society.

The cup of tea — or rather, a small tin of it — stands before me as I write. It has just come back from the analyst's. It is quite harmless, and, of course, utterly useless for any of the diseases for which it is recommended. Its basis is a herb that resembles the South American maté; it also contains thyme, cardamoms, cloves, and the dried petals of a few common flowers. It might perhaps have slightly digestive properties, but that is all.

Now, if this stuff had been purchased from a chemist of doubtful reputation, with the object of exposing its proprietors to prosecution for selling drugs under false pretences, there would not be very much in the story. But I did not come by it in that manner; it was presented to me, with due ceremony, by one of the leading lights of the Ayurvedic fraternity, a man of the greatest respectability, who — mark this well — thoroughly believed in its magic properties. And that *is* a story — a very good story, or perhaps we should say, a very bad one.

The story becomes even better — or worse — when we take into consideration the following facts:

Firstly, this cup of tea is typical of the whole Ayurvedic mumbo-jumbo, with its blend of astrology, witchcraft, and religion, and its highfalutin claims to have rediscovered ancient secrets which are far in advance of Western medicine.

Secondly, the cup of tea is being brewed in ever-increasing quantities. The Ayurvedic system is spreading like wildfire throughout modern India; new hospitals are being erected as fast as they can put them up; students are being enrolled by their thousands; *in many parts of India the number of Ayurvedic doctors is between twenty and thirty per cent greater than the number of allopathic, or 'Western' doctors.*

Thirdly, the main impetus for the growth of this gigantic quackery is, quite simply, nationalist fervour. It is the medical expression of Swadeshi. Ayurveda, whatever else it may be, is not British; it is purely Indian, and therefore must be supported. The mystical bent of the Indian mind — even in science — is so marked that we should not be justified in accusing its advocates of sharp practice, though some must surely be aware that its claims are unjustified; and if they or their families are suffering

from anything worse than a slight headache they do not hesitate
to consult a 'Western' physician.[1] Naturally, they do not advertise
these lapses from the true faith; it would not be good for trade;
and in the meantime they continue to treat the ignorant millions
of India with a variety of dopes which are tragically ineffective.

II

This is not the place for a lengthy description of the principles
of Ayurveda; several volumes would be needed. The main body
of the 'science' — if it can be dignified by such a name — is to be
found in the ancient Vedic scriptures, which were, of course, composed in Sanscrit. For over two thousand years Sanscrit was the
exclusive perquisite of the Brahmins, the most conservative body
of men that any nation has ever produced since history began. It
may therefore be gathered that Ayurveda did not advance very
far along the lines of pure research. It did, however, accumulate
to itself over the centuries a considerable debris of extraneous
superstitions, which had no connection with the original Vedic
hymns. For instance, it borrowed a good deal of the jargon of
astrology. It also allowed authority to two ancient Hindu
physicians by name Charaka and Susruta, whose works, translated
into Arabic by Ar Razi, are among the curios of medical literature.
Anything that sounded likely to appeal to the credulity of the
peasant was incorporated in Ayurveda; it became a sort of witch's
cauldron; and its brew, though flavoured strongly with a religious
essence, was sharpened by scraps of black magic, local fairy
tales, and even, from time to time, oddments from Western consulting rooms. The brew, none the less, remains largely poisonous
and — to Western Ideas — wholly bogus.
    This is the system which, in the name of nationalism, is rapidly
assuming responsibility for the health of one-fifth of the human
race.

[1] One classic example, of course, was afforded by Gandhi himself. Gandhi had
spent a large part of his life inveighing against European doctors, whose hospitals
he described as 'institutions for propagating sin'. Yet when he himself developed
appendicitis he forgot all about his Ayurvedic counsellors, and was operated upon
by a British doctor.

III

We can best appreciate what Ayurveda is by stating, as concisely as possible, what it is not. The things it does not attempt to do are even more significant than the things it does. Here are some of its more glaring omissions.

1. It disdains the microscope and ignores the whole field of bacteriology; its diagnosis is therefore mere guess-work.
2. It rejects surgery, and gives the cancer patient a pill.
3. It knows nothing of injections, either intravenous or intramuscular; the syphilitic is compelled to swallow crude arsenic, to the delight of the spirochete but the dismay of his liver.
4. It has no disinfectants adequate to deal with any but the simplest cases of sepsis; to prevent the spread of cholera it hangs a bunch of flowers over the doorway.
5. Anaesthetics, needless to say, are quite unknown to it, and when it requires an analgesic it relies on crude opium.
6. It deliberately rejects countless remedies that have unquestionably proved their worth in Western medicine, and it rejects them in favour of methods that can only be described as wishful thinking. Rather than use British sulphonamide preparations for pneumonia, or a Canadian product like insulin for diabetes, the Ayurvedic doctor's 'therapy' allows his patient to die on his hands.

One could write pages about the glaring deficiencies of Ayurveda; for the average man, these few sentences should be enough.

However, in fairness to Ayurveda, let us admit that just as witch-doctors in Western Africa have discovered herbs which are effective for local fevers, so the Ayurvedic physicians have evolved, through the centuries, certain simple remedies for common complaints.

It would hardly have been possible for them to have failed to do so. They can relieve constipation, they can temporarily abate the fever of malaria, they have several good tonics, an excellent cold cure, and a secret remedy for dysentery which is often very effective. In two cases they have actually anticipated Western medicine. They were the first to use gold in the treatment of consumption, and they were the first to use a certain oil, whose name I forget, in the treatment of leprosy. These discoveries were made many centuries ago, and if they had been followed up in the spirit of Western research, the world might have been saved much misery. But Ayurveda, as we have seen, was a secret Brahmin society. Its exponents were gripped fast by the superstition that if a secret was given to the world it would 'lose its virtue' (or, more likely, cease to be a source of profit) and therefore the seals were put on the bottles, the herbs were locked away, the sacred books were jealously guarded, and Time, in Indian medicine, stood still.

We have indicated, briefly but accurately, the pros and cons of Ayurveda. But we have forgotten one branch of this 'science' which has shown remarkable progress. It is not a very honourable branch but it plays so large a part in Ayurveda that it must be mentioned.

I V

In the manufacture of aphrodisiacs, Ayurveda reigns supreme.

On my desk lies the catalogue of one of the many firms of Ayurvedic chemists. These firms are legion; they have a huge mail-order business; and their long lists of testimonials offer impressive proof that the mystic approach to medicine is something which the Indian likes, demands, and is ready to pay for.

However, there is nothing mystic — and probably nothing exaggerated either — about their claims to stimulate the sexual appetite.

Concerning a certain ointment we are told that it will 'infuse young men with horse-like vigour'. The Westerner might feel alarmed by the prospect of developing such equine propensities; not so the Hindu.

Of a certain syrup it is written 'it causes the fountain of desire to spurt, just like the brilliant sun in the serene sky'. And as though this were not enough, for a dollar . . . 'it has the effect of cooling the brain as well' (it is somewhat difficult to reconcile those apparently conflicting properties).

There is a powder which acts so swiftly that 'we can say, in bold language, it churns up the blood'. 'Bold' is certainly the word. And another powder, for very old men, which will 'drive away their weakness as the dim darkness fades away with the rise of the sun in the eastern sky'. The picture of these vigorous ancients is not very attractive.

Under the heading 'For Help in Merriments' comes a positive spate of inflammatory mixtures. One trembles to think of what happens to those who take them. There is one which is said to make even the most jaded persons 'lusty with electric tremors' . . . a condition which, one would have thought, would lead sooner or later to the police court. But as it also 'induces a lofty attitude to life' the findings of the magistrate might be robbed of their terrors.

These things have been mentioned not for their 'amusement value' but because they have a profound significance. In India, where the shadow of death lies over so vast an area of the continent, where so many industries fade and languish, the trade in aphrodisiacs grows from year to year, absorbing an utterly disproportionate amount of the nation's income.

It is a disturbing thought . . . as though a death mask were twitching.

v

So extraordinary was the prospect of this apparent witchcraft, being openly practised by thousands of obviously respectable doctors in the middle of the twentieth century, that I took the earliest possible opportunity of studying Ayurvedic hospitals, teaching centres and dispensaries. Like all human institutions they varied widely; in fact, a few of them, particularly those in Hyderabad, had features which commanded admiration, for instead of slavishly adhering to Ayurveda, they were honest enough to incorporate the lessons of the West. But the average was appalling. And from that average the following composite picture is offered of a visit to a typical Ayurvedic centre.

Hardly have we crossed the threshold than an incident occurs which sets the tone of the whole place. One of the attendants rushes forward, flings himself into the dust, and feverishly pats the sandalled feet of the doctor who was showing us round. (This is a favourite Indian gesture to indicate humility and respect; many low-caste Indians precipitate themselves in this manner at the feet of a native policeman of whom they have inquired the way.) A few minutes later, this same attendant will be seen mixing medicines in the dispensary. Has he washed in the mean-time? A glance at his hands suggested that he has not.

However, perhaps it is foolish to feel squeamish about it. Is it not written in the books of Ayurveda, 'when we think of the medical culture of the Aryan sages, we forget ourselves with joy and feel proud of being born in India, the land purified by their foot-dust'?

There is sure to be plenty of foot-dust in this institution, and plenty of other dust as well, and whether it has any purifying qualities is an open question. The amount of it is certainly a tribute to the popularity of Ayurveda.

In the entrance, the professor pauses and points to the closely packed crowd that is milling round the consulting tables.

'All this,' he says, 'is but one of the many results of Swadeshi!' There is a fanatical ring in his voice as he pronounces that word. 'It is one of the signs that we are surging towards freedom!'

And surging towards a great many other things, we reflect, surveying the flushed and spotted faces of the wretched patients. No sort of attempt appears to have been made to segregate persons who are obviously suffering from infectious diseases. In front of us are five or six young men across whose bare chests and shoulders is plainly stamped the rash which indicates secondary syphilis. These unfortunates are about to be given a cup of tea or a few pinches of crude arsenic, and then dismissed as 'cured'!

We feel like going up and saying 'for heaven's sake run away from these deluded men . . . turn your back on it all and go to a western doctor who will tell you the worst, and save you and your children from endless horrors'.

But what can be done? The position is delicate in the extreme. The Ayurvedic doctors are suspicious of all Western investigators;

in order to obtain a true picture of their practices it is necessary to feign not only interest but active sympathy. The least sign of adverse criticism is likely to make them shut up like oysters. And so one is obliged to murmur 'splendid!' when all the time it would have been easier to shout 'shame!'

As it is, there will probably be no need for us to speak at all; the professors see to that. As we go round the building a cease-less torrent of words pour from their eager lips — words in which they claim that Ayurveda is capable of almost any miracle short of raising the dead from the grave — and they come pretty near to claiming *that*!

VI

Meanwhile we are being loaded with wreaths of flowers. These will be presented by successive batches of students whom we visit in their lecture rooms. As we enter each room several students spring to their feet, and burst into a song of welcome, at the end of which they hang a wreath round our necks. We feel we are playing the role of Judas, and would willingly have foregone the flowers, particularly as they prove to be full of insects which crawl down the spine. However, it is too late to turn back now.

The perpetual patter of mumbo-jumbo shows no signs of stop-ping. Ayurveda, they are saying, possesses the supreme remedies 'for the heart' ... 'for the blood' ... 'for the brain', etc., etc., all somewhat vague, to put it mildly. If the student attempts to infuse a little reality into the conversation, the following is the sort of dialogue we may expect:

'Have you a cure for diabetes?'

'Oh, yes.'

'Does it bear any resemblance to insulin?'

'Oh, no!'

'Is it as effective as insulin?'

A pause.

'Well *is* it?'

'Perhaps not.'

'Is it *at all* effective?'

'Well . . .'

'I had always understood,' we continue, 'that until the invention of insulin, diabetes — particularly in the case of persons under twenty — was incurable and generally fatal.   Is not that the case?'

'Well, perhaps . . .'

'But *isn't* it?'

Here the superintendent probably intervenes, saying that they must admit that Ayurveda is not 'perhaps' very effective in cases such as diabetes, and that 'if the patient does not respond' to the treatment, they would 'probably' advise him to 'go elsewhere'.

It needs no extensive knowledge of medicine to suggest that when they had finished with him he would probably have sunk into the diabetic coma from which there is no awakening.   However, what is the use?

Here is the record of a conversation I had with two Ayurvedic experts on the subject of syphilis. (This was before I had been presented with the cup of tea.)

'Oh, we have wonderful cures for syphilis. Many cures. And *we* use arsenic, too.'

'But I thought you didn't give injections.'

'We don't. We give it orally.'

'Arsenic? Orally?'

'Yes. Neosalvarsan. In very small doses, of course.'

'And how long does it take to effect a complete cure?'

'Two or three months.'

I blinked at this extraordinary statement.

'Two or three *years*,' corrected the elder doctor.

The discrepancy did not seem to worry the younger doctor.

'In any case,' he said, 'we cure it.' And he proceeded to tell me of the case of somebody's servant who had come to the hospital with secondary syphilis, whose blood three months later had given a negative reaction to the Wasserman test.[1] As if that — even if it were true, which is improbable — was proof of a permanent cure!

I happen to have made a fairly close study of the ravages of this

[1] Why the Ayurvedic doctors permit themselves to borrow an essentially Western process like the Wasserman methods of diagnosis, is a mystery. The fact remains, they do.

disease and of the efforts which Western medical science has made to check it. Long ago I had reached the same conclusion as C. MacLaurin, who summed up his study of European history with the devastating generalization . . . 'war and syphilis have been the two chief scourges of mankind'.[1]

It was MacLaurin who originally set me on the track of this scourge, a knowledge of whose evil workings is essential not only to the contemporary historian but to the novelist, the journalist, the priest . . . and indeed to all who study the hearts of men.

The war had only increased the urgent need for public knowledge. The seaports of Britain showed an increase of over 100 per cent; the munition factories provided figures almost as startling; and the flames of the curse were fanned by the influx of large numbers of workers from Ireland, where, unfortunately, the policy of the church has been firmly set against any tendency towards sexual enlightenment.

This 'hush hush' policy had been fought for many years by several of us in Fleet Street, and it was a happy moment, when, early in the war, I persuaded the editor of a great and influential newspaper to publish an article — the first of its kind — in which the word 'syphilis' was plainly printed in black and white, instead of being cloaked by the cowardly euphemism . . . 'a certain loathsome disease'.

The irresponsible credulity of the Ayurvedic doctors, therefore, was a little too much for my party manners. I murmured a few vague 'Reallys' and 'How interestings', observed that it was very hot, and took my leave.

Apart from the strong impetus given to Ayurveda by the rise of nationalism, it has been quick to exploit the element of the picturesque in which it is so rich.

'We use powdered pearls!' they exclaim.

'And the navels of unicorns, no doubt,' we feel like retorting.

'Jewels play a great part in our system,' they cry; 'rubies and emeralds and many semi-precious stones.'

I myself have tasted a spoonful of the celebrated mixture of powdered pearls, which is mixed into a glistering white paste with sugar and rose-water. After taking it I felt, for a moment,

[1] *Post Mortem,* by C. MacLaurin (Jonathan Cape).

like a sort of inverted Cleopatra, but had no other adverse symptoms. They said it was 'good for the heart'. Then there is a fragrant compound made from figs and pomegranates and the petals of rose leaves; I had a dollop of that. I declined, however, a stuff which was made from silk-worm cocoons; it looked as if life was not yet quite extinct in it.

However, there is one testimonial I *can* give them. Once, when I was in Bengal, an elderly Ayurvedic doctor, hearing that I was interested in his 'science' wrote to tell me that he would shortly be sending me a bottle of medicine which would solve all my greatest problems.

In due course the bottle arrived. I undid the wrapping and read the directions on the label.

But no . . . really *no*. This was too much.

It was an aphrodisiac. More than that, it was the sort which infused one with 'horse-like vigour'.

I was on the point of throwing the bottle out of the window when I changed my mind. I decided to give it to Hussein; a little extra vigour would do him no harm, judging from the languor with which he pressed my trousers.

On the following day, when Hussein called me he said, 'I drank sahib's bottle last night'.

'*All* of it, Hussein?'

'Yes, sahib. Very good medicine, sahib.'

He laid out my trousers. They certainly were pressed better. But his hands were very shaky, and he looked suspiciously dark under the eyes.

So perhaps there is something to be said for Ayurveda after all.

CHAPTER VIII

GAOL-BIRD

THE voice of the woman at the other end of the telephone was light and musical and full of laughter.

'I was in gaol,' she said, 'when you first arrived, which is why we have not met before. However, I'm out again, for the moment at least; so you will come to tea? This afternoon, then, at five-thirty.'

I hung up, and scribbled on the telephone pad the words 'gaol — Naidu — shock'. This memorandum had a simple object; I wanted to remember the shock which those words had caused — 'I was in gaol' — coming as they did from a cultured and charming woman like Mrs. Naidu. Constantly, in India, as we noted earlier in the book, one is stunned by the impact of these shocks, only to find, a few weeks later, that they are shocks no longer; they are accepted, absorbed into the general fabric of life. However, 'I was in gaol' still evokes a feeling of surprise, particularly as it is associated with that charming voice, so very sweet and — if she will forgive the suggestion —so very Mayfair.

Before we go to call on Mrs. Naidu let us take a brief stock of our bearings. We are back in Hyderabad where, you may remember, we began our search for Indian art. A great deal has happened in the meantime, to ourselves, to India, and the world at large, but this is not yet the place to record it. For the moment it is sufficient to observe that it is the month of October, that Lord Linlithgow's long and anxious reign as Viceroy is drawing to a close, and that the political situation is quiet, apart from the ominous rumblings caused by the famine in Bengal, a disaster which we shall later be investigating on the spot.

As we pause on the threshold of Mrs. Naidu's house, a word must be said about her importance on the Indian scene. Apart from Dr. Ambedkar, she is the first major political figure who has made her appearance in this book. The omission has been deliberate. It seemed to me quite futile to plunge into Indian politics before making any attempt to understand the Indian people. The utter lack of any factual and atmospheric background is the cause of the unreality of so many debates about India, whether they are in the House of Commons or the columns of the American press. Nothing could be more ludicrous than the spectacle of elderly British liberals gravely applying the principles of Western democracy to a country in which democracy has about as much hope of surviving as a clump of Scottish heather in the desert of Thar. Nothing could be more grotesque than the determination of American publicists, such as the bucolic Miss Pearl Buck, to talk about the Indian 'people', as though there were no difference between a Gond aboriginal, a Bombay boxwallah, a Punjab Chaprasi, a Madrasi lawyer, a Travancore untouchable, a Sikh warrior, a Pathan moneylender, Mr. Gandhi and His Highness The Aga Khan.

Any debate on the intricacies of Indian politics by men who have never been east of Suez must inevitably be as futile as would be a debate of the affairs of London County Council by men who had never been west of Karachi.

However, we have now reached a stage where we have at least a rough idea of the background against which the major figures of Indian politics move and have their being. Among these figures Mrs. Naidu stands out, and always has stood out, in high relief. Sixty-four years old, she has lived—to put it mildly—a full life. She was the first Indian woman to be elected President of Congress; wherever the fight had been the thickest she was to be found, fluttering a gaily-bordered Saree, with feminine defiance, in the face of the British raj. She had been swept into *lathi* charges, had held Gandhi's hand at some of the most crucial moments of his career, and ... while finding time to produce a considerable family, had written a great deal of enchanting poetry. One feels a temptation to say, with Pater, that 'all these things had been to her as the sound of flutes', but perhaps that would be going a little too far. The fact remains that she still gives the impression of being a young woman. She has allure, and she knows it.

11

Punctually at five o'clock the ex-gaol-bird sat cross-legged on a divan, talking with a bubble and brilliance that was reminiscent. of Lady Oxford at her best, in the old Bedford Square days, when yellow tulips were two shillings a dozen and sherry was just a drink, and not an Event.

'This house is like Sanger's circus', she announced. The warning was necessary. Behind my chair there suddenly bobbed up a very thin daughter with a deep Girton voice. 'What has happened to you?' she demanded. 'When I heard you speak at Oxford you were plump and brilliant; now you are thinner than I am and you haven't said a thing.' Another not-so-thin daughter rushed into the room proclaiming fiercely, 'If you've come here for a lesson in anti-Imperialism you've certainly come to the right place!'

'Be quiet, my dear,' intervened Mrs. Naidu. 'Mr. Nichols hasn't had his tea yet.'

There was a son who seemed wrapped in yogic meditation; and another son with a black beard, who proved to be an Ayurvedic doctor; he lay back in his chair, exploding with general Ayurvedic principles, such as . . . 'The solar system has five centres in us: one, reasoning; two, the eyes; three, the liver; four, the creative power; five, the solar plexus'. As I was trying to cope with some. very slippery cucumber sandwiches at the time I may not have quoted him quite correctly, but that was the general idea. There were various other people, including Mrs. Naidu's husband, who looked amiably puzzled by the general uproar, which was increased by the fact that every other minute a servant entered with an envelope containing money for the Famine Relief Fund. Mrs. Naidu slit open each envelope with a whoop of joy, and waved rupee notes over her head . . . 'This is from X, he's a darling, *much* more than he can afford.' 'Look at this from Y . . . if she thinks she's going to get away with ten rupees, she's very much mistaken. Ring her up, darling, and ask her to tea.'

Last but not least there was a Siamese cat, of such overpowering elegance and charm that it was only by the strictest mental concentration that I was able to avoid giving all my attention to it.

At last the circus seemed to fold up its tents and depart — how, I never quite realized, for nobody went through the formality of saying good-bye. I was left alone with Mrs. Naidu, the chief performer.

'What shall we talk about?' she asked.

'Gaol, if you don't mind.'

'Why should I mind? I've nothing to be ashamed of. And some of it was very entertaining.'

We will skip the whys and the wherefores of the mass Congress arrests. (They took place on August 8th, 1942.) They will be the subject of endless debate, and when history gives its final verdict it will record an emphatic vote in favour of the British Empire. If it had not been for those arrests the whole of India would have been plunged into bloody chaos within a week; the Japanese would have swept through the gates carrying fire and slaughter, and the war would have been indefinitely prolonged. Mrs. Naidu, naturally, does not agree with this view. She maintains that the majority of Congress were innocent lambs, who had no subversive intentions; and as far as she herself is concerned she may be quite right. We will not go into all that. It is more interesting to consider her merely as a cultured, charming woman, swept into gaol as the result of her convictions.

It was in Bombay, on the night of August 7th, 1942. A few hours earlier there had been a great Congress meeting, attended by all the leaders, from Gandhi downwards. This meeting had been marked by a number of fiery speeches; there was thunder in the air, and Mrs. Naidu, with feminine intuition, was the first to sniff that thunder.

'Late in the evening,' she said, 'I had a hunch. I said to Patel,[1] "I believe we're going to be arrested". "Don't be silly," he said. "Why?" "I don't know," I said, "but I'm sure we are. And very soon too; to-night or to-morrow." He kept on asking me why, and I remember I said, "Because the British always get in a panic if we even begin to blow our noses".

'Well,' she continued, 'that night, or rather, early the following

[1] Sardar Patel, the Party Boss, and virtual dictator of the eight Congress ministries.

morning, it happened. I went to bed as usual, and then the hunch came back so strongly that I got up, had a cold bath, and began to pack. And sure enough, at 4 a.m., the bell rang, and there they were. When they saw me, all dressed up and waiting for them, they looked so astonished that I couldn't help laughing. "But, madame," they cried, "how did you know? We were only told ourselves an hour ago." "Just a hunch," I answered, and they had to believe me, because there was no way in which I could possibly have received any information; the house had been guarded all night and all the telephone wires had been cut.

'When we reached the station,' she went on, 'it was about dawn. I was feeling quite gay; I'd had time to dress properly, and my hat was on straight — and anyway, it was all in the day's work. But some of the others were very disgruntled; they had been completely taken by surprise. Gandhiji had been saying his prayers and I must say that the police were very courteous and stayed outside till he had finished. But I don't think Patel had been saying *his* prayers —and judging by the expression on the faces of some of the others, they hadn't been saying them either.

'There were forty of us, and we had a lovely special train. The Chief of the C.I.D. came up to me, looking very anxious, and said, "I do hope there is not going to be any trouble". "So do I," I said. He asked me, "Will you sit with Mr. Gandhi in the train and keep him quiet?" I *had* to laugh again. I said that I would be honoured to sit with Gandhiji but really there wouldn't be any need to keep him quiet; he certainly wouldn't try to jump out of the window or pull the communication cord or anything like that. And, of course, Gandhiji was as quiet as a mouse; he wasn't even angry; all he kept on saying was, "But it's so *silly*, so very *silly* . . . just when I was about to negotiate with the Viceroy".

'Meanwhile,' she continued, 'I was wondering where they were taking us; it's a curious feeling, being whirled off in the early hours of the morning to a completely unknown destination. I hoped it would be to the old prison where I'd been ten years before, and where I'd planted 108 trees, or was it 109? Anyway, I'd be glad to see those trees again. As you know, they took us to the Aga Khan's so-called palace . . .'

'Why "so-called"?' I interrupted.

'Well, you know, it's not really so much of a palace, not when you think of the Aga Khan. Another nut? Or one of those things with cherries?'

'No thank you.'

'And really' — in the same breath — 'we were quite comfortable. The rooms were pleasant and the food was good, and the British were most polite. But' . . . and here a dangerous gleam came into her eyes . . . 'what they didn't seem to realize was that we would far rather have starved on a rubbish heap, in freedom, than have been kept inside in luxury. We were utterly isolated, but *utterly*. Not a fly came in from outside; we saw nobody but the doctor, and he always looked at us in a sort of terror as though he thought we were going to be tactless enough to die or fade away or do something generally embarrassing. And for three weeks we had not a scrap of news. All the papers were banned, and there was no radio; even our families had no idea where we'd been taken. We were guarded like precious jewels in a casket . . . are you sure you won't have another cup of tea?'

'No thank you.'

'It's cold and it's black, but it *is* tea. Still, if you insist. Where was I?'

'Being guarded like a jewel in a casket.'

'So I was. Well . . .'

We can skip the next part of the story; prison life is inevitably monotonous, even when it centres round so sparkling a personality as Mrs. Naidu. Now and then, of course, there were brighter moments; one of them occurred when C. Rajagopalachari, himself an ex-President of Congress, came to visit Gandhi. The last time C.R. had seen him Gandhi had been reading *The Hound of Heaven*, and Mrs. Naidu had been sitting by him trying to explain what it all meant.

'Well,' said C.R., 'have you finished that dog poem yet?'

Perhaps the most dramatic thing she told me was about Gandhi's famous fast of February 1943. A number of acid things have been said about that fast; it has been suggested that the state of the Mahatma's health chart varied according to the political situation, that when the Viceroy looked like yielding, Gandhi grew rapidly worse, and when it was quite evident that the Viceroy was adamant, Gandhi took a marked turn for the better. I do not credit these suggestions; they are ungenerous, they are also unnecessary. No doubt the fast was indefensible; it was barefaced blackmail and whatever its outcome it could have no effect on the general situation except to confuse the issues. None the less, our contempt for this form of political masochism does not justify us in assuming that it was a fake.

Mrs. Naidu, at least, had a very different story to tell. She said that towards the end of the seventh day, Gandhi, to all appearances ... died. He had been sinking rapidly since the morning; they were gathered round his bedside, fearing the worst. As the dusk deepened, the worst seemed to happen; his breathing ceased, his pulse faltered and stopped. 'It was as though a light had gone out of the world,' she said. *How* he came back, by what miracle the frail, wizened body reasserted itself, she could not explain; she was too moved by the memory of it. All she could suggest was that it was a supreme effort of will. She is probably right; India is full of men who have ventured far into the valley of the shadow, and have turned and retraced their steps.

I V

The curious feature of the foregoing account is that the things which Mrs. Naidu did not mention are really more significant than the things which she did.

She was very frank; she did not attempt to conceal her hatred of 'British Imperialism'; if she had had any complaints of the prison regime, not only as it applied to herself but to others less fortunately situated, she would certainly have proclaimed them. But she did not.

Charges of actual brutality, needless to say, one would not expect. Even the most hysterical opponent of British rule has not yet seriously charged us with emulating the methods of the Nazi concentration camps.[1] But one might well have expected to be told

[1] The number of occasions when physical violence has been cited against the British, even in times of riot and civil commotion, is astonishingly small. Apart from one or two unhappy episodes, of which Amritzar is the most notorious, the charges boil down to a few bruised heads and broken limbs. And even these, it must be remembered, were usually caused by *Indian* policemen, defending themselves against greatly superior odds.

of discourtesy, of the irritations of petty officialdom, of inadequate diet, and of attempts at mental intimidation. The fact that Mrs. Naidu made no such charges justifies us in assuming that there was never any occasion to make them.

When British critics point accusing fingers at the overflowing prisons of India, when they draw invidious comparisons between our avowed principles and our actual practice, they are ignoring several vital factors — apart altogether from the fact that a large proportion of the prisoners were self-confessed saboteurs, who, in any other country at war, would have been shot out of hand.

The first of these factors is that large numbers of the prisoners positively *forced* themselves behind the bars. It was not a question of how to bring them in but how to keep them out. It was the 'thing' to go to prison. It was smart, it was chic. The shadow of the prison bars had the same *cachet* as the scars of the Heidelburg student. Most of all, a spell in prison was an excellent financial investment. For the politician, of course, it was essential, and for the journalist, nearly so; but even for the smaller fry it was time well spent. There were always plenty of employers waiting with open arms for 'safe' young men — young men who realized that their true interests lay in the exclusion of British capital from the motherland.

Honest Congress politicians do not deny this. Why should they? It was a very ingenious way of embarrassing the British raj; apart from the sheer physical difficulty of finding accommodation for so many voluntary *detenus*, at a time when every available building was overflowing with the military, the quotation of the prison figures had a very adverse effect on British prestige abroad.

Had the true facts been known, it would not have been only British prestige that was affected. There is something profoundly disquieting, to the Western observer, in this mass-masochism. It may be suggested that the Indians had no alternative. Even if we grant this suggestion (which I do not) such conduct is unthinkable in the youth of any other country. It is neither virile nor creative. But it is profoundly Hindu. It is an aspect of a spirit which is to be observed in many walks of Hindu life.

The other important factor which is ignored by our critics is the large proportion of prisoners who came from classes so impover-

ished that prison life, by comparison with their own, was a luxury.
They had no political affiliations. Gandhi, Jinnah, Nehru —
these were names that meant nothing to them. All they knew was
that they were hungry and homeless. Normally, they would have
avoided prison like the plague; it had an evil name, and after they
came out of it they would have been even more despised and
rejected than before. But now, for reasons which they did not
pretend to understand, prison had suddenly become 'respectable'.
Their elders and their betters were clamouring to get inside. And
inside, as they well knew, was good food, and clean beds, and no
cares for the morrow.

To the arguments of their empty stomachs was added the glory
of martyrdom; the result was inevitable; they threw their stones,
flashed their knives, and swarmed through the gates, their faces
wreathed in smiles.

PART THREE

CHAPTER I

HEIL HINDU!

THIS is probably the first presentation of India in which Gandhi makes his entrance in the third act. Usually he comes on with the rise of the curtain, and dominates the play till its final fall; and even during his brief exits you can hear him making noises off.

'But then Gandhi is India' . . . you may tell me. 'We have been told so over and over again. So it must be true.'

On the contrary, it is blatantly untrue. Gandhi is violently repudiated by the overwhelming majority of 100 million Muslims, who regard him, quite rightly, as their most dangerous enemy. Gandhi is no more 'India' to them than Laval is France to the Free French. Of course, you do not hear much about these Muslims; they have little cash to spare for propaganda, nor have they Gandhi's genius for publicity. But they surely have some right to be heard, and in a later chapter we shall hear them.

In the meantime, let us switch some belated limelight on to the elderly *prima donna* of the Hindu political stage. We cannot meet him in the flesh because, during the whole of my stay in India, he was in gaol. The phrase 'in gaol' is somewhat misleading, because the gaol was one of the Aga Khan's palaces, and he could have walked out of it at any moment he chose, by signing a half-sheet of notepaper. He would not have been signing away his soul, he would not have been betraying himself or anybody else, nor would he have been influencing in the smallest degree, either for better or for worse, the cause of India's independence. He would simply have been signing a guarantee not to sabotage the war effort, not to lay his country open to the Japanese, not to stab the British and American armies in the back. That was all he was asked to do, and he would not do it. He preferred to stay in gaol, polishing his halo, while his myriads of admirers confused the issue with a smoke-barrage of verbal incense that swept round the whole world, even creeping into the legislatures of Britain and the U.S.A., tickling the throats of parliamentarians and senators, and causing them to cough up a

157

collection of sheer nonsense unparalleled in the annals of democratic institutions.

It is the almost invariable custom of writers who criticize Gandhi
to soften their remarks with all manner of qualifications; they say
'we think his policy would not work — but of course we realize
that this is because he is a saint'; or they say 'we differ from his
reading of the facts — but we do not for a moment question his
high regard for Truth'. It is almost as though they were afraid of
the little man, as though he might suddenly swoop out of the ether
and strike them dead.

I do not choose to follow this example. I have no incense to
spare for Mr. Gandhi, except the small pinch which one grudgingly
tosses at the ugly feet of any other dictator, as a reluctant tribute
to his theatrical qualities. For the rest, apart from the fact that in
Britain's most dangerous hour he chose to stab us in the back in
a manner strongly resembling Mussolini's thrust at falling France,
he seems to me a typical Hindu politician, of quite inordinate
vanity, narrow, ignorant, and supremely intolerant. As for his
much-vaunted regard for Truth . . . well, really, Mr. Gandhi
should look up that word in the dictionary and then, if he is wise,
he will change the subject as rapidly as possible.

But I do not propose to change the subject. Since this book of
mine will inevitably be attacked by Gandhi's apologists, let us
refer, for a moment, to the manner in which Gandhi himself
attacked another book which was not to his liking, by name
Mother India. When *Mother India* was published, it shook the world
like a clap of thunder. The thunder rolled on and on, the storm
showed no sign of abating, and Gandhi had to do something about it.
So he wrote an attack on the book, six and a half columns long,
and he called it 'The Drain Inspector's Report'. As an example of
the work of a man who professes so high a regard for 'Truth' it is,
to say the least of it, surprising.[1]

In impassioned language he branded the work as a hotchpotch
of lies; it was 'doubly untruthful' . . . it was a 'crime committed
against me' . . . 'I warn American and English readers against
believing this book'.

[1] For a fuller account of this affair see *After Mother India*, by Harry H. Field
(Jonathan Cape, London).

His sharpest comments were reserved for the account of the interview with himself in which he gave a message to the world. He suggested that this was a tissue of untruths. '*I do not remember* having given the message Miss Mayo imputes to me, and the only one present who took any notes at the time has *no recollection* of the message imputed to me.'

Unfortunately—most unfortunately for the Hindu George Washington—irrefutable documentary evidence exists to prove that this message which Gandhi and his associates so suddenly and so conveniently forgot, was not only given, but revised and approved by Gandhi himself, typed by his secretary, signed by himself, and dispatched to the authoress with a covering letter . . . beginning, ironically enough, 'Dear Friend'.

All this — we are asked to believe — Gandhi 'forgot'. Well, well . . . that may be the case. But surely so convenient a *lapsus memoriae* somewhat invalidates his claim for the Washington stakes?[1]

In 'The Drain Inspector's Report', which is really a museum piece for the student of the Gandhi version of 'Truth', he committed himself to a great many more . . . shall we say . . . 'misstatements'. He not only challenged Miss Mayo, he challenged history itself. One of Miss Mayo's most moving passages described an ovation given to the Prince of Wales, on his arrival in Bombay. The whole Press, not only of India but of Britain and the U.S., was plastered with pictures and accounts of this ovation, which was so spectacular that it made a first class news-story. Here is how the *Times of India* — hardly an irresponsible journal, and one of the three papers which Gandhi reads every day — described the event:

'The police were almost helpless; they could not keep back the crowds which surged forward to get a closer glimpse of the Prince. Traffic regulations went to the winds. The crowds surrounded his car and cheered . . . such cheering as has never been heard in Bombay before. Even the wearers of Gandhi caps took them off

---

[1] A photograph of this damning letter, signed by Gandhi, is reproduced in *After Mother India*, p. 29 Here is the anthor's account: 'At Mr. Gandhi's request, delivered by one of his attendants at the close of the interview, the notes of his message, having been typed out in full, were sent back to Mr. Gandhi for revision and amplification. In due course Miss Mayo received back an approved typescript which Mr. Gandhi had caused to be retyped, together with his covering letter.'

and waved them wildly in the air. The rich man in his motor car, the poor man in his rags; Hindus, Mahommedans, Parsees, Europeans — all joined in this final demonstration of loyalty and affection. So large were the crowds that it took the Prince's motor car ten minutes to cover the last hundred yards.'

Now, at the time when this outstanding event occurred — the high light in a tour on which all the world's cameras were focused — Gandhi had his sharp little ear to the ground and his sharp little eye on the horizon, listening to the slightest echo and watching the faintest shadow of the Prince's movements. Why? Because he was trying to organize a boycott of the Royal visit. And so it is difficult to believe that he can have remained in total ignorance of this demonstration. Yet that is what he *does* ask us to believe. Moreover, he bluntly implies that it never happened at all. He writes:

'She describes an ovation *said* to have been given to the Prince of Wales, of which India *has no knowledge*, but which could not possibly escape notice *if* it had happened.'

So that if we are to believe Mr. Gandhi, on this occasion, we can only do so by assuming either that he was under a very lengthy anaesthetic or in a state of protracted trance.

In this review, Mr. Gandhi employs the customary Hindu ruse of inserting little words into the mouths of his opponents, and then challenging them. (I have referred to this habit in the chapter entitled 'Gentlemen of the Press'.) On this occasion the word inserted was 'always'. Says Gandhi:

'She has described the visit to me and informed her readers that there are *always* with me two secretaries who write down *every word* I say ... this statement is not true.'

Maybe it is not, but then Miss Mayo never made it. Mr. Gandhi made it; the word 'always' is his own invention. Miss Mayo courteously referred him to the text, to point out his delicate emendation of her words. Needless to say Gandhi did not acknowledge her letter.

'The Drain Inspector's Report', to repeat, is a museum piece for all students of the Gandhi mind. It is a masterpiece of evasion, duplicity, and false implication. And it is completely typical of the man who, by reiterating the word 'Truth' until it sounds like the

squawk of a parrot, has bluffed half the world into believing that
the tinsel with which his own hands have crowned himself, is, in
very truth, a halo of divine radiance.

II

However, it is not with Gandhi the man that we are here concerned, but Gandhi the dictator, and the Fascist organization
which he has created, called Congress, which obeys the slightest
crack of his whip.

One of the strangest paradoxes of modern history is that Congress
should be the darling of warm-hearted Western liberals, who would
faint with horror if it were suggested that they were themselves
tainted with Fascism. For Congress is the only 100 per cent, full
blooded, uncompromising example of undiluted Fascism in the
modern world.

Firstly, it is Fascist in principle. The Nazi insistence on the
superiority of one race, and the necessity of keeping its blood pure,
is matched by the Brahmin's unrelenting claim to dominance and
the necessity of maintaining the laws of caste. Just as every Nazi is
a superman, so every Brahmin is 'Bhudeva', which means 'God on
earth'. And Congress is, of course, a predominantly Brahmin
organization.

Secondly, it is Fascist in practice. It is a Gandhi dictatorship.
So many examples might be quoted in proof of this assertion that
it is difficult to choose the most telling. Perhaps the clearest was
his personal frustration of the British attempt to introduce responsible Provincial Self-government. The Act of 1935 granted
large measures of autonomy to the Provincial Governments; it was
completely negatived by the Congress party caucus dominated
by Gandhi. The Provincial Governments were as clearly dominated by the will of Gandhi as the Italian corporations by the will
of Mussolini; if any made even a gesture of independence, the axe
descended.

Thirdly, it is Fascist *by open confession.* Which makes the attitude
of the aforesaid liberals all the odder. History appears to be once
more repeating itself. Just as many people refused to take *Mein*

L

Kampf at its face value, blinding themselves to the fact that it was an ultimatum to the world, so these same people refuse to take the open declarations of Congress leaders at *their* face value. Perhaps that is because Congress has two voices, one for the East and one for the West. And the latter is very much the gentler of the two.

Let us amplify this statement that Congress is Fascist 'by open confession'.

Before me is a book called *The Iron Dictator*. On the dust cover is a melodramatic drawing of a ferocious face, twisted into the sort of grimace that Mussolini used to affect when he was braying for the moon. The face is a portrait, and a very good one, of the book's subject, Sardar Patel.

Patel is the chief party boss of Congress; he was described by John Gunther as 'Congress's Jim Farley, the ruthless party fixer and organizer'. This title is proudly quoted by the author, who amplifies it with a sub-title of his own 'Gandhi's Greatest General'. Mark that word 'General'; it echoes rather strangely in such close connection with the name of the meek-voiced apostle of peace. Gandhi — Jim Farley — party bosses — generals ... how can all these gentlemen be in the same boat? How indeed? The fact remains that they are.

The Iron Dictator has had a very wide sale in India; you see it on nearly every bookstall. It has frequently been recommended to me· by Congress enthusiasts; it may be fairly taken as representing the average Congress mentality in the same way that Rosenberg's theories are representative of the Nazi 'philosophy'.

We open it and turn to page 93. This contains a description of how 'Gandhi's Greatest General' deals with his political opponents. It is the fate which awaits all Congress members who do not toe the line. The enemy, in this case, was an eminent Bombay minister called Nariman, who was somewhat too 'ideological' for Patel's taste. Patel therefore decided that he must be got out of the way. Says the author with evident approval:

'Patel's system was not based on democracy — it was a reaction against democracy. Anybody who did not agree with it had to be eliminated ... Either one agrees with him and is incorporated in his machine or one disagrees with him and is sent to the wall. He has ruthlessly (but tactfully) eliminated opponents out of his path.'

Ruthlessness and tact — where has one heard of that sinister combination before? Does it not recall a certain episode in the life of Hitler? But yes ... and in case we have forgotten, the author hastens to remind us:

'*Nariman not only disagreed with Patel but like the storm-troopers Ernst and Roehm he had personal differences with the Dictator. The storm troop leaders were shot by Hitler. Nariman was not shot, but merely eliminated...*'

A convenient word, 'eliminated', and one with which we shall constantly meet in our investigations of Congress procedure.

As if to make certain that we do not overlook the resemblance between the two dictatorships, Congress and Nazi, the author bluntly asserts: 'It was never an ideological difference, it was a difference in method and stress.' He illustrates this by comparing Patel with one of his most famous rivals, Chander Bose. '*The difference between Patel and Bose is the same as the difference between Hitler and Rudolf Hess.*'

Of these two gentlemen, most of us would probably register a reluctant vote for Hess. But then, we are not Congressmen.

It would be necessary to quote the whole book to build up an accurate picture of this towering, swashbuckling, ruthless politician, who is one of Gandhi's very closest collaborators. Perhaps he best expressed his personality — and his fitness to be judged as a responsible statesman — in a single sentence which he made just before his arrest. It was at the time of the Cripps mission. The Japanese were sweeping towards the frontiers. Inside those frontiers millions of voices were being raised in discord — 'lie down and let them trample over us' — 'get up and fight' — 'resist' — 'do not resist!' Poor Cripps!

Above all those voices rose the voice of Patel. At the last great Congress meeting he made a thunderous speech.

'*He demanded that the British should hand over the power to ANY-BODY — to the Muslim League, or to the Hindu Mahasabha, or even to criminals and dacoits. We would rather be ruled by the dacoits than by the British.*'

That had the true Goering note, and the audience yelled approval with true Nazi fervour. Those well-meaning British sentimentalists who so constantly blacken their own country's reputation in the eyes of the world may perhaps, for once in a way, be faintly distressed by being estimated so much lower than the dacoit. The dacoit is the cut-throat, the strangler of little children, the sneak-thief, the raper of women in the dark. One had hoped that Stafford Cripps was a cut above all that. Those champions of India—Mr. Sorensen, M.P., and Miss Ethel Mannin, the 'fearless novelist' — appear to think otherwise.

It is a pity.

However, perhaps they never heard of Patel's outburst; perhaps his preference for dacoits was never reported to them. It is more than likely. Patel does not often get into the news — not into the liberal organs of the West. The Congress publicity experts (who could teach Goebbels a number of tricks) see to that. It would create an unfortunate impression if Gandhi were shown clasping the hand of quite so ferocious-looking an individual as 'His Greatest General'. And so Gandhi usually poses in the neighbourhood of goats, small children and lotus pools. These, being comparatively dumb, cannot give the show away.

III

One has only to keep one's eyes open, in India, to see all the signs and portents of Fascism sticking out a mile. Even if one had made no study of the Congress tactics and the Congress record, the resemblance to the Fascist countries is unmistakable.

Consider the question of uniform. The Khaddar dhoti[1] and the Gandhi cap[2] are the counterparts of the Nazi shirt and the swastika; no orthodox congressman cares to show himself in any other costume on official occasions. Even if he had been educated in the West, even if in his private opinion the dhoti is a hideous and embarrassing garment which would make a scarecrow of the Apollo Belvedere, he must stick to it. Or rather, it must stick to him, which it does with a vengeance in the period of the monsoon.

Gandhi's understudy on the North-West Frontier is a blustering giant of a man called Khan Ghaffar Khan. He is widely known throughout India as 'the frontier Gandhi'. His first action, when

[1] Indian costume of hand-made cloth, draped about the legs and wound round the waist.
[2] A sort of Glengarry of white cotton.

he decided to throw in his lot with Congress, was to dress up all his followers in red shirts. The frontier Gandhi's Redshirts are supposed to be apostles of gentleness and non-resistance. When thousands of fanatical six-footers squat down firmly in front of a few harassed British policemen armed with bamboo canes, the 'gentleness' becomes somewhat academic.

The Congress Flag, green, yellow and white, is saluted by the Hindus with the same fervour as the swastika was saluted in Germany. It is a *party* flag, pure and simple. Time and again it has been torn down by the Muslims with the same ferocity as, in Germany, the swastika was torn down by the Communists. Yet many misguided Westerners appear to regard it as the flag of India!

The German 'Heil Hitler' has a striking equivalent in the Indian 'Gandhiji'. The terminal 'ji' is in theory an expression of endearment, in reality it has become a test of orthodoxy. If one did not say 'Heil Hitler' in Germany one was asking for trouble, and if one does not say 'Gandhiji' in India, one gets it.

A little while ago I was addressing a gathering of Indian students. I referred to Gandhi as Gandhi. 'Gandhiji, Gandhiji!' cried some angry voices in the crowd. For once in a way I had the right answer.

'My own leader,' I said, 'is Mr. Winston Churchill. I consider him a great enough man to be described as "Churchill". I am paying Gandhi the same compliment.'

It was a compliment that was not appreciated.

The resemblances between Gandhi and Hitler are, of course, legion.   .

In January 1941, the German radio station at Zeesen, in a special broadcast to India, proclaimed ... '*The German people respect Mahatma Gandhi as much as Adolf Hitler. Herr Hitler has the same principles as Mahatma Gandhi.*'[1]

We need not take that too seriously; Hitler would discover himself to have the same 'principles' as Marx or Tolstoy, if it suited his convenience. In any case, we do not need Hitler's testimony; the resemblances between the two dictators are too obvious to be stressed.

---

[1] Quoted in *Freedom or Fascism* (Radical Democratic Party of India, New Delhi, 1942).

All the world is familiar with the picture of Hitler retiring to Berchtesgaden to escape from the adoration of the multitudes (for whom he has openly expressed his profound contempt), seeking happiness in solitude, listening to the still small voice of his celebrated 'instinct', which is translated into commands that must be obeyed without question.

Look upon that picture and on this. Romain Rolland, one of Gandhi's most passionate advocates, writes: 'The Mahatma is literally sick of the multitude that adores him; he at heart distrusts numbers; he is happy only in solitude, hearing the "Still Small Voice" that commands.'

The distrust in numbers, the refuge in solitude, the sacred 'Voice' and the necessity to obey it . . . to what goal do these tendencies conduct? Democracy or Fascism? The answer, surely, is too obvious to be stated.

'God has chosen me as his instrument.' Gandhi has said this on a number of occasions.[1] So has Hitler. So has Mussolini. It is not on record that Roosevelt or Churchill have staked similar claims, and some of us prefer their reticence. We do not all take kindly to astute politicians who make a corner in God — and even Gandhi himself would not deny that he is a very astute politician indeed, though of course he would put it in his own way.

The acid test is his insistence on infallibility. It is the first and last justification of all dictators.

'L'etat c'est moi', said Louis XIV.

'I *am* the German people,' said Hitler.

'The Duce is always right,' said Mussolini.

'I *am* the Hindu mind,' said Gandhi.

Where, precisely, is the difference? I am not the only person who would like to know the answer to that question. The Muslims would like to know it too. Anybody in doubt as to the ceaseless apprehension with which they regard the supernatural eminence of the Hindu political idol should study some of the Muslim League publications, for example a brilliant piece of creative analysis entitled *Nationalism in Conflict in India*.[2] Here is the author's comment on the present situation:

[1] See *Gandhi in India*, an Anthology (Tripathi Ltd., Bombay).
[2] Muslim Printing Press, Daryagenj, Delhi, 1943.

'There is the closest similarity between the Congress and the Nazi associations. Hitler commands the same respect and allegiance in Germany as Mr. Gandhi in India. He is more than a hero, a national saviour, or even a God to the Germans. The same is the case with Mr. Gandhi. He is both a spiritual and political leader of the Hindus and pretends to speak with divine authority. Nobody can dare to criticize him and yet remain a member of the Congress. A host of prominent Congress' leaders had to leave the Congress as they had incurred the displeasure of the Mahatma. Mr. Nariman, Dr. Khare, Mr. Subhas Chander Bose, Mr. Roy, and Mr. Rajagopalachari, all at one time held positions of immense influence in the Congress, but their difference of opinion with one man alone in the Congress, Mr. Gandhi, led to their permanent expulsion.'

IV

Late in the day — maybe too late — a few of India's best brains have woken up to the true nature of Congress rule, and the Fascist menace behind it.

Just as the Nazi movement was joined, in its early days, by numbers of decent Germans who honestly believed that it might prove an instrument of national regeneration, so the Congress movement had the support of a number of decent Indians who saw in it the true hope of independence . . . and more than independence, of unity and social progress.

When the German liberals were disillusioned, they were kicked out of the party, and — unless they could flee the country — shot. When the Indian liberals were disillusioned, they also were kicked out of the party, but owing to the fact that India is guarded by British law, they were not shot. Their voices ca

Let us listen to some of these Indian voices, warning their fellow-countrymen of the Fascist road along which they are so eager to race.

One of the most compelling of them is the voice of M. N. Roy.

All the old political clichés have been used about Roy. 'Stormy petrel', 'enfant terrible' and the like. In his early days, his main interests lay in Russia. He had a passionate interest in the Communist experiment which he appears to have believed could be repeated, *mutatis mutandis*, in India. Why he left Russia is not quite clear, though it is obvious that in some respects he had been disillusioned. All that concerns us is that in 1930, surrounded by glamour and mystery, he reappeared on the Indian scene, where he promptly proceeded to get into everybody's hair, from the lion's mane to the Brahmin's bun.

Why has Roy this remarkable talent for getting into people's hair? For two reasons. Firstly, because he is rock-bottom honest, and rock-bottom honest Indian politicians are rarer than diamonds. Secondly, because he is a socialist who realizes that behind all the fog and fury of religious and political controversy lies a crazy economic structure that is hideous and worm-eaten and tottering. He wants to knock this structure down, Congress wants to bolster it up.

Roy has been called 'The Karl Marx of India'. The tag will do as well as any other, though he is so electric a personality that one might as well try to tie a label on to a flash of lightning. This personality he expresses through a small but influential political group called the Radical Democratic Party. The official organ of the party, published in New Delhi, is *Independent India*. Apart from his contributions to this paper, Roy is a prolific writer, hammering away with brutal insistence on the hidden alliance between Gandhism, Congress, and Fascism, an alliance which, though it is vehemently denied, is not only unquestionable but inherent in the very structure of the two movements.

He is not sparing of personalities. This is what he writes of Jawaharlal Nehru, Indian's Number 2 politician, and Gandhi's inevitable successor.

'Theoretically anti-Fascist, Nehru has been acting as the leader of Indian Fascism, and temperamentally none is better suited for the role. He is a classical "National-Socialist", being neither a nationalist nor a socialist. His nationalism is cancelled by his loudly professed internationalism, and his socialism is belied by nationalist fanaticism. If Gandhi is the spiritual guide of Congress, Nehru is its effective leader, and as such, he is the leader of Indian Fascism.'[1]

[1] *Freedom or Fascism*, by M. N. Roy (Radical Democratic Party, December 1942).

Such an opinion will come as a shock to the tens of thousands who have read Nehru's best selling autobiography with its picture of a sensitive, cultured man constantly thwarted by the brutality of British Imperialism.

One of the few outstanding ex-Congress leaders who was not in gaol in 1943 was C. R. Rajagopalachari. He spent most of the year in a futile effort to bring about some sort of reconciliation between Jinnah and Gandhi. I had a long talk with 'C.R.' in Madras, and he struck me as a man of the subtlest intelligence whom I should certainly employ as counsel in any case which demanded . . . shall I say . . . a 'sinuous' interpretation of the facts. He is, of course, a Brahmin of the Brahmins, fanatical prohibitionist, and one of the ablest interpreters of the Gandhi oracle. He asked me not to quote what he said, and I shall respect his wishes. But that need not deter us from quoting his public utterances. In a recent speech at Lucknow University he gave the frankest possible exposition of his reverence for the Germany of Frederick, von Moltke and Hindenburg; he held up to the admiration of Young India 'that wonderful outcome of scientific organization, the German army'; and he demanded, if Germany could 'rise' and 'revive' after the last war (an odd way of describing the German descent into the Nazi abyss) why Indian nationalism should despair of following her example.

As Roy says: 'Germany, not the Germany of Goethe, Lessing, and Beethoven, nor of the rebels of 1848, nor of Haeckel, Helmholtz, Koch, Virchow, Planck, etc., but the Germany of the Kaisers and of Hitler, has always been the beloved of the Indian nationalist. In contrast to this curious sympathy, Indian nationalism has never felt any sympathy for France, the land of great revolutionary traditions.'

He continues:

'The cult of an omnipotent State, which prevailed among the Prussians, found full and explicit warrant in the teaching of Hegel. The logic of tyranny was gilded by the ethical beauty of sacrifice. The state was God. In the name of that abstraction, millions must be prepared to work, to suffer and to perish. That is exactly the ideal which Mr. Rajagopalachari placed before the youth of our country. The rise of the modern German nation, in his opinion, represented the realization of that ideal. "Why then should we despair?" One has only to know the Hegelian metaphysical doctrine of State in order to visualize "the power of the spirit", which, according to an accredited leader of Indian Nationalism, saved Germany and will save India also. That mystic power is not a moral force, but brute force in the most highly organized form. That is the political implication of the Gandhian creed of non-violence. We must thank Mr. Rajagopalachari for having practised the other part of the creed, namely, truth.'

V

It is almost impossible for even the most skilled observer to discover when Gandhi is sincere and when he is not. His mind is a jungle of contradictions and complexes in which the explorer is soon hopelessly lost. Maybe that is his intention. If, in the course of a long career, one makes a sufficient number of violently conflicting statements, one can always look up the files and say, 'I told you so'. Which is what Gandhi does, whenever he is in a tight corner.[1]

However, let us give him the benefit of the doubt, and assume that there are occasions when he actually means what he says. We are still faced with the incontrovertible fact that what he says invariably leads, directly or indirectly, to Fascism.

Consider his economic 'policy', if it can be dignified by such a term. It begins, ends, and has its entire being in the *charkha* ... the spinning wheel, which is linked in his mind with the conception of 'non-violence'. If only the peasants will weave their own cloth, in their own homes, and go on weaving it, and accept the most intolerable impositions of the rich Hindu landlords with non-violence, then all will be well. All the economic evils of India will disappear and Swaraj will be automatically won.

If any man were to preach such moonshine in any other country but India he would be regarded, not as a statesman or an economist, but as a low comedian. The doctrine of *charkha* is

[1] For some of his more startling *volte faces*, read the chapter entitled 'Gandhi's Professions and Performance' in the Muslim League publication *Nationalism in Conflict*.

about as practical as the suggestion that unemployment would disappear in the U.S. if only the American housewife knitted her husband's socks. *Charkha* has, of course, a minor value, in that it is a blow aimed at the Lancashire cotton industry, but that it is in no way a serious menace to big business is proved by the fact that Gandhi's most ardent supporters are the Hindu mill-owners and the millionaires of the steel combines, whose profits are largely dependent on sweated labour. Naturally, they are delighted by Gandhi's propaganda, which aims at convincing the peasant that — apart from the hated British raj — he is best as he is, that there is no need for him to strike for better pay, nor acquaint himself with the true facts of his exploitation. The crude and blatant exponents of Hindu capitalism could wish for nothing better than this vast pool of serfs, sunk in ignorance and superstition, sworn to non-violence, with all their grievances conveniently concentrated on the British bogy. For the Fascist boss, such a state of affairs is as near to Paradise as he is ever likely to attain. But for the Indian people, Gandhism is mass suicide. In the words of Roy:

'Gandhism was created by the ignorance, the blind faith, and hero-worship of the backward Indian masses. Gandhism is the expression of the worst in our people, of its ignorance, its cowardice, its defeatism, its backwardness.'[1]

It is the same with the other great plank in Gandhi's programme, his so-called 'non-violence' ... a doctrine which, in practice, has invariably and inevitably led to violence on a quite unprecedented scale. People talk as though Gandhi had invented this menace to world peace; we can acquit him of this charge. Non-violence is as old as the Hindu hills; it is part and parcel of the fatalism, the pessimism, the negativism in which the whole Hindu faith is shrouded. The purest example of it in modern India may be seen in the spectacle of the Hindu moneylender's method of extracting payment for a bad debt. Instead of going to law, or facing up to the debtor and giving him a sock on the nose, he sits on his doorstep and weeps in the hope that his client may thereby be shamed into a settlement.

Perhaps Gandhi is sincere in his devotion to non-violence; perhaps he is not; it does not much matter, either way. In a man

[1] *Gandhism, Nationalism, Socialism*, by M. N. Roy (Bengal Radical Club).

so weirdly muddle-headed, sincerity or the lack of it, ceases to be of any consequence. Here is one of his latest 'definitions' . . . if one can use such a phrase to describe so vague a blur of confused thought.

'If a man fights with his sword single-handed against a horde of dacoits armed to the teeth, I should say he is fighting non-violently. Supposing a mouse fighting a cat resisted the cat with his sharp teeth, would you call that mouse violent? *In the same way, for the Poles to stand bravely against the German hordes vastly superior in number and strength was almost non-violent.*'[1]

Any man who could tell you precisely what that means, and even more, what it doesn't, would be something of a genius. Apparently Gandhi wishes to imply that a Polish machine gun, in the process of mowing down 50 Nazis, was 'almost non-violent' because there were not a sufficient number of other machine guns on its flanks. In other words, *violence when employed against superior odds automatically becomes non-violence!*

'A very convenient theory' as one critic observed, 'for the rebels in an unarmed revolt!'

Very convenient indeed. It must have been a perpetual solace to the non-violent nationalists who so often poured non-violent petrol over policemen and lit it with non-violent matches, and the non-violent mobs who . . . always provided that they were in a majority of a thousand to one . . . battered British and Canadian boys to death with non-violent bludgeons.

Over the bodies of these victims of his policy Gandhi could still smile his toothless smile and say 'Well really you know, all this is *almost* non-violence!'

However, even Gandhi, in the months preceding his imprisonment, had begun to drop the mask. He was convinced that Britain was finished and that Japan had won the war. He was anxious to stand well with the little yellow men who, he thought, would shortly be his new masters. Needless to say, he did not confess this in so many words, for he always speaks with one eye on America, and if America had caught him in an overt flirtation with Japan, the consequences to his prestige would have been

---

[1] Quoted in *Congress Responsibility for Disturbances* 1942-3 (Government of India Press).

catastrophic. But he went as far as he could. He handed to Japan, in advance, a blank moral cheque which they could use to justify their assault on India. He suggested that the Japanese were only too anxious for peace but that they were reluctantly compelled to aggression because India was defended by the British.

'The presence of the British in India is an invitation to Japan to invade India,' he said. '*Their withdrawal removes the bait.*'

In other words, had there been a Maginot line running down the whole Burmese frontier, armed to the teeth with a hundred divisions, with adequate air support, Gandhi would have immediately blown it up, because it was a 'bait'. And once the bait was removed, and the rich fields lay open and undefended, the Japanese would, of course, have right-about-turned and marched home, singing lullabies.

If Gandhi really thought this, it is difficult to see how any sane man can deny either that his influence was a menace to the cause of the United Nations, or that it was a priceless asset to the Axis. Even his greatest lieutenant, Jawaharlal Nehru, at one of the last meetings of the Congress Working Committee, was reluctantly compelled to admit that the draft of policy which Gandhi was ordering them to adopt was, in effect, an Axis manifesto.

'The whole background of the draft is one which will inevitably make the world think that we are linking up with the Axis powers,' he said. '*The whole thought of the draft is one of favouring Japan.*'

After such a revealing confession from India's Number 2 leader it is hard to follow the mental processes of those who claim that Gandhi's release would immediately lead to an intensification of India's 'War Effort'. We might well ask 'War effort against whom? Japan . . . or the Allies?'

I am the very last person to deny tolerance to the genuine war-resister, the truly non-violent man, even though bitter experience has convinced me that the road to world peace runs through less romantic country, and must be guarded by police as well as by principles, and paved with laws as well as good intentions. But Gandhi's 'non-violence' seems to me bogus from first to last. Not only does it conduce — as he knows it must conduce — to bloodshed, but in its very principles it makes a hundred compromises with brute force.

We suggested, a moment ago, that he had begun to drop the mask just before he was sent to gaol. Let us amplify this statement by a few extracts from his own speeches and manifestoes:

'We shall *do or die!*'

'This is an *open rebellion!*'

'If rioting does take place, it cannot be helped.'

'Consider yourself a free man and act as if you are free.'

'This move will be felt by the whole world. It may not interfere with the movement of British troops, but it is "sure to engage British attention".'

All very non-violent, of course! All nicely calculated to stay the hands of any hot heads who might be tempted to resort to the force which Gandhi pretends to abhor! Particularly when it is read in conjunction with the Congress bulletins which were flooding India like an avalanche. Those bulletins carried Gandhi's inspiration to its logical conclusion. For example, they were blatantly pro-Japanese:

'Japan has consistently and persistently pronounced that she has no interest nor lust for conquest of India except that the Britishers are driven out and India becomes free at once.'[1]

They were quite open in their incitement to murder. They demanded the immediate 'Formation of Guerrilla Bands to give surprise attacks on the Tommies.'[2] 'They also issued instructions that "Britishers' cooks are to be organized to cook bad food for their masters"[3] . . . a polite way of describing mass-poisoning.

Theft, arson, riot, and every form of sabotage were openly advocated, irrespective of the slaughter of innocent persons which these acts might entail. For had they not always, as their divine authority, the great master of 'non-violence', with his subtleties, his equivocations, his 'Pharisaical glosses'? In his newspaper *Harijan*, at the time of his arrest, the following masterpiece of evasion had appeared 'as an answer to an earnest question'.

Q. What may be permitted for disorganizing Government within the limit of non-violence?

[1] *Bombay Congress Bulletin*, August 17th, 1942.
[2] Leaflet entitled 'Workers of India', issued in the name of the A.I.C.C. Office, August 27th, 1942.
[3] Ibid.

A. I can give my personal opinion only. It will be non-violence without blemish.

So far so good. And the next sentence?

Cutting wires, removing rails, destroying small bridges cannot be objected to in a struggle like this.

'*Small* bridges.' An exquisite phrase, Mr. Gandhi! When is a bridge 'small' and when is it 'not small'? And of what consolation to the victims of a railway disaster are the pious words with which their non-violent assassins tore up the tracks?

V I

Meanwhile, through the windows of the palace at Poona, where he is confined, incense drifts round the figure of Gandhi, proffered by genuine anti-Fascists all over the world. It is the most ironical paradox of the twentieth century — this anti-Fascist worship of the man who was prepared to sell the pass to Fascism!

What of the future? What are the limits — if any — of the mischief he will be able to cause? Are there likely to be any major changes in his policy? Although the answer to these questions must be largely a matter of guesswork, it should be possible to give a reasonably accurate forecast of the trend of events.

I myself think that his *practical* influence — in spite of the aforesaid clouds of incense — is sharply on the wane, and is not likely to reassert itself even under the most favourable conditions. By the time these words are published he will be seventy-five. He has stepped out of gaol to find a very different world from the world he left behind. Britain is no longer *in extremis*, struggling with her back to the wall; the little yellow men are no longer waiting to be welcomed on the doorstep, with their smiles and their promises.

Most important of all, the tremendous gap between his mystic mumbo-jumbo and the hard but exciting realities of the modern world is more than ever apparent. This gap has always been a worry to the more intelligent members of Congress. Nehru openly admitted it in his famous *Autobiography* — indeed, the most vivid part of that book is the account of the exhausting mental struggle which he has constantly been obliged to wage in his

endeavour to reconcile the conflicting claims of loyalty to the
Mahatma and the integrity of his own vision of the modern world.
Spinning wheels and non-violence on the one side, with, of course,
the sacred cow in the background ... ('I bow to no one,' said
Gandhi, 'in my worship of the cow') ... all the spells of medieval-
ism, in a mad hotchpotch, wrapped up in a parcel labelled 'take
it or leave it'. And on the other side, a shrinking world, moving
with ever greater velocity, a world of thrilling social experiment,
streamlined and sceptical. How could a man like Nehru fail to
be torn, as so many of his colleagues were torn? Only by a series
of uncomfortable compromises and over-ingenious sophistries
could they dodge the awkward fact that the Gandhi cap is a very
bad fit indeed for a man with a modern brain.

So it has been, on a wide scale, with the youth of India. Every
day that Gandhi has been in gaol has seen a rapid increase in the
number of young Indians who either voluntarily or involuntarily
are being brought into the orbit of the war effort, which means
into the orbit of the twentieth century. From thousands of
villages young men are flocking to the army centres where, for
the first time in their lives, they are taught the rudiments of
hygiene and discipline, and are given their first sight of the magic
of modern machinery. This latter point is of very great importance.
One of the most brilliant pieces of organization which Britain has
achieved during the present war is the gigantic War Exhibition
which has been moved from centre to centre, during the past
eighteen months, in an effort to teach India the issues of the war
and the manner in which it is being waged. The Exhibition is not
merely a collection of tanks and propaganda posters; it is a complete and self-sufficient picture, on an enormous scale, of modern
engineering, aviation, transport, agriculture, radio, cookery,
social service, botany, medicine, etc. etc.

In spite of the frenzied efforts of Congress to boycott it, the
Exhibition has been an unqualified success, particularly with the
younger men. It has marked a turning point in their lives. They
have come from sleepy villages which, if Gandhi had his way,
would go on sleeping, and suddenly the whole wonder box of
modern science is thrown open before them. They stare in amazement and growing delight and soon they are lost, irrevocably

seduced, walking in a new world from which even the hypnotic voice of the Mahatma can never recall them.

For into this new world the Mahatma does not fit — not by any stretch of the imagination. Those young men, whether Gandhi knows it or not, and whether *they* know it or not, are lost to him for ever. And by the end of 1944 it is calculated that there will be over 40 million of them.

Summing up, we may say that the realities of the situation — apart altogether from the fact of his advanced age — have inevitably robbed Gandhi of his bitterest sting. Non-violence has been exposed, once and for all, as the violent humbug which it really is. And though some of his followers may still pay lip-service to the ideal of *charkha*, most of them will soon cease even to pretend that it is of the least value in solving India's problems.

Meanwhile, of course, the incense will continue to drift around him, the halo will be polished brighter and brighter by millions of adoring hands, and when eventually he departs from this world, it is a safe bet that he will be canonized and sit for ever enshrined among the myriad gods of the Hindu pantheon.

M

CHAPTER 11

HATE FOUNDS AN EMPIRE

WE are now approaching the most important and also the most urgent problem in this book, for we have come to the borders of Pakistan.

Pakistan is an Empire. True, at the moment it is only an empire of dreams, but in the minds of the Muslim it is none the less real for all that.

Literally it means Land of the Pure — ('pak' pure; 'stan' land). In geographical terms it means a great block of land in the north-west of India, consisting of Baluchistan, Sind, the Punjab, and the North-West Frontier, together with a block in the east, consisting of the greater part of Bengal.

It is proposed that these areas, which are predominantly Muslim, should be separated once and for all from the rest of India, which is predominantly Hindu, and should proclaim themselves an independent state. This proposal has the fanatical support of the Muslin League, a compact and fighting organization which commands the allegiance of at least eighty-five per cent of India's Muslims. Its leader is, of course, Mr. M. A. Jinnah.

This dream empire may one day come out of the clouds, and place itself on the world's map with a bang. I am one of those who believe not only that this will happen, but that it *must* happen. If it does, an entirely new situation will have arisen in Asia, which will shatter the existing balances of power, and drastically modify the policies of every country in the world.

It seems fitting, therefore, that we should cross the borders of this Empire, and study it in detail.

But before we do that, we must first study the background against which the dream was born, the background of communal discord between the Muslims and the Hindus, which Pakistan seeks to resolve. We have had scattered evidence of it throughout this book but we have not yet isolated it for special consideration. The time has come to do so.

II

The City of Bombay, compared with most of the big cities of India, is quiet, orderly, and 'civilized'. It is well-policed; the streets are brightly lit; a woman can wander through it alone at all hours of the night and day without running any serious danger of being molested.

Most important of all, the communal question is comparatively quiescent. At a time when many other cities have been drenched in the blood of Hindus and Muslims, Bombay has gone quietly about its business.

And this is Bombay's record from February 1929 to April 1938 — the last years for which statistics are available.

In 1929 there were two communal riots. In the first 149 were killed, 739 seriously injured, and it lasted for 36 days. In the second 35 were killed, 109 were injured, and it lasted for 22 days.

In 1930 there were two riots, and in 1932 another two. They were apparently of similar proportions, but the only details available are for the second 1932 riot, in which 217 were killed, and 2,713 seriously injured. This lasted for 49 days.

There were riots in 1933, 1934, and 1935, but they were on a smaller scale. In the chief 1936 riot 94 were killed, and 632 seriously injured. This raged for 65 days.

1937 was comparatively quiet; in the chief riot only 11 were killed, and 85 seriously injured, and it was over in a mere 3 weeks.

But in 1938, in one riot alone, which lasted only two and a half hours, 12 were killed and over 100 injured.[1]

Since then the situation has steadily deteriorated. And Bombay, remember, is one of the *quieter* parts of India, as far as communalism is concerned.

'Placed side by side with the frantic efforts made by Mr. Gandhi to bring about Hindu-Moslem unity, the record of Hindu-Moslem relationship from 1920 to 1940 makes most painful and heart-rending reading. It is a record of twenty years of civil war, interrupted by brief intervals of armed peace.'[2]

This fact — of such vital importance to the world — is con-

[1] These statistics are taken from *Thoughts on Pakistan*, by Dr. B. R. Ambedkar (Thacker & Co., Bombay). This book, to which I am much indebted, is essential for any student of Pakistan, or, indeed, of modern India.
[2] Ibid., p. 180.

veniently ignored by all those bemused liberals who are hyp-
notized by the word 'India' and by the compact geographical
unity of the area in which these passions hold their sway. If they
could only come down from their clouds, and fly over the country
— as the airmen say — at 'tree-top height', they might change
their opinion. The last Mopla rebellion at Malabar, for instance,
would not look very pretty in close-up, with its enormous piles of
Hindu dead, its heaps of pregnant women ripped wide open, its
burning temples, its pillage and destruction.

These dreamers at home, who so glibly proclaim that communalism is 'fostered' by the British might hesitate before spreading this lie if they investigated conditions on the spot. The cause
of the last serious riot in Kohat, for example, was publication of
an anti-Islamic poem! That little piece of literature caused the
death or serious injury of 155 men and women, nearly a million
rupees worth of damage to property, and the flight of thousands
of terror-stricken evacuees.

All over India it is the same story. A fancied slight to one of
the Hindu gods, a sneering reference to the Muslim's Allah, a
brick thrown at a religious procession, or even the impudent pipe
of a flute at the hour when the Muslim turns to Mecca — and hell
is let loose. Out come the rifles and the daggers, the pitch-forks
and the knuckle-dusters; for weeks and months the countryside is
gripped with terror.

In the end, of course, it is always settled by a handful of British
boys, like the platoon of 25 men of the Royal Sussex Regiment
who recently dispersed a crowd of 25,000 fanatics at Karachi.
This seething mob had gathered to avenge the execution of the
Muslim murderer of a Hindu who had insulted Islam. They were
on their way to the heart of the city, to pillage, loot, and murder.
The police had already been overwhelmed, so the British boys
were called in. They were ordered to fire; 47 people were killed;
and, of course, the Congress screamed to high heaven that this
was another example of the tyranny of 'Imperial might'.

One boy per thousand religious fanatics — 'Imperial might' —
that's pretty good, when you think it out.

The evidence of Hindu-Muslim hatred at murder heat is so
overwhelming, so universal, and above all, so *contemporary* that it

would be an insult to the reader's intelligence to insist upon it. If there are any persons still inclined to question this evidence they must be referred to the statistics. They are so damning that they cannot be 'cooked', even by the most fanatical Hindu.

This, then, is the background of Pakistan, a background of blood — blood in the past, blood in the present — and, unless the dream comes true, a great deal more blood in the future.

III

'But all these troubles will die down' — you may tell me. 'Men have resolved their differences in other nations, why should they not resolve them in the Indian nation?'

To answer this question with any accuracy we must first define what we mean by the word 'nation'. Renan did this so perfectly in his famous essay on Nationality that we will not attempt to better his words.

What constitutes a nation? Renan says:

'A nation is a living soul, a spiritual principle. Two things constitute this soul; one is in the past, the other in the present. One is the common possession of a rich heritage of memories; the other is the actual consent, the desire to live together, the will to preserve worthily the undivided inheritance. *To have common glories in the past, a common will in the present; to have done great things together, to will to do the like again — such are the essential conditions for the making of a people.*'

How does India stand up to this test? Consider the first of Renan's conditions — the common possession of a rich heritage of memories. What do the Muslims remember? They remember that, before the British came, they had been top dog for 800 years; they had lorded it over the Hindus by right of brain and brawn. And the Hindus have not forgotten all the unpleasant details which that overlordship entailed. In the words of Bhai Parmanand in his pamphlet 'The Hindu National Movement': 'In history the Hindus revere the memory of Prithi Raj, Partap, Shivaji and Be-raji Bir who fought for the honour and freedom of their land against the Muslims, while the Muslims look upon the invaders of

India, like Mohammed bin Quisim and rulers like Aurungzeb, as their national heroes.'

Yes, both Hindus and Muslims have a 'rich heritage of memories', but they are all memories of hate.

Moreover, these memories are not only in the past but very much in the present. It is often asserted that the ideal of Pakistan is a mushroom growth, that hitherto Muslims and Hindus have managed to live together, however uneasily, and that therefore this summary divorce is too drastic a measure. This argument ignores the facts of contemporary history. It is true that in the past the Hindus and the Muslims have refrained, however reluctantly, from mass murder and have contented themselves with incessant guerrilla warfare. It is also true that as long as Britain was responsible for law and order, this state of affairs might have continued indefinitely. But with the approach of national independence, communalism has flared up in a spectacular manner . . . in fact, *the demand for Pakistan has increased in precise ratio to the granting of self-government.* Why is this? The reason is indisputable. It is because self-government has meant very largely Hindu government, and the Hindus, as soon as they obtained power in any shape or form, proceeded to abuse it. They gave the Muslims the bitterest possible foretaste of the fate they must expect, if and when the British leave India.   •

The facts were as follows: By the act of 1935 representative self-government on a free electoral basis was established in eleven provinces. We need not confuse ourselves with the details of the ¹ Act; it is sufficient to observe that though there were certain necessary safeguards, it was a tremendous step forward. The Act provides a perfect 'nursery' for a young nation on the threshold of independence; the institutions it created should have been ideally suited for the purpose of fitting Indian politicians for complete and unfettered responsibility.

The Act received the royal assent on August 2nd, 1935; elections for the new legislatures were held in the winter of 1936-7; Congress found itself in a large majority in seven out of the eleven provinces. As soon as it was in power in these provinces, it dropped the mask. Instead of inviting the Muslims to share the fruits of office, instead of attempting any form of coalition, it rigidly ex-

cluded them from all responsibility. But it did not confine its
autocracy to political matters; it proceeded to attack the Muslims
in every branch of their material and spiritual life. A great campaign was launched to enforce the use of Sanskritized Hindi at
the expense of the Persianized Urdu;[1] the schools were dominated
in a manner so ruthless that it would have aroused the admiration
of the Nazis, Muslim children being compelled to stand up and
salute Gandhi's picture; the Congress flag was treated as the flag
of the whole nation; justice was universally corrupted and in some
provinces the police were so perverted that to this day the Muslims
refer to them as 'the Gestapo'; and in business matters the dis-
crimination against Muslims, from the great landowners and
merchants to the humblest tillers of the soil, was persistent and
pitiless.

The best proof of these allegations is the fact that when war
broke out and the Congress ministries resigned, Mr. Jinnah, the
President of the Muslim League, called for a Day of National
Thanksgiving to mark the end of the tyranny, and this day was
fervently celebrated all over India by the vast majority of the
Muslim population.

So much for Renan's first condition — the 'rich heritage of
memories', binding men in love, companionship, and common
pride. It would appear that the Muslims and the Hindus are
hardly qualified to make any strong claim to such a heritage.

IV

And Renan's second condition . . . 'the longing to live together,
to do great things together'?

This question has already been largely answered by the foregoing facts, but since it cannot be answered too emphatically, we
will pause to reinforce the argument.

The Hindus and the Muslims are 'longing to live together' in
precisely the same degree as the French are longing to live with
the Germans or the Americans are longing to live with the

---

[1] The Muslim resentment of this campaign cannot be fully appreciated unless it
is realized that the Koran is written in the Persian script.

Japanese. To quote Dr. Ambedkar, who certainly should know:
'It is like a race in armaments between two hostile nations. If
the Hindus have the Benares University, the Muslims must have
the Aligarh University; if the Hindus start one movement the
Muslims launch another; if the Hindus have the R.S.S.[1] the
Muslims reply by organizing the Khaksars.[2] This race in social
armament and equipment is run with the determination and
apprehension of nations which are on the war path. The Muslims
fear that the Hindus are subjugating them; the Hindus feel that
the Muslims are engaged in reconquering them. Both appear to
be preparing for war.'[3]   .

A longing to live together?

So far we have principally considered the Muslims' insistence
on their difference from the Hindus. But in spite of Gandhi's
perpetual theme song of the unity of 'India' and the common
nationality of 'Indians', there are vast bodies of *Hindu* opinion that
are equally insistent on the differences between Hindus and
Muslims.

Here, for example, is the typical viewpoint of Hindu orthodoxy
as represented by the Mahasabha, a powerful political party which
contains many of the best brains of right wing Hinduism. In a
recent presidential address, Mr. V. D. Savarkar aroused great
applause by asserting:

'In India we Hindus are marked out as an abiding Nation by
ourselves. Not only do we own a common fatherland, a territorial
unity, but what is scarcely found anywhere else in the world, we
have a common Holy Land which is identified with our common
fatherland. Our Patriotism therefore is doubly sure. We have
common affinities — cultural, religious, historical, linguistic, and
racial, which through the process of countless centuries of association have moulded us into a homogeneous Nation. The Hindus
are no treaty nation — but an organic national being.'[4]

Where, precisely, do the Muslims fit into this somewhat exclusive
picture? The answer, of course, is that they don't. The Mahasabha
neither likes them, wants them, nor acknowledges them. As far

---

[1] Hindu Volunteer Corps.   [2] Muslim Volunteer Corps.
[3] *Thoughts on Pakistan*, p. 242.
[4] Speech at Calcutta Session of Hindu Mahasabha, December 1939.

as the Hindus are concerned the Muslims can go and ... well, you know what they can go and do. And this smouldering hatred even rang from Savarkar the tortured admission that India was 'not an unitarian and homogeneous nation', but the product of centuries of cultural, religious, and national antagonism. '*Let us bravely face the unpleasant facts,*' he proclaimed. '*There are two nations in India, the Hindus and the Muslims.*'

So far, so good. It was something to obtain such a confession from a representative Hindu leader of such wide responsibility. But unfortunately, in the same breath that M. Savarkar concedes the Muslim claim to separate nationality, he denies them any practical means of expressing it. He, and the party he leads, are violent opponents of Pakistan. 'Oh yes,' they say, 'the Muslims are a nation, just as much as we are, but we don't propose to grant them anywhere to live. Oh yes, they are *in* India, and unfortunately there are 100 millions of them — heretics and outcasts to a man — but India is *ours*, and we intend to keep it so. Oh yes, it is true that they were the dominant power for many centuries, and that they were the only people apart from the British who ever gave India even the semblance of unity, but all that happened in the past and we have no intention of allowing it to happen again. Thanks to the British we are now top dog. We are three to one in numbers and twenty to one in cash. And when the British have gone we shall be even more top dog. *And* how!'

That is a precise and accurate analysis, in irreverent language, of the orthodox Hindu point of view. And though Gandhi would raise his hands in horror at the suggestion that such ideas should ever enter his sainted head, they very evidently enter the head of his big business supporters, who have only too frequently been rash enough to give public expression to them.

So we arrive, finally, at this conclusion.

The Muslims claim, with passionate fervour, that they are a separate and independent nation. And they are right.

The Hindus — or at least a formidable percentage of them — claim with equal fervour that they are a separate and independent nation. And they are right.

But when the Muslims wish to give logical effect to their aspirations, and form a national home, the Hindus protest to high heaven, the batteries of the Congress press start firing at full blast, all over the world richly subsidized young Hindus burble passionately about the Unity of India, and Gandhi takes to his bed and refuses even to smell a banana.

What does it all mean?

It means — of course — vested interests. The old bogy which is also, unfortunately, a fact, the sinister fact that is behind so much of the world's malaise.

For not the first time we will permit India to accuse herself. Here is the verdict of an authoritative spokesman of the Muslim League:

'The real reason why the Hindus are so much opposed to Pakistan is that it strikes at the root of their vested interests, and shatters all their dreams of exploiting the entire sub-continent of India. Their emphasis on India's unity and indivisibility is a political stunt to stifle the national consciousness of Muslims for their full share in the political and economic field.'[1]

No man who is aware of the extent to which Congress is dominated by the big bosses of Hindu business can possibly doubt the truth of this assertion. Naturally, Hindu capital wants to be complete master in its own house. Naturally, it wants to tighten the screw on the teeming masses, particularly the Muslim masses. It would ... and will ... fight to the death to retain and extend its economic control over the areas which it is proposed to snatch from its grasp. There is already great wealth in those areas, and more is on the way. Bengal offers golden opportunities for industrialization, and would serve as a ready market to the agricultural provinces of the west which, in their turn, are rich in untapped resources — ore, minerals, forests, to say nothing of millions of acres of some of the finest soil in India, particularly in the Punjab.

Yes, the vested interests of Hindu capital will struggle against Pakistan to the last gasp. And they will use every artifice of diplomacy and propaganda to make the world ring with protests against the 'mutilation' of the Indian 'motherland'. They will weep, they will wail, they will bribe, they will threaten — and, to

[1] *Pakistan and Modern India*, with a foreword by Quaid-I-Azam (Malabar Hill, Bombay).

add to the confusion, they will have at their command the services of men of undoubted integrity, whose fervid Hindu nationalism has totally blinded them to the facts. Such a one is Pandit Jawaharlal Nehru, who at a time when the streets were running with blood and the whole country was on the verge of a civil war of appalling dimensions, calmly wirelessed to America that *'except for a small handful of persons there is no difference between Hindu and Muslim in race, culture, or language'*.[1] No amount of exclamation marks could do justice to this staggering assertion, nor to the fantastic understatement with which he followed it: 'There is now a demand on the part of some Muslims for partition of India, and it must be remembered that this demand is hardly four years old. Few take it seriously.'

'Some' is an odd expression for 85 millions! 'Few take it seriously' is a queer way of describing the surging, live-or-die passion of a great nation!

Well, you have been warned. You know what to expect, as the outlines of the dream empire take shape, and are traced more clearly on the world's consciousness. Pakistan will be attacked, lied about, subjected to an unparalleled barrage of misrepresentation. None the less, I believe that it will survive the test. I believe the empire will be born.

And now, let us pay a call on the potential emperor — Mr. M. A. Jinnah. In view of the strategic position which he occupies, it is hardly an exaggeration to describe him as the most important man in Asia.

----

[1] *New York Times Magazine* of July 19th, 1942.

CHAPTER III

DIALOGUE WITH A GIANT

THE most important man in Asia is sixty-seven, tall, thin, and elegant, with a monocle on a grey silk cord, and a stiff white collar which he wears in the hottest weather. He suggests a gentleman of Spain, a diplomat of the old school; one used to see his like sitting in the window of the St. James's Club, sipping Contrexeville while he read *Le Temps*, which was propped against a Queen Anne toast rack stacked with toast Melba.

I have called Mr. Jinnah 'the most important man in Asia'. That was to ensure that you kept him spotlit in your mind. Like all superlatives the description is open to argument, but it is not really so far from the truth. India is likely to be the world's greatest problem for some years to come, and Mr. Jinnah is in a position of unique strategic importance. He can sway the battle this way or that as he chooses. His 100 million Muslims will march to the left, to the right, to the front, to the rear at his bidding, *and at nobody else's* . . . that is the point. It is not the same in the Hindu ranks. If Gandhi goes, there is always Nehru, or Rajagopalachari, or Patel or a dozen others. But if Jinnah goes, who is there?

By this I do not mean that the Muslim League would disintegrate — it is far too homogeneous and virile a body — but that its actions would be incalculable. It might run completely off the rails, and charge through India with fire and slaughter; it might start another war. As long as Jinnah is there, nothing like this will happen.

And so, you see, a great deal hangs on the grey silk cord of that monocle.

I first met him on December 18th, 1943. He said he could give me half an hour, and gave me nearly three. In that space of time he surveyed a very wide field; the gist of his remarks, however, the living essence, is in the following dialogue, which he has been good enough to edit.

Here we are then, sitting in a quiet room looking out on to a garden, discussing one of the most important problems in the world, with the man most competent to solve it.

II

SELF The most common accusation of your critics is that you have not defined Pakistan with sufficient precision — that there are many details of defence, economics, minorities, etc., which you have left deliberately vague. Do you think that is a just criticism?

JINNAH It is neither just nor intelligent, particularly if it is made by an Englishman with any knowledge of his own history. When Ireland was separated from Britain, the document embodying the terms of separation was approximately *ten lines*. Ten lines of print to settle a dispute of incredible complexity which has poisoned British politics for centuries! All the details were left to the Future — and the Future is often an admirable arbitrator. Well, I've already given the world a good deal more than ten lines to indicate the principles and practice of Pakistan, but it is beyond the power of any man to provide, in advance, a blue-print in which every detail is settled. Besides, Indian history proves that such a blue-print is totally unnecessary. Where was the blue-print when the question of Burmah's separation was decided at the Round Table Conference? Where was the blue-print when Sind was separated from Bombay? The answer, of course, is 'nowhere'. It didn't exist. It didn't need to exist. The vital point was that the principle of separation was accepted; the rest followed automatically.

SELF How would you describe the 'vital principles' of Pakistan?

JINNAH In five words. The Muslims are a Nation. If you grant that, and if you are an honest man, you must grant the principle of Pakistan. You would have to grant it even if the obstacles were a hundred times more formidable than they actually are. Of course, if you do *not* grant it, then . . . He shrugged his shoulders and smiled . . . Then, there is an end of the matter.

SELF When you say the Muslims are a Nation, are you thinking in terms of religion?

JINNAH Partly, but by no means exclusively. You must remember that Islam is not merely a religious doctrine but a realistic and practical Code of Conduct. I am thinking in terms of *life*, of everything important in life. I am thinking in terms of our history, our heroes, our art, our architecture, our music, our laws, our jurisprudence . . .

SELF Please, I would like to write these things down.

JINNAH (*after a pause*) In all these things our outlook is not only fundamentally different but often radically antagonistic to the Hindus. We are different *beings*. There is *nothing* in life which links us together. Our names, our clothes, our foods — they are all different; our economic life, our educational ideas, our treatment of women, our attitude to animals . . . we challenge each other at every point of the compass. Take one example, the eternal question of the cow. We eat the cow, the Hindus worship it. A lot of Englishmen imagine that this 'worship' is merely a picturesque convention, an historical survival. It is nothing of the sort. Only a few days ago, in this very city, the cow question became a matter for the police. The Hindus were thrown into the greatest agitation because cows were being killed in public. But the cow question is only one of a thousand. (*A pause*) What have you written down?

SELF I have only written 'The Muslims are a Nation'.

JINNAH And do you believe it?

SELF I do.

JINNAH (*with a smile*) What other questions have you got there?

SELF The first is economic. Are the Muslims likely to be richer or poorer under Pakistan? And would you set up tariffs against the rest of India?

JINNAH I'll ask you a question for a change. Supposing you were asked which you would prefer . . . a rich England under Germany or a poor England free, what would your answer be?

SELF It's hardly necessary to say.

JINNAH Quite. Well, doesn't that make your question look a little shoddy? This great ideal rises far above mere questions of personal comfort or temporary convenience. The Muslims are a tough people, lean and hardy. If Pakistan means that they will have to be a little tougher, they will not complain. But why *should* it mean that? What conceivable reason is there to suppose that the gift of nationality is going to be an economic liability? A sovereign nation of a hundred million people — even if they are *not* immediately self-supporting and even if they *are* industrially backward — is hardly likely to be in a worse economic position than if its members are scattered and disorganized, under the dominance of two hundred and fifty million Hindus whose one idea is to exploit them. How any European can get up and say that Pakistan is 'economically impossible' after the Treaty of Versailles is really beyond my comprehension. The great brains who cut Europe into a ridiculous patchwork of conflicting and artificial boundaries are hardly the people to talk economics to us, particularly as our problem happens to be far simpler.

SELF And does that also apply to defence?

JINNAH Of course it applies to defence. Once again I will ask *you* a question. How is Afghanistan defended? Well? The answer is not very complicated. By the Afghans. Just that. We are a brave and united people who are prepared to work and, if necessary, fight. So how does the question of defence present any peculiar difficulties? In what way do we differ from other nations? From Iran, for example? Obviously, there will have to be a transition period. We are not asking the British to quit India overnight. The British have helped to make this gigantic muddle, and they must stay and help to clear it up. But before they can do that, they will have to do a lot of hard thinking. And that reminds me — I have something I would like to show you.

·

He excused himself and left the room. I lit a cigarette and waited. And suddenly I realized that something very remarkable was happening, or rather was *not* happening. I was not losing my temper. Jinnah had been almost brutally critical of British policy (though I have not quoted his remarks in the above dialogue), but his criticism had been clear and creative. It was not merely a medley of wild words, a hotchpotch of hatred and hallucination, in the Hindu manner. It was more like a diagnosis. The difference between Jinnah and the typical Hindu politician was the difference between a surgeon and a witch doctor. Moreover, he was a surgeon you could trust, even though his verdict was harsh.

'The British must realize,' he had said to me before we tackled the problem of Pakistan, 'that they have not a friend in the country. Not a friend.'

A Hindu politician would have said that at the top of his voice, with delight. Jinnah said it quietly, with regret. Here he was again. In his hand he carried a book.

JINNAH You will remember I said, a moment ago, that the British would have to do a lot of hard thinking. It's a habit they don't find very congenial; they prefer to be comfortable, to wait and see, trusting that everything will come right in the end. However, when they do take the trouble to think, they think as clearly and creatively as any people in the world. And one of their best thinkers — at least on the Indian problem — was old John Bright. Have you ever read any of his speeches?

SELF Not since I left school.

JINNAH Well, take a look at this. I found it by chance the other day.

He handed me the book. It was a faded old volume, *The Speeches of John Bright*, and the date of the page at which it was opened was June 4th, 1858. This is what the greatest orator in the House of Commons said on that occasion:

'*How long does England propose to govern India? Nobody can answer that question. But be it 50 or 100 or 500 years, does any man with the smallest glimmering of common sense believe that so great a country, with its 20 different nationalities and its 20 different languages, can ever be bound up and consolidated into one compact and enduring empire confine? I believe such a thing to be utterly impossible.*'

I handed back the book.

JINNAH What Bright said then is true to-day . . . In fact, it's far *more* true—though, of course, the emphasis is not so much on the 20 nationalities as on the 2 . . . the Muslim and the Hindu. And why is it more true? Why hasn't time brought us together? Because the Muslims are *awake* . . . because they've learnt, through bitter experience, the sort of treatment they may expect from the Hindus in a 'United India'. A 'United India' means a Hindu-dominated India. It means that and nothing else. Any other meaning you attempt to impose on it is. mythical. 'India' is a British creation ... it is merely a single administrative unit governed by a bureaucracy under the sanction of the sword. That is all. It is a paper creation, it has no basis in flesh and blood.

SELF The ironical thing is that your critics say that Pakistan itself is a British creation — that it is an example of our genius for applying the principle of 'divide and rule'.

JINNAH (*with some heat*) The man who makes such a suggestion must have a very poor opinion of British intelligence, apart from his opinion of my own integrity. The one thing which *keeps* the British in India is the false idea of a United India, as preached by Gandhi. A United India, I repeat, is a British creation—a myth, and a very dangerous myth, which will cause endless strife. As long as that strife exists, the British have an excuse for remaining. For once in a way, 'divide and rule' does not apply.

SELF What you want is 'divide and quit'?

JINNAH You have put it very neatly.

SELF You realize that all this will come as something of a shock to the British electorate?

JINNAH Truth is often shocking. But why this truth in particular?

SELF Because the average, decent, liberal-minded voter, who wishes Britain to fulfil her pledges, and grant independence to India, has heard nothing but the Congress point of view. The Muslims have hardly a single spokesman in the West.

JINNAH (*bitterly*) I am well aware of that. The Hindus have organized a powerful Press and Congress—Mahasabha are backed up by Hindu capitalists and industrialists with finance which we have not got.

SELF As a result they believe that Congress is 'India', and since Congress never tires of repeating that India is one and indivisible, they imagine that any attempt to divide it is illiberal, reactionary, and generally sinister. They seriously *do* believe this. I know that it is muddle-headed, but then a democracy such as ours, which has to make up its mind on an incredible number of complicated issues usually *is* muddle-headed. What they have to learn is that the only liberal course, the only generous course, the only course

N

compatible with a sincere intention to quit India and hand over the reins of government.. . . .

JINNAH And the only *safe* course, you might add, is . . .

SELF
JINNAH } Pakistan!

III

The essence of Pakistan — at least of its spirit — is found in the foregoing dialogue. To give a complete exposition of the details of the plan, in a book of this size, would be quite impossible. It would need a sheaf of maps and pages of statistics, and it would carry us far afield, over the borders of India, and involve us in a great deal of unprofitable speculation.

It is fairly certain, however, that the reader who takes the trouble to go really deeply into the matter, with a mind unwarped by prejudice, will come to the conclusion that Pakistan offers no insuperable difficulties, economic, ethnographic, political or strategic, and is likely, indeed, to prove a good deal easier of attainment than a large number of similar problems which the world has successfully resolved in the past fifty years. It is, of course, a major surgical operation, but unfortunately there are occasions in the lives of nations, as of individuals, when major surgical operations are not only desirable but vitally necessary. And this is one of those occasions. The constant friction between the Hindu and Muslim nations has produced something which strongly resembles a cancer in the body politic. There is only one remedy for a cancer, in its advanced stages, and that is the knife. Gandhi's faith cures, British soothing syrup, the ingenious nostrums which are proffered by eager hands throughout the world — all these are useless. They only aggravate the patient's condition and make his ultimate cure more difficult. To the knife it will have to come in the end, and surely one knife, used swiftly and with precision, is better than a million knives, hacking in blind anarchy in the dark?

What is strange, in the whole Pakistan controversy, is not the support which it is slowly gaining among all realistic men but the opposition which it still evokes from sincere well-wishers of India.

This is, of course, due to the strength and persistence of Congress propaganda, backed by Hindu big business. The Hindus have almost a monopoly of propaganda. By subtle and persistent suggestion they have managed to persuade the world that they *are* 'India', and that any attempt to divide 'India' is a wicked 'plot on the part of the British, acting on the well-established principle of divide and rule'.

Most liberals of the West have fallen for, this propaganda, hook, line, and sinker. Consequently we have the extraordinary spectacle of 'advanced' British politicians rising to their feet in the House of Commons, and solemnly and sincerely pleading the cause of Indian 'Unity' *in the joint cause of Indian independence* — sublimely ignorant of the fact that their insistence on this so-called 'unity' is the one and only thing that keeps the British in the saddle!

Unite and Rule.

Divide and Quit.

Those words should be prominent on the desks of all those who offer their opinions on India and her problems.

An even more remarkable aspect of the success of Congress propaganda is that it has been accepted by vast bodies of men and women who really are genuinely disturbed by the grievances of oppressed minorities in any other part of the world but India. They will call urgent committee meetings to discuss a fancied slight to the Slovaks, they drive themselves nearly crazy worrying over the Hungarians in Roumania or the Austrians in Northern Italy, but they remain completely apathetic to the wrongs of 100 million Muslims, whose claims to nationality and independence are far more ancient and far more urgent. If these people were not so obviously sincere, they might well be accused of perfidious Albionism on a scale almost unparalleled in history.

I wish that there were space to speculate on the probable results to the world of the adoption, by the British Government, of the policy of 'Divide and Quit'. I myself believe that it would be salutary not only for India, but for Britain and all mankind. It would be a natural step forward in the March of Time. It would cleanse the world's bosom of much perilous stuff. And if it were done quickly, cleanly, and without compromise, it might reap for Britain golden rewards, not only in the things of commerce but in the things of the spirit, by reminding us of our kinship with the great Muslim world, with which, if we would only admit it, we have so profound an affinity.

POSTSCRIPT

A friend who has read this chapter made the following comment: 'Jinnah, as you have enunciated him, sounds convincing, but to what extent does he really represent Muslim opinion? Is the Muslim League, in actual fact, identical with Muslim India? If it is, then Pakistan wins; if it is not, and if there is any considerable body of Muslims who oppose the League, your whole argument falls to the ground.'

This is an important point, and it deserves an answer. It can be given very briefly.

If the Muslim League does *not* represent Muslim India, one may politely inquire who *does*? If there is any other organization challenging its right to speak for the Muslim masses, what is it? Where is it hiding itself? And why, if there were even the faintest shadow of opposition to the League in the Muslim ranks ... why, oh why is even the Congress unaware of its existence? Why does Congress confine all its complaints, so loudly and bitterly, to the *League*? Why does Congress proclaim, day in and day out, that it is with the *League* that they must reach a settlement? Why does Gandhi address all his pleas, his admonitions, and his scoldings to Jinnah, the leader of the League?

The answer, surely, is sufficiently obvious; it is because the League *is* Muslim India. There are no discordant voices for the simple reason that the League is the complete expression of the Muslim will.

For those who like statistics, the figures are overwhelmingly convincing. With only one exception,[1] EVERY SINGLE BY-ELECTION FOUGHT BY THE MUSLIMS ANYWHERE IN INDIA DURING THE LAST SEVEN YEARS HAS BEEN WON BY LEAGUE CANDIDATES. They were cent per cent pro-Pakistan, their programmes contained not the faintest shadow of the suggestion of compromise or prevarication, and they swept the board, every time, everywhere, in Bengal, in

[1] A curious case in the United Provinces, where local and personal prejudices confused the issue.

Assam, in the North-West Frontier, in Sind, in all the provinces, in fact, which Pakistan will eventually absorb. In the Central Legislature itself, out of 30 Muslim seats, 28 are held by vehement Leaguers.

If that is not the expression of the Muslim people's will, it would be legitimate to inquire what was!

CHAPTER IV

HUNGER

AND now it is time to study the manner in which the British are
tackling those problems. Anything like a general survey being
beyond the scope of this book, it will be best if we concentrate on
one event which has lately gained widespread attention throughout the world — the recent famine in Bengal.

We choose to discuss this for several reasons. First and foremost
because it was so shocking and heart-rending a business that the
world's conscience should be constantly reminded of it. Every
calendar of every British and Indian politician ought to be marked
with a little memo, towards the beginning of each summer, to
remind him of the horror of 1943 and the need to guard against
its repetition.

But there is another reason why it is important to re-enact the
tragedy. By large sections of opinion, at home and abroad, it was
regarded as a blot on the British record. The warm-hearted,
muddle-headed British public, who invariably take an almost
masochistic delight in putting themselves in the wrong, before
they have made even the most cursory attempt to examine the
evidence, excelled themselves on this occasion by the positive
relish with which they shouted *mea culpa*. People who could not
even find Bengal on the map — let alone give an adequate description of the method of its government — echoed every scanda-
lous accusation of the Congress propagandists and automatically
assumed that any statement made by British officers on the spot
must be a lie. Indian students at British universities, who must of
necessity have been in total ignorance of the facts, were elevated
into oracles, while British public servants, with twenty years'
experience, were condemned almost unheard. It was an outstanding example of a national trait which is usually called .
'fair-mindedness', though on occasions like this there would be
some excuse for describing it as pathological.

However, it is not primarily to plead the cause of any group of politicians, British or Indian, that I am writing this chapter, but to speak for the pitiful masses who, in the heat of local controversy, were often almost forgotten.

11

Hunger is a cruel caricaturist.

It takes the slim body of a child and puffs out the stomach with a single bloated line, till you will say that it was swollen with phantom foods. Of all the tragic figures in Bengal none were more poignant than the children. As they shuffled down the streets their faces were like tight-stretched masks and their limbs like withered twigs; but always those grotesque stomachs swelled out in front of them, as though in mockery of their plight.

This freakish effect of starvation was not to be seen in the adults; their stomachs were merely non-existent—patches of brown skin stretched between the lower ribs and the thighs. But they too bore all the marks of caricature; they were like cartoons come to life. In the past few years we have all seen posters illustrating the plight of the oppressed peoples of Europe, we have become bitterly familiar with drawings of skeleton mothers clasping dying children in their arms, of young bodies shrunk to the bone, staring sightlessly at lurid skies. Well, Calcutta was like that. You kept saying to yourself 'this is not life, this is some frightful pageant; and surely, it is grossly overproduced. How can cheek-bones stick out so sharply? How can ribs be so bleakly defined? How can shoulders give that hideous effect of loose cloth draped over a gaunt framework?'

'No — this is not life, it is melodrama, and very crude melodrama too.' So one reasoned. And indeed, no theatrical producer would have dared pile on the horror so thick.

The rats, for example. Surely, if this had been a play or a film, the rats would have been smaller? As one stood under the arches of Chowringhee, late at night, with the bodies of the destitute huddled all around in attitudes of spectacular abandon, the rats looked like great dogs, slinking about in the shadows. As the weeks went by, and as the last remains of strength slowly ebbed from the wretches in the gutters, the rats grew bolder; they did not hurry when they crawled over the body of a child; they paused ... you saw their bright eyes twinkle, as though in anticipation.

No film director would have passed films like that; he would have been accused of parody.

Yet this was no parody; it was plain fact. Of all the stories they told me, before visiting Calcutta, the one which sounded least convincing concerned the fights for food-refuse which were alleged to be taking place round the municipal dustbins. This story was printed so often, and always with such a wealth of harrowing detail, that it sounded bogus. Yet it was precisely this story that I saw being played in real life within a few hours of arrival. I was walking down a side-street when there was the cry of a child. I looked back. There on the pavement the child lay sprawling; it had been hurled away from a bin by its father who was himself plunging one hand into an indescribable collection of garbage, while with the other hand he fought off the rest of the family. They were snarling and wailing like exhausted animals and from time to time lifted some loathsome scrap of refuse to their lips.

III

I went to Calcutta at the height of the famine because Mrs. Naidu had said in Hyderabad, that 'this crisis has done more to undermine the prestige of the British raj than fifty years of Congress propaganda'.

Mrs. Naidu, needless to say, welcomed this fact — if fact it was. The qualification is necessary because some of Mrs. Naidu's facts, which were typical of the Congress propaganda, were somewhat akin to wishful thinking. For instance, she was apparently convinced that one of the major causes of the famine was the greed of the army. Such a suggestion will not bear a moment's examination, firstly because the British army did not eat rice, and secondly because the Indian army would have been eating rice in any case, whether they were in uniform or out of it. The atmosphere of the Naidu household was thick with such 'facts'. Another concerned the food eaten by the Italian prisoners who were interned somewhere in the Central Provinces. Listening to the Naidus one was almost convinced that the Italians were responsible for the deaths of tens of thousands of Indians.

However, it is distasteful to criticize the members of a family who were so kind to me. When I left Hyderabad, Mrs. Naidu's son—the Ayurvedic expert—came to see me off at the station. Just as the train was leaving he handed me a little package. It proved to contain a copper plate, pierced in three places. Wrapped round the plate were some directions to the effect that if it were hung over the stomach, three inches above the navel, it would prove efficacious in warding off cholera, which was raging in Calcutta at the time. This seemed so singular a remedy that some days later I asked a European doctor if it could possibly be of any value. He said that it might serve to divert a bullet but that as far as discouraging the cholera germ was concerned it would be as effective to wear a piece of blotting-paper.

However, all this is keeping us from the stricken areas, so let us speed along with the train, and see for ourselves whether Mrs. Naidu was right in her contention that a resounding blow had been struck against the British raj.

The train was not due to arrive in Calcutta till about noon, but as soon as I pushed up the blind in the early morning, and looked out at the wayside station where we had halted, it was evident that we had already arrived in a land of the dying. All along the platform, wherever there was any shade, crowds of living skeletons were huddled together. They were quite silent and almost motionless. Occasionally a child would stir uneasily, and now and then one of the skeletons would very slowly lift up the food-tin which it was holding and stare into its empty depths, as though hoping by some miracle to find food in it. One little girl just outside my carriage kept on putting her finger into the tin, rubbing it round and round, and then sucking it.

I am not one of those who hold — with Bernard Shaw — that it is wrong to give money to beggars. Obviously, private charity would be superfluous in an ideal society, but since society is not yet noticeably ideal it seems not only heartless to ignore distress when one has the means to relieve it, but positively cruel to accompany the denial by some smug generalization of Fabian doctrine. It is difficult to imagine Christ greeting a beggar with a lecture on economics.

And so, when the little girl began to rub her finger round and round the tin I took down my suitcase and began to fumble hastily around to see whether there might be something in it which she could eat. The result was not very happy — a small tin of tongue, a bottle of tomato juice, a tin of sardines, and some canned beans. Still it was something, and one could add a rupee or two.

I tried to open the window. As usual it stuck. I tugged harder; it suddenly seemed vitally important to give this food to the little girl.

'Can I help?'

It was my travelling companion, a pleasant-faced young Hindu who had joined the train late the night before, and had clambered straight into the upper berth.

'If you wouldn't mind . . .'

He climbed down and went to the window. Then he noticed the tins, and paused.

'Were you thinking of giving those to the people outside?'

'Yes. It's all I have.'

'It wouldn't do any good. They couldn't eat it.'

'I should have thought they'd eat anything?'

He shook his head. 'No. They only eat rice.'

I looked out at the little girl. Surely at least she could have had some of the beans?

'All the same,' I said, 'I wish we could open this window. I have a little money . . .'

'But they could not buy anything with it. There *is* no food here. That is why they are all at the station, to board trains that will take them to Calcutta.'

The train was beginning to move, and just at that moment the window flew open of its own accord. There would still have been time to hand out my pathetic presents, but somehow it didn't seem any use. As the rows of silent skeletons streamed past the window I began to wonder if *anything* was of any use, short of a miraculous deluge of manna from the hard and burning heavens.

I turned to my Hindu friend. 'Did you mean it literally, when you said they only ate rice?'

'Quite literally. Food means that and nothing else. It doesn't mean meat, nor fish nor eggs nor potatoes; it doesn't mean corn, nor millet, nor even *bajri*, which bears many resemblances to rice. It means rice first, last, and all the time, morning, noon, and night. If you gave them anything else most of them wouldn't know what to do with it. And even if they managed to eat it, it wouldn't agree with them. If you feed a rice-eater on anything but rice he develops a host of stomach troubles, from dysentery downwards.'

This young Hindu proved an instructive travelling companion. He was himself employed in a branch of the Food Administration, and he told me one thing about the shortage which seemed so fantastic that at first I thought he must be romancing. Subsequent inquiry proved that he was telling the truth, and so here is the gist of his story.

It concerns the population problem. In the last twelve years the population of India has increased by sixty million. (If the average Englishman realized that this is almost equivalent to the entire white population of the British Empire, he might sit up and take notice. He might see several warning shadows looming on the horizon. So, for that matter, might the average citizen of the United States!)

But the province of Bengal has increased at an even greater rate than the rest of India. Why? For the reason described above as 'fantastic'. *Simply because the proportion of Muslims and Hindus in the province is so nearly balanced that all devout parents are engaged in a crazy race to produce children at any cost.*

The children will have no food? No clothes? No jobs? No possible prospects? It is of no consequence. All that matters is that another baby should be on the way at the earliest possible opportunity. Only thus can Allah be praised and Vishnu propitiated.

And so, you see, statistics in India are not quite as simple as statistics in some other parts of the world. There is witchcraft working behind the figures, and when you examine them closely they dance and flicker in strange variations.

I began to realize that my trip to Calcutta might prove instructive in more ways than one.

IV

Calcutta at last. And always that terrible sense of caricature to which we referred at the opening of this chapter.

It seemed to permeate every branch of society. On one of my first days in the city I went to lunch with a young man who was doing a fine job in the relief kitchens. He lived in a luxurious modern flat; we had delicious cocktails; the company was elegant and distinguished.

'We never eat rice in this house,' he said. 'Not since the famine. I have told my cook not to buy it under any circumstances.'

And at precisely that moment the butler entered with a tray of caviare on toast. It was not his fault; the caviare would have been of no use to the skeletons outside. But the sense of caricature was acute.

Everywhere it was the same. The friend with whom I was staying had a bowl of goldfish. It was pleasant to sit on the balcony and watch them swimming round, cool and glittering and aloof. And then one day I noticed on the table by the bowl a little packet labelled 'Finest Goldfish Food'. The contrast was trite and obvious . . . the well-fed goldfish and the starving children . . . but one's mind was beginning to develop morbid fancies, in which even the obvious seemed swollen and distorted, like the slim figures of the goldfish themselves.

All down the main shopping centres there were restaurants and food-shops. Outside them, propped against the wall, huddled in the gutters, sprawled over the steps, were the silent skeletons. If you wanted to buy some chocolate to send home to England you had literally to step over the bodies. I only did it once—the whole thing was too painful and embarrassing. After a few days the very sight of food was hateful.

My first attempt at private charity was not a success. One day, from the balcony where my friend kept the goldfish, we saw a woman on the pavement below, stretched face downwards with a child lying across her shoulder. Both were nearly naked and both were in such an extremity of starvation that one could have taken the skin of their backs and twisted it round like an old rag. We were just sitting down to tea and I said to the bearer, 'We really can't sit here and eat while there are people like that outside'. So we cut two large pieces of walnut cake, poured out a jug of tea, added some fruit and a couple of rupee notes and sent the bearer down with it. He was a Pathan, with a deep contempt for Bengalis, and he did not at all relish his errand, which he regarded as beneath his dignity. However, he took down the parcel and we watched the result.

It took the woman several minutes to rise to a sitting position. Then, very slowly, she held up the cake and sniffed it. Then she let it fall in the gutter, where it attracted the attention of a couple of crows. Meanwhile the child was also stirring. He too held up the cake and sniffed it, and for a moment it seemed as though he was going to eat it . . . but no, he only crumbled it up in his tiny fingers. The tea they neglected completely. After a while the woman listlessly gathered up the fruit and tied it, together with the two rupee notes, in a bundle of filthy rags. All these actions were performed in slow motion. An hour later she was still fumbling with the rags. Then, with the most painful effort and many false starts, they staggered to their feet and shuffled away.

On the following morning, the daily official list of famine casualties read as follows:

Admission to hospital of sick destitutes	137
Died in hospital	84
Bodies removed by Sanitation Squads	76

I wondered in which class would be numbered the two poor wretches we had tried to help.

v

No useful purpose will be served, in these pages, by prolonging a description of the agonies of this famine. The reader might be taken on a tour of the relief kitchens or into some of the villages, where conditions were even worse. Or into the offices of the ministers and the business men of all parties, with whom I discussed the problem exhaustively. He would only be harrowed and confused.

But apart from its human interest, this tragedy arouses two questions, and for that reason it is essential to examine, however briefly, its causes.

Those questions are, firstly, to what extent was the Central Government responsible? The manner in which we answer this question will decide in what degree we must regard the famine as a blot on our Imperial record.

Secondly, to what extent was the Provincial Government responsible? The manner in which we answer this question will decide in what degree India may be regarded as capable of self-government.

Let us tackle this problem as swiftly and concisely as possible.

There were three main causes of the famine. Here they are in order of their importance. However diffident I may feel about some of the opinions expressed in this book I am not in the least diffident about these. These are facts which admit of no argument.

The first and far the most important cause was Nature herself. The crop of August 1942 was one of the worst on record; it was followed in October by devastating cyclones. In the meantime the whole of the Burmah crop had been lost in the fortunes of war. As if this were not enough, the spring of 1943 was marked by devastating floods, which disrupted communications already over-burdened by war transport.

Whatever form of government had been in power — even if there had been a Central Government entirely composed of geniuses and a Provincial Government entirely composed of saints — there would have been famine, and the man who denies it is, quite bluntly, a liar.

The second cause of the famine was the corruption, incompetence, and irresponsibility of the Provincial Government.

Judging from the debates in the House of Commons, it would appear that many members of the opposition were totally unaware that there was such a thing as a Provincial Government in Bengal at all — a government, moreover, that was overwhelmingly Indian in composition, entrusted with powers that should have been adequate to deal with the situation, and, even if they had not been adequate, could have been reinforced by prompt appeal to Delhi. (The appeal, as we shall see, was not made till it was too late.) The speeches of the British Labour members, in particular, were incoherent outbursts of sentimentality which reflected the realities of the situation rather 'less accurately than the 'Indian Love Lyrics' of Miss Amy Woodford Finden.

What is the record of this Provincial Government — this *Indian* government, elected by free and open suffrage in conditions of the widest publicity?

Well, it was headed during the most critical months by a gentleman called Mr. Fazlul Huq. Since my own views of Mr. Huq's activities might possibly be regarded as prejudiced, it will be sufficient to quote the opinion of him delivered by the Lord Chief Justice in Calcutta High Court on August 24th, 1943, when his Lordship described Mr. Huq as 'unfit for public office'. He was summing up in an 'unsavoury and disquieting' affair which was known as the Jiaganj Rice Looting Case. Mr. Huq's connection with this case was — to quote the Chief Justice — that while he was Chief Minister of the Province he 'criminally interfered with the legitimate transport of rice, of which there was a grave scarcity in the province'.

Here is the end of the summing up, quoted from the *Calcutta Statesman* of August 25th:

'It was clear that Mr. Fazlul Huq, while Chief Minister, had used his position to influence the course of justice for political reasons. If the legitimate and proper transport of food could be interfered with and the malefactors protected by the Chief Minister, then there was an end of law and order in the province. At the time this rice looting took place Mr. Huq was Minister for the Home Department; the looted rice was intended for Berhampore Jail; the administration of jails was a matter with which the Home Department was charged. *But neither his solemn oath nor public responsibility prevented him from doing this nefarious work.*'

'As far as his Lordship was aware there was no punishment in law for the breaking of the promissory oath taken by Mr. Huq when he assumed office as Chief Minister. *But a clean violation of it branded a man as unfit for public office.* If solemn promissory oaths by persons who took office in the State were to be disregarded as mere formalities, there was no possibility of good government. His Lordship observed: "*Mr. Huq is left to the contemplation and judgment of his fellow-men*".'

One would have thought, after these acid comments, that Mr. Huq would have retired to the country and devoted the rest of his life to the cultivation of hydrangeas. Not at all. His career appears to have been in no way prejudiced. Bengal politics are like that.[1]

Let us turn to the official documents. One of the most remarkable journals I have ever read is the *Official Report of the Assembly Proceedings in the Bengal Legislative Assembly*. This may be described as the Bengal *Hansard*, but it bears about as much real resemblance to *Hansard* as the Marx Brothers bear to the Barrymores. So numerous are the interruptions, the uproars, and the calls to order that the pages give the impression of farcical dialogue rather than of sober debate.

However, occasionally a member does manage to utter a few consecutive sentences, and one of these occasions was on July 5th, 1943, when the Minister for Civil Supplies, the Honourable Kwaja Sir Nazimuddin made a statement on the food situation (see volume 45 of the *Assembly Proceedings*). If the vociferous critics of the British Government had taken the trouble to study this statement they might have been less hasty in their strictures. For here, the Minister admits in so many words that he had deliberately spread the impression that all was well when, in fact, famine was already stalking towards Bengal in seven-league boots. Listen to him:

'I have found criticisms levelled against me that I had stated that there was no shortage when actually there was serious shortage in the Province ... but it appeared to me that insistence on shortage would only increase panic and stimulate hoarding and push up prices. *I therefore refused to discuss the question ... I was able*

[1] An interesting sidelight on the mentality of Mr. Huq, who, it must be emphasized, is one of the most prominent and successful politicians that Indian nationalism has produced, is afforded by the advertisement columns of the *Bombay Chronicle Weekly* for November 7th, 1943. This contains a glowing tribute from Mr. Huq to Raj Jyotishi, 'the great astrologer and renowned Taptrick'. Among Jyotishi's contributions to mankind is the sale of powerful jewels and charms whose wearers are guaranteed 'promotion in service, prosperity in business, peace of mind, family happiness and immunity from incurable diseases'. The jewels are described as 'protection from all evil stars'. In justice to Mr. Huq it must be admitted that he is by no means the only Indian politician who boasts of his reliance upon astrologers and magicians; Jyotishi's list of Indian clients is formidable, and includes many of the most distinguished champions of Indian nationalism. *Chacun à son goût*, but it is a little difficult to reconcile this jiggery-pokery with adult representative institutions.

to state with a clear conscience that *there was or would be sufficient and there was no need for panic.*'

In the light of such statements it is difficult to understand the violence with which British members of Parliament assailed Mr. Amery for *his* lack of foresight.

Another outburst greeted Mr. Amery when he suggested that one cause, at least, of the famine was hoarding and black marketing. It was suggested that this was a 'libel on the Indian character' . . . 'a cowardly attempt to shift responsibility from his own shoulders'.

Was it? Listen to the Indian version of the matter, as exposed in the same speech of Sir Nazimuddin.

'Hoarding and black marketing and other anti-social activities were widely prevalent; one of the major factors we had to deal with was greed brought about by the speculative rise in prices.'

He went on to explain that between the 10th and the 12th of June a special drive was launched against hoarders. The results of this drive were staggering. 'It is difficult to estimate the amount but it can easily be put down in the region of seven to eight million maunds.'

In Western measures this is roughly equivalent to six hundred and forty million pounds. Considering that this vast amount was unearthed in the space of forty-eight hours it would seem that hoarding was not so alien to the Indian mentality as it had been inferred.

Another outburst from the theorists occurred when one or two British spokesmen hinted that things might not have been so bad if the various Indian provinces had adopted a more good-neighbourly policy . . . if there had been some signs of fraternal unity among the Indians themselves. 'Another libel!' cried the critics. 'An unwarranted sneer at the Indian character!'

Unwarranted? Once again, let India speak for herself. Nazimuddin described how, in order to relieve the situation, it was essential to restore free trade between Bengal and the more fortunate neighbouring provinces and states.

'What followed,' he states, 'is well known. The neighbouring Provincial Governments *did everything possible to defeat free trade*, and requisitioned all visible stocks to provide their own security

o

services with cheap food-grains.' He added that, 'I hope and trust that even now these Governments will shed their parochial instinct and come to our assistance'.

His hope was not justified. So much for brotherly love!

That is the one thing for which one will search in vain throughout these riotous volumes of the *Assembly Proceedings* . . . fraternity. Not once — not for a single moment, not in a single paragraph — is there the least evidence that the members are prepared to forget their personal squabbles in the cause of a wider humanity. Those of us who used to follow the debates in the French Senate before the war were often sickened by the irresponsibility, the egotism, and the corruption of the deputies, who had utterly forgotten the greatness of France in the furtherance of their own petty interests. But the French deputies were a collection of saintly altruists compared to the politicians of Bengal. Reading these debates one has the impression that the very atmosphere of the Chamber was impregnated with some strange poison in which public decency faltered and died.

And the nature of this poison — though the whole of Bengal rises up and contradicts me — was the old, old curse of India . . . religious bitterness. Hardly one of the members was able to visualize the starving multitudes outside as men and women, they thought of them only as Hindus and Muslims. This is so bitter an accusation that I would not make it on my own authority. We must allow India the unhappy privilege of convicting herself from the mouths of her own people.

Here is an extract from a speech by the well-known liberal leader, Pandit Kunzru, delivered at a mass meeting held at the Calcutta University on October 15th, 1943 (the quotation is from the report in the *Hindustan Standard* of October 17th).

'Even at the present time when the Hon'ble Food Minister is seeking the co-operation of all classes, he has appealed to the peasants *in the name of the Muslim League* to desist from withholding food grains from the market! Could there be a greater tragedy for Bengal than such an attitude in this situation, appealing only to a *section* of the people, and rousing feelings detrimental to the best interests of the population of Bengal?'

It is significant that this attack on the Muslim League aroused greater enthusiasm than any other part of the Hindu Pandit's speech.

And now for the Muslim side of it. Writing in the *Calcutta Statesman* of October 12th, 1943, the Muslim correspondent 'Shahed' makes the following observations:

'The Muslim leaders have repeatedly begged the Hindu Opposition to assist them in ending this tragic and shameful episode in Bengal's history. Even after the most atrocious libels uttered against the Ministry during the recent food debate in the Assembly, Mr. Suhrawardy made an appeal to the libellers to co-operate. The answer was, "We will not listen to murderers!" '

To sum up, the debates in the Bengal Assembly, through the long months of the crisis, afforded a sickening example of passion, prejudice, and irresponsibility.[1] Reading them it is difficult to believe that these are grown-up men discussing an urgent and vital problem; they sound like naughty children. It is impossible to acquit either side of blame, but it is only fair to admit that the Muslims did *try* to achieve some sort of façade of unity. They may not have offered the olive branch very gracefully but they did at least produce it. To quote again from 'Shahed's' article:

'The Muslims are prepared to forget; their leaders are even now prepared to work hand in hand with their Hindu traducers, if only the latter will likewise bury the past, and above all, *abandon tactics to gain communal and political ends*, and regard the issue of Bengal's starving people as the only issue that matters.'

Our summary is growing to unwarranted lengths. But the matter is too important to be skimped.

We have seen that the two main causes of the famine were firstly the malignant forces of nature, and secondly the incapacity of the Indian Provincial Government to cope with the resultant situation.

---

[1] Time and again the vital business of debate is interrupted in order to rehash some futile religious wrangle. The interested reader will do well to refer to volume LXIV (No 3), p. 454 onwards, where he will find the opening acts of a typical Indian political drama. It arose from the demand of some Muslim students at the Pabna College, for a small room in which to say their prayers. As soon as the request was granted, the Hindu students gathered outside the room at prayer time and made loud noises with musical instruments. The result may be imagined; the whole college was in an uproar; and the controversy spread to the Assembly itself. The reports of the debates give the impression that these matters were very much more important to the delegates than the fate of their starving countrymen.

That brings us to the third reason — our own shortcomings, the failure of Delhi.

It can hardly be questioned that the future historian will consider this third reason of minor importance, compared with the others. We have already seen that no attempt was made by the Provincial Government to enlist Delhi's aid until they had got themselves into such a mess that there was no other way out. And by now we should know enough about Indian nationalism to realize that there would have been an outburst of protest if Delhi had overriden the Provincial Government by making any gesture that could have been interpreted as 'premature'.

That does not absolve us from all responsibility. But in admitting responsibility we are at least entitled to a fair defence. For example, one of the accusations most frequently levelled at us is that there were no adequate statistics to guide the authorities in their endeavour to distribute food throughout the province. That is quite true; the available statistics were hazy and out of date. The methods of obtaining them were absurdly primitive. What usually happened was that the District Officer would call for his Choukidar (a sort of village caretaker) and say, 'What sort of yield shall we have from the line by the river to the village boundary?' And the Choukidar would put his hand over his eyes, and after gazing about him for a few minutes would report that there would be 200 bighas[1] of a twelve-anna crop and 100 bighas of a fourteen-anna crop. That was all that happened, and if the margin of error was less than 25 per cent he was lucky. Obviously, in territories where even at the best of times there was a 5 per cent deficit for the whole population, such methods were courting disaster, sooner or later.

But if we admit facts like these let us at least set them against their proper background. What does that background show us? It shows us a population of sixty million in the province of Bengal alone, largely illiterate, increasing at a rate which would tax the resources of a land flowing with milk and honey. A population, moreover, so violently torn by religious discord that the mere absence of civil war is a remarkable tribute to our administration. And in charge of this vast and turbulent people, lacking even the

[1] A bigha is about a third of an acre.

rudiments of homogeneity, are a mere handful of Europeans, who receive singularly little co-operation from their Indian colleagues to whom, in increasing measure, they have handed over power.

Blame us, if you will, but blame us for not achieving miracles. That is the only charge to which we need honestly plead guilty.

Most of the British failures in India — and nobody suggests that there have not been failures — have been due to an excess of gentleness rather than to an abuse of strength. We have known the right thing to do but we have not always done it, for fear of offending Indian susceptibilities.[1] The Bengal famine might never have happened if the thinly scattered ranks of British officials had been able to count on the co-operation of a large number of educated Indians, acquainted with the intricacies of local agriculture and village life. No such body existed. True, there were thousands of unemployed graduates in the big cities who would have been perfectly fitted for the work, but they refused to contemplate it. It was too dull, irksome, and disagreeable; it was much better left to the British. They preferred to eke out a scanty livelihood as hangers-on at the law courts, hack journalists, stenographers, and even errand-boys. Once the average Indian graduate has escaped from his village, wild horses will not drag him back again.

Well, *somebody* will have to drag him back again if the rural districts are ever to show any advance in education, agriculture, sanitation, and the rudimentary decencies of life. We might have dragged him back ourselves, if we had had the courage to pass an act compelling the Indian graduates to spend at least a year or two, after obtaining their degree, in studying rural administration. We did not possess the courage, and now that we have granted provincial autonomy, we no longer possess the power. This vital act will have to be passed by the Indians themselves.

And then, the sparks will begin to fly.

I repeat, the only charge to which we need plead guilty is the

[1] The classic example of this tendency is afforded by the appalling custom by which high caste Hindu women burned themselves on the funeral pyres of their husbands. We wanted to abolish this, of course, and we did, but refrained from doing so because of our traditional policy of non-interference with national institutions. Incredible as it may sound, many high caste Hindus still deplore the abolition of suttee. I have heard them refer, with wistful regret, to the grand old days when women had 'the courage to do it'. If the British quit India it is a fairly safe bet that suttee will return.

charge that we did not achieve miracles. And when Lord Wavell came to Delhi, we nearly did. Why? Because once again we had the courage to rule as we thought fit, without timidity or sub-servience to Nationalist criticism. Wavell treated the whole prob-lem from a military angle, issuing crisp, decisive orders and showing, from the outset, that he would 'stand no nonsense'. And the vast majority of Indians breathed a sigh of relief. Now, at last, something would be done. Now, at last, the interminable wrangles in the Assembly would echo into limbo, and be silenced by the clear-cut commands of British officers. True, the Press was not noticeably co-operative. There were sneering references to Wavell's eyeglass, which was described as yet another example of 'Vice-regal pomposity'. (He wears it to conceal the fact that one eye was blinded in battle.) There were many suggestions that the only reason the British were concerning themselves with the problem at all was because they feared the famine might adversely influence their military position.

However, if one read between the lines, one detected a sense of gratitude. It was the same sort of gratitude which has so often caused crowds of religious rioters to cry, 'Thank God they're here!' when British troops have arrived to restore order. Needless to say this gratitude is never expressed in print; the humble masses who are saved from bloodshed are not of the class who write letters to the papers. All the outside world knows of these matters is that some Congress leader has been hit on the nose with a bamboo rod, and this is reckoned as yet another black mark against Imperial brutality.

But the Indian knows — the real Indian, the peasant in his paddy field, who only prays to be left in peace. The Indian knows, and the Indian will remember. Let us hope that he will not have too bitter cause to remember — and to regret — in the stormy days that lie ahead.

CHAPTER V

WHITE AND OFF-WHITE

IF you were to take the entire population of Great Britain, men, women, and children, and dump them down in the middle of India, they would still be outnumbered nine to one.

That is a graphic illustration of perhaps the most singular feature of British rule, the fact that it is the rule of a mere handful. In peace time (apart from the tiny standing army, which was only just adequate to perform essential police services) the ratio was about 10 thousand British subjects to 40 million Indians.

The phrase 'Quit India' makes one think of a mass exodus, a sort of transfer of population, spread over many months and involving an immense disruption of transport. Actually, it could all be accomplished over a week-end, and every man, woman, and child could be removed from the country in a single convoy of modest proportions.

Never was so much done for so many by so few. The word 'done' is substituted for the word 'owed' because it is the purpose of this chapter to assess the British as frankly as we have assessed the Indians, to inquire what sort of people they really are and how far they are worthy of their responsibilities.

Those ancient figures of comedy — the pukka sahib and his memsahib — do they really exist? Do they yell for *chota pegs* at sundown, in the manner of E. M. Forster? Do they 'go out in the midday sun', in the manner of Noel Coward? Do they indulge in illicit passions against a background of tamarind and sandalwood, in the manner of Somerset Maugham?

The answer to these questions, like the answers to most of the questions in life, is 'Yes and No'.

There are, of course, some quite frightful people, particularly in the female line, vulgar, sex-ridden women who spend most of their lives in the long bar of the hotels, trying to look like ladies and cocottes at the same time, without any noticeable success in either direction. They are petulant and domineering, and complain loudly if they are asked to do any war work; even half an hour at a canteen seemed to make them feel that they were being crucified. There was a good deal of bitterness among the troops in all the big cities because practically nothing was done for their comfort. An occasional 'society' revue (in which the quality of the 'society' was as questionable as the taste of their material) was about the sum total of the efforts of the majority of the ladies in Bombay and Calcutta.

HELP THE WAR EFFORT BY GOING RACING

Believe it or not, that is a headline which is splashed across the Bombay newspapers every week. People coming from war-time England, when they first saw that notice, found it difficult to believe their eyes; it seemed impossible that so atrocious a lapse from taste could have been passed by any responsible Editor. The Bombay race-course is seven miles from the centre of the city; every Saturday during the season it is surrounded with a sea of expensive thirty-horse-power cars, burning petrol which has to be brought thousands of miles through perilous seas. From these cars step the English ladies of Bombay, smiling gaily, because their hats are new and their consciences are clear. Are they not 'helping the war effort'? Does not the sum of two per cent — yes, a whole *two* per cent — of the tote go to war charities? What more can a girl be expected to do on a hot Saturday afternoon, after a whole week of dry martinis?

I suggested to various members of the European Association that such an advertisement was unspeakably vulgar, and that it would be unthinkable in Britain, or indeed in any country that had the remotest realization of being at war. I told them that it was an insult to our Russian allies, and an affront to the men of the merchant navy. They replied:

'But the Indians go to the races. Why shouldn't we?'

'At least we might try to set an example.'

'But it *is* helping the war effort,' they answered.

We left it at that. Bitter experience had proved that the members of the Bombay European Association are a collection of liverish nobodies, sunk in suburban complacency, ignorant, petty, and pretentious.

However, fortunately for the Empire, they are by no means typical of the British in India. To use a phrase which they would probably use themselves, the average British men and women are a 'pretty decent lot', particularly those who live in remote districts, far from the cities — though they themselves would probably agree that they are not brilliantly exciting. It is difficult to keep one's sparkle at a temperature of 100 in the shade, on a small salary, with no intellectual companionship but one's houseboy, with no news except a few copies of *Life*, four months old and partially eaten by ants . . . above all, with no thanks, either from the Indians or one's fellow-countrymen.

The one quality that is common to all of them is courage. Whatever else you may deny to this tiny handful of men and women who are scattered over the country like a pinch of alien dust on a gigantic desert, you must grant them courage. You must grant it to the young policeman, yesterday a schoolboy, bewildered by the fierce religious hatreds of a mob which he must try to control almost alone, a mob of thousands on whom he must not fire except in extremity — and 'extremity' does *not* mean when his face is bloody with broken glass. You must grant it to the little garrisons of the North-West Frontier, living in the perpetual shadow of the sniper, the human sport of the men who kill, quite literally, for fun, since that is the tribesman's way. Forty years ago Kipling flashed his searchlight on the life and death of those youths who guard the northern gateway:

> A scrimmage in a border station,
> A canter down some dark defile . . .
> Two thousand pounds of education
> Drops to a ten-rupee jezail.

Those lines are as true to-day as when they were first written.

Courage you must grant to the judges, steering a straight furrow through a jungle of falsehood, trickery, and vituperation; to the doctors, sticking to their principles in an enervating atmosphere of superstition and hostility; to the business men, fighting a ceaseless battle against rivals to whom the most elementary principles of business integrity are alien and incomprehensible.

Above all, you must grant it to the women. Apart from the

handful of pampered nonentities whom we encountered on the race-course, there are thousands of others, nurses, missionaries, wives of country officials, who deserve the very highest respect. Theirs may not always be a very sensational variety of courage; it may be only the sort which enables them to scan the aforesaid pages of *Life* without bursting into tears. For out of those pages comes the sound of music and laughter and the swish of crepe-de-chine, and these things have been long denied them. That sort of courage is really more remarkable in the long run than the 'British phlegm' which these women invariably display in a crisis, the almost unnatural calm which seems to cloak them, like an armour, when a train is held up or a mob is storming the gates. Whichever variety of courage you prefer, they have it in abundance.

11

There are three main criticisms to be made of the British in India, if we consider them as individuals rather than as cogs in the Imperial machine.

Firstly, they never say 'thank-you'.

Riding in my first Indian train, from Gwalior to Delhi, I asked a very red-faced Colonel the Indian for 'thank-you'. The coolies who had carried the luggage were waiting to be paid; it was very hot and they had worked quickly and well; it seemed ungracious merely to tip them and send them off.

'Thank-you?' ejaculated the Colonel. 'Thank-you?'

'Yes,' I repeated. 'Thank you.' (If you say the word 'thank-you' often enough it sounds quite peculiar, like a sort of Chinese fish.)

'But my dear fellah,' he spluttered, 'you *don't.*'

'Don't say thank-you?'

'Certainly not. Nevah. It isn't done.' He shook his head violently, and began to climb the steps into the carriage. Then he turned his head: 'S'matter of fact, doubt if there *is* such a word. Been in India thirty years. Know Hindi. Know Urdu. Never heard anybody say it. Thank-you!' And he retired into the railway carriage, making old-fashioned noises.

I gave the coolies an extra tip to make up for the lack of a 'thank-you' and there is no need for the cynic to tell me that they greatly preferred this *bakshish* to any social graces by which it might have been accompanied. Their wages are so miserable that they would let the sahibs spit in their faces for an extra anna. Sometimes the sahibs come very near to doing it.

None the less, the incident seemed important. The British have got a lot out of India, but they have never said 'thank-you'. The Indians have got a lot out of the British, but *they* have never said 'thank-you' either. It is a pity; these things do help. I know that there are all sorts of awful little rhymes which people print on calendars, about the importance of giving sunny smiles to cripples and saying 'thank-you' to withered old apple-women (whatever apple-women may be). And I often suspect that the creators of these moral sweetmeats find it much easier to part with a smile than a sixpence. There are some of us, however, who like to smile *and* give sixpence.

'Thank-you. Thank-you. What is the word for thank-you?'

I went through India asking this question, feeling stranger and stranger, wondering if I was the victim of some odd personal complex. Nobody else — British or Indian — ever seemed to feel the lack of this word. Servants staggered into hotel bedrooms with monstrous tin trunks on their heads. Nobody said 'thank-you'. Waiters yawned at midnight tables while the sahibs guffawed over their brandy. Nobody said 'thank-you'. People picked up things that had been dropped, made way in buses, gave directions in strange, winding streets. Never a 'thank-you'. It made me feel more and more dumb and churlish. I found myself inventing a 'thank-you' of my own — an odd sort of hiss accompanied by a smile and a nervous twitch. It appeared to alarm those who were its recipients, but it salved my conscience.

It was the Princess of Berar who first told me the word for 'thank-you'. Of all the women in India she was the one who really needed it least, for she was so beautiful that she had only to smile to make a man feel that he was being paid the most eloquent compliment. However, she was not an Indian at all; she was the daughter of the ex-Caliph, and she had royal manners as well as royal blood. She had experienced the same feeling of discomfort over the lack of a 'thank-you', and she made me a present of two words. You will not find them in any of the elementary textbooks for Europeans. Presumably, they are so rarely used, that nobody thought it worth while to mention them. The first word is 'mihrbani', though that may not be the correct spelling. It means something like 'graciousness'. The second word is 'shuggrea', and that means, apparently, 'sweetness', or something like it. I used to say both words in loud ringing tones to the dirtiest and most degraded beggars in the vicinity, to the horror of the sahibs and the high-caste Hindus, but to the evident delight of the degraded ones, who had never heard such words cast in their direction before.

III

The second main criticism to be levelled against the British who live in India is that they do not live in India at all. Their heart is in the Highlands — or in Kensington High Street. They make not the smallest effort to understand the country and their only thought is how soon, and how profitably, they will be able to get out of it.

These people used to say to me, *ad nauseam*:

'What? You're going to write a book about India when you've only been out here a year? Good Lord man, I've been out here over *twenty* years, and I don't know a thing about it yet!'

To which one was tempted to reply . . . 'Evidently not. And if you stay out here another twenty you'll still be as ignorant.'

There is something very irritating to the trained reporter in this suggestion that it is necessary to live in a country for twenty years before one is qualified to express an opinion about it. The trained reporter would probably see more in a single railway journey than the amateur would see in a year of residence.

Here are some elementary questions about India and the answers that the average Englishman will give to them.

'*Have you ever seen an Indian film?*'

'Good Lord, no. Fearful things, Indian films.'

Yet India's films provide an admirable short-cut to an understanding of the national psychology.

'*Have you read the* Bhagavat Gita?'

'Who's that? What d'you say?'

'The *Bhagavat Gita.*'

They have never even heard of it. It is as though an Indian
coming to England had never heard of the New Testament.

I met a large number of English padres, but only two had
heard of the Abbé Dubois' *Hindu Manners, Customs and Ceremonies,*
and even they had not attempted to read it. Yet Dubois is a
quite indispensable classic; he is the *one* author whom no student of
India can afford to ignore.

'*Have you ever slept the night in an Indian village?*'

'No *thanks.* Too many bugs.'

How can you ever enter into the heart of India till you have
shared at least *one* night with the peasants, living as a peasant?
Admittedly, I did not do it often, but even a short experience
taught me more than a dozen books. I learned, for instance, the
strange sense of oneness which the Indians have with the animals;
it seemed quite natural that four little goats should be sleeping in
one corner of the hut, that a cluster of hens should be brooding in
another, and that from time to time a bullock should push a solemn
head through the door. It was not possible to get much sleep, and
the bites were legion, but there were many compensations. The
wail of the flute as the dusk was falling, the lovely silhouettes of
the women at the well, charcoal black against a jade-green sky,
the bowl of curds and fresh fruit which they brought me before
going to bed, and the wreath of frangipani that they placed around
my neck. I hung it on the wall when they had gone, and watched
the candlelight flicker on the silver tinsel with which they had
threaded it.

And then — the sudden dawn, very rich and red, a regular
blood orange of a dawn; and the singing of the peasants as they
set off to the paddy fields. There are few things more beautiful
than a paddy field in the early light; it is like a quilt embroidered
in many shades of green, from the pale stretches of the out-
plantings, thinly sown against the red earth, to the vivid squares
of glowing emerald which mark the crop to come.

To sacrifice such an experience because of the danger of a few bugs seems, to say the least of it, unenterprising.

'Have you any real Indian friends?'

'Friends? Well — I know some quite decent Indians. S'matter of fact, some really *quite* decent Indians. But I wouldn't exactly call them *friends*.'

That is perhaps the major tragedy; the gulf does exist, and most people, however hard they try, are unable to bridge it.

The immortal garden-party which opens the pages of E. M. Forster's *A Passage to India* is not a thing of the past; it is still being held on a thousand Indian lawns. Admittedly, the ranks have drawn closer, the white and the dark — the figures intermingle, saree and muslin, Gandhi cap and panama, and there are not so many awkward pauses in the conversation, for the British hosts are not quite so sure of their position nowadays, while the Indian guests *are* quite sure of theirs. None the less, it is really the same garden-party; rob it of its extra airs and graces, turn on it the searchlight of an impartial critical intelligence, and you will find that it is the same scene; the white is not really mixing with the dark, the saree is not really blending with the muslin . . . the East is not meeting the West.

Mind you, it is not· all the fault of the British — not by any means. Very often, when the British hold out their hands, the Indians refuse to shake them. Here is an example. Most of the clubs in the hill-stations are mixed; members meet on terms of perfect equality; provided that they pay their subscriptions, no questions are asked, no privileges given.

So far, so good — in theory. But in practice, what happens? The Indian men refuse to allow their wives and daughters to come to the club. They come themselves, night after night, they dance with the wives of British officers, but their women folk stay at home. And that annoys the British, particularly the young male British. Even in the houses of comparatively 'advanced' Indians the women are often locked away out of sight as though one would jump on them if offered the opportunity.

Needless to say, this is a mere pinprick, but it is the same sort of pinprick as the Indians themselves experience when they are the victims of colour-prejudice at home. It is therefore salutary that we British should have a taste of it, if only to be reminded how irritating it can be.

Perhaps the most important question we might ask is:

'What do you think of the Anglo-Indians?'

By his answer to this question the 'pukka sahib' will probably reveal his true mentality.

IV

There are about 140,000 Anglo-Indians[1] in India, and they are perhaps the most luckless community in the world.

They are neither one thing nor the other. They are doomed to lose, whether the ball spins black or red or zero. So intolerant is human nature, so arrogant and illogical the mind of man, that they are equally despised by both their half-brothers, the British and the Indians.

Worst of all, they are despised by themselves.

Their one idea, which amounts to an obsession, is to deny their coloured blood.

It would be funny if it were not tragic. I once knew an Anglo-Indian nurse. She was a nice girl, patient, efficient, and pretty in her dusky way. There could not be a moment's doubt about her origin, which betrayed itself in her hair, her eyes, the palms of her hands. But to hear her talk you would think that she could trace her pedigree back to the Plantagenets.

'These *Indians*!' she would cry, in contempt, when the bearer brought the wrong medicine or the sweeper was lazy in his work. 'Really — these Indians! One can do *nothing* with such people!'

Her father was British, her mother Indian. She used to show me snapshots of herself with her father. The mother was hardly ever in the pictures; only once did I catch a glimpse of her, a dark little figure hovering in the background. The page of the album was quickly turned when that snapshot came into view.

[1] The phrase Anglo-Indian is a polite euphemism for 'half-caste'. In nine cases out of ten the father is British and the mother Indian; there are very few instances of British women marrying Indian men. The figure of 140,000 is certainly an understatement, for Anglo-Indians are reluctant to proclaim themselves as such, and show endless ingenuity in concealing their coloured origin.

'I have been out here far too long.' That is one of the favourite phrases of the Anglo-Indian girl. 'I've absolutely lost touch with home.' They have never been 'home' at all, poor creatures, but they would die rather than admit it.

'I have Spanish blood in my veins.' That is another favourite. It helps to account for the dark skin and the black hair. Some girls even pick up little Spanish phrases which they introduce into their conversation. They tell you that they learned them from their grandmothers.

'Four shades whiter in four weeks!' So run the headlines of one of the innumerable advertisements for skin whitening products. The Anglo-Indian girls spend a large proportion of their incomes on these preparations, which are marketed with great ingenuity. 'Don't for one moment imagine that because you were born with a dark skin you can do nothing about it,' proclaims the inventor of a popular bleacher. 'The technique of beauty treatment has been revolutionized with the introduction of X . . . the skin tonic which acts scientifically on the pigment cells.'

I am not qualified to comment on the efficacy of these productions, but even if they do all that is claimed for them, the Anglo-Indian girl would still be easy to 'spot'. For instance, she cannot disguise her voice; it has a curiously shrill 'overtone', particularly when she laughs. And though she may be a natural blonde, there is always a tawny shadow to her skin, as though there were honey in her veins. Sometimes it is very beautiful, like ivory by candle light, but it is emphatically of the East.

The great ambition of these girls is to marry an Englishman — by hook or by crook — to be taken out of the country, anywhere, anyhow, as long as they can escape from the dubious halfway-house in which life has cast them. Since the war this ambition has naturally been enormously stimulated. British and American soldiers have been besieged by offers of marriage, often accompanied by considerable cash inducements.

One cannot blame the girl who makes such an offer — particularly if she has a little imagination, and realizes that otherwise her road must inevitably lie downhill. She has seen the fate of her sister who has not achieved matrimony with a white man; it is not pleasant. It is either a lonely spinsterhood, with pride as a poor recompense for poverty, or a reversion to type . . . a marriage into an Indian household. And that is usually a step to be bitterly regretted, for her Indian relations despise and distrust her, they can never regard her as 'one of us'. If a son is born to her, and if, as sometimes happens, he is as white as his grandfather, his position is doubly invidious. Even by the Anglo-Indian Catholic schools he is regarded as an outsider. He grows up disillusioned, embittered; with the approach of manhood he takes a perverse delight in degrading himself, drinking with the scum of the city, fighting in the native brothels, hanging round the docks and the wharves, spitting out oaths in the lowest Hindi, like a tragic Kim who has lost his way in life.

For the men of the first generation, who can boast of an English father, it is not so bad. To ensure that their status is respected — officially if not socially — a fair proportion of posts is reserved for them in the public services, particularly in the police and on the railways. Some of them, by exceptional merit have risen to positions of eminence and wealth. For the greater part of the Anglo-Indian community, however, the future is none too bright; and though one has every sympathy with them, it must be admitted that their troubles are partly of their own making. Owing to their deep-rooted inferiority complex they are fanatically insistent upon their superiority to their Indian cousins; they lose no opportunity of setting themselves apart; they carry their protestations of 'loyalty' to a ludicrous extreme; they are *plus royaliste que le roi.*

To a certain extent this unhappy state of affairs must be considered a reflection on British rule. It is a consequence, or rather a survival, of the 1857 mentality, when Indians were 'a lot of damned natives' and when the idea that we were trustees for their well-being was still the monopoly of a few eccentrics. The Dutch never adopted this attitude, which has proved as unprofitable as it is inhumane; from the first they encouraged inter-marriage between the two races, with the result that the Eurasian community in the Dutch colonies is virile and self-respecting, and has, indeed, been one of the most stabilizing influences in the Dutch dominions.

What would have happened if we had followed the Dutch example? If by a supreme effort of imagination, we had married the East to the West, and created an immense Anglo-Indian community with genuine rights and privileges? It is one of the most fascinating speculations in which the historian could indulge. But unfortunately it must remain a speculation; it is too late for any such experiments to-day. The tide of British power is ebbing fast, and the Anglo-Indians are left stranded on the beach, scanning the empty seas for a friendly sail ... a sail which will never come.

CHAPTER VI

LOOSE ENDS

IN a book of this nature it is quite inevitable that there should be considerable gaps. To admit this is not to make any concession to the 'live-in-India-for-thirty-years' school of thought. If one lived in India for three hundred years there would still be endless deficiencies in one's knowledge. An army of scholars, working for many lifetimes, would only be able to skim the surface of a country so complex and so imponderable. The best that any single man can do is to give a rough sketch emphasizing those features that strike him as most significant.

That has been my endeavour. Even so, there are too many uncertain lines in our sketch, too many shadowy spaces that need to be 'blocked in'. This chapter is a rough effort to strengthen those lines and fill in those spaces.

We will begin by repairing an omission that is only too common in books about India.

THE STATES

A casual perusal of the Indian debates in the House of Commons would suggest that most of the speakers were quite unaware that nearly two-fifths of the territory of the country is not under British rule at all, but is under the rule of the Princes, whose subjects number no less than eighty millions.[1] If they mention the States at all they speak of them with airy patronage, as though they were circus exhibits, that could be whisked off the stage by the wave of the Congress wand. They seldom if ever inquire either if it is desirable that they should be whisked, or . . . assuming that it *is* desirable . . . how the whisking is to be done, nor by whom, nor with what consequence so drastic a measure is likely to be fraught.

---

[1] There are 562 States in India, but at least a third of them are of minor importance, while over a hundred are so tiny that they would more fittingly be described as 'estates'. States like Hyderabad, Mysore, Kashmir, etc., however, are larger and more densely populated than many European countries.

Is there anything to be said for the States? Surely, if we are practical men, that is the first matter that we should endeavour to decide. We can best decide it by paying a visit to one of them.

II

Towards five o'clock in the evening, if you are looking out of the window of a train travelling from Bellary to Bangalore, which is the second City of Mysore State, you will suddenly notice a remarkable change in the landscape. It is not a floral or topographical change; it is a social change. After endless vistas of broken-down villages, stony fields and half-starved cattle, the eye is refreshed by neat thatched houses, green acres, swelling pastures, and herds of beasts that would do credit to the home counties. The change is so startling that the inquisitive traveller is impelled to ask what has happened. The answer is:

'We have just crossed the border from British India; we are now in the State of Mysore.'

The reaction on the Englishman who learns this news for the first time is . . . or should be . . . disquieting. He says to himself: 'If there is this extraordinary contrast between the prosperity of Mysore and the poverty of British India, which we have just left behind us, then there must be something seriously wrong with British India.' We will examine this reaction shortly; it is natural and healthy and demands an answer. At the moment, however, let us look more closely at these blooming fields and these flourishing villages; for if they stand up to closer scrutiny they should give pause to those Indian commentators who so lightly assume that the States are worthless anachronisms, bundles of rubbish that must be fed to Congress flames.

Alighting at Bangalore we find a modern city, well lit, well paved, and — for India — almost clean. The indescribable filth which litters the pavements of most Indian cities, the stagnant gutters, the fly-blown piles of excrement . . . all these are absent. Even the tragic army of dogs, those bundles of disease and misery, do not make their appearance. We learn that the Maharajah, although a devoutly religious man, has actually had the courage to run in the face of religious sentiment to the extent of having numbers of these unhappy creatures put out of their agony.

In Mysore city it is the same tale — hospitals, research institutes, schools of arts and crafts — instead of being few and far between, they crowd together. And when you leave the city and drive out into the country, you drive on broad well-surfaced roads through fields of abundance. As far as the eye can see stretch fertile acres, plentifully nourished by an immense irrigation system. When you leave the road, and set off on foot, the villages through which you pass are — for India — almost clean. It is necessary to make this qualification: the word 'clean' in India has a very different interpretation from the word 'clean' in any other country.

'These signs and portents' — you may suggest — 'are only the casual impressions of a tourist. It would still be possible, behind this pleasing façade, for autocracy and oppression to flourish in their most odious forms.'

That is possible, but it does not happen to be the case.

In the sphere of government we find the same high level, both in theory and in practice. To sneer at Mysore's representative institutions merely because the executive is not fully responsible to the legislature is as foolish as to deny all merit to the House of Lords. In theory, the House of Lords is not easily defensible (a number of admirable institutions in many countries have no theoretical justification), but in practice, at least to-day, it serves a valuable purpose. And although, in Mysore, the executive is in somewhat the same position as was the House of Lords at the beginning of the present century, it rarely ventures to cross swords with the popularly elected legislature, which is conscious of its power.

Any man who assumes that democracy cannot live or flourish in the atmosphere of an Indian State should disabuse himself of this illusion by studying the debates of the Mysore Legislative Council; few democratic assemblies could rival the high quality of their eloquence nor the ample reserves of their common sense. Just before I arrived in the State there had been heated discussions in the Council concerning the Collective Fines Bill, a measure which aimed, as its title suggests, at imposing a collective fine on all the inhabitants of those villages which had been concerned in riots ... (the bill was really copied from a similar measure in British India). The pages of *Hansard* could not show a debate that was better balanced nor more moderate in temper than this, though feeling ran high.[1] The result of the debate was thirty-four for the Ayes, twenty-one for the Noes. Several significant amendments were championed by the opposition; all were incorporated. It was an inspiring example of enlightened democracy — or perhaps one should say enlightened aristocracy (though the two are not necessarily opposed).

I saw Mysore from almost every angle — beginning at the top, in the Palace. Oh, that palace! By day it is as indigestible, architecturally speaking, as a wedding cake, which it strongly resembles; it consists in layer upon layer of sugary decoration and cream-puff ornament. But at dusk the whole gigantic edifice is suddenly transformed, for they switch on the lights, and at once we are in fairyland. The absurd confectionery of the building melts away and we see only its skeleton, or rather its ghost, tricked out in a thousand necklaces of light that seem to float against the violet sky, suspended by invisible fingers.

The Maharajah himself is a young man of considerable culture and transparent sincerity. He did not seem particularly 'pro-British'; he made several shrewd and frank criticisms of our policy; but he was certainly 'pro-Mysore'. Most of his ministers would have distinguished themselves in any British Cabinet — though that, perhaps, is a double-edged compliment. They were chosen from widely different ranks of society. Several of them went out of their way to express to me their determination that Mysore should never fall into Congress clutches.

'We will not tolerate Vakil Raj'[2] was their way of putting it.

I also saw Mysore from the bottom. I came to know the villagers, their wives and their children, in their homes, on their fields, during their hours of work and of play. And also during their hours of prayer, for on a certain hill not far from the city there was a holy man, a Yogi, who for thirty years had lived in a cave ... or rather, a tiny hole in the rock. Pilgrims came to see him from far and wide; I used to stand in their ranks, and nobody

[1] *Mysore Legislative Council Debates*, vol. 48, No. 11, July 2nd, 1943.
[2] Lawyer rule.

worried or stared. Sometimes when it was late, and the pilgrims had departed, I used to crawl into the cave and sit with him alone, hunched up under the low, incense-stained roof. He was one of the most beautiful old men I have ever seen, attenuated and elongated like an El Greco, and we had long conversations in a mixture of languages and signs. It must be granted that he never said anything of particular interest, his remarks being largely confined to statements of facts with which one was already acquainted, such as 'War is terrible' and 'Man is wicked'. However, it really did not matter what he said, he was so exquisite to look at, and I only wish that he had been in a museum, in a glass case, properly lit, so that one could have enjoyed him from every angle.

III

As a whole, Congress is 'anti' the States;[1] it asserts that they are 'bulwarks of British rule', and it has managed to spread the impression that they are actually British inventions. They are, of course, nothing of the sort, and any man who makes such an assertion is only exposing his ignorance of the rudimentary facts of history.

'When, after the decay of Mogul power in the middle of the eighteenth century, the East India Company began to intervene in the political affairs of India, they had to solicit the favour of Indian rulers, like the Nizam and the Marathas, to seek their alliance in order to keep the French power in check. The Company was not at that time a political power, and the same circumstances which favoured the growth of its power also operated to strengthen and establish on an independent footing the rule of the local chieftains who owed nominal allegiance to the Mogul Emperor at Delhi. Thus, though the majority of the bigger Indian States are not survivals of old Indian monarchies, they are *not* the creations of British policy.'[2]

---

[1] In Chap. II, however, we saw that Gandhi is out of step with Congress on this matter, though he has expressed so many conflicting opinions that it is impossible to decide what he really thinks.

[2] *Indian States*, by K. M. Panikkar (Oxford University Press).

It is worth noting that on no occasion have the Congress publicity mongers sunk so low, in perfidy and misrepresentation, as
when they are dealing with the States. A single example, out of a
thousand, will suffice to illustrate this point. One of the most
widely circulated of all Congress publications is a booklet entitled
'Fifty Facts about India'.[1] It purports to be a reply to a booklet
of the same name published by the British Information Services
in America, and it bears the sub-title 'Political and Economic Hell
in India'. As an example of barefaced lying it has never been
matched, nor even approached, by Dr. Goebbels. It bristles with
statements like, 'A speaker in Hindustani can go anywhere in
India and make himself understood', which is about as accurate
as the assertion that Japanese is completely comprehensible to all
Irishmen. However, it is with its comments on the States that we
are here concerned. In spite of the fact that Mysore is the most
economically advanced area in the whole country, that Travancore, Cochin and Baroda show the highest standard of literacy,
that Hyderabad is making great strides in education and industrial development, and that in many other States there are
signs of progress which are unknown in Congress-dominated India,
it lumps them together as 'sinks of reaction and incompetence and
unrestrained autocratic power exercised by vicious and degraded
individuals'. That there have been vicious and degraded princes
is true; and that the British Government has always exercised its
right to depose them, when their depravity or inefficiency was
established, is equally true. Such a one was the Prince of Alwar;
to find his equal in sheer cruelty and beastliness would be difficult, for he could have given lessons to Nero and the Marquis de
Sade. One Indian woman, who, to her cost, had known him well,
told me of the horror with which she had seen him beat a polo
pony to death after a match in which he had not distinguished
himself. And the description of this monster, in 'Fifty Facts About
India'? Here it is:

'*The Prince of Alwar was deposed because he was a patriotic Indian.*'
The statement is beyond comment.

[1] Hamara Hindustan Publications, Bombay.

IV

We mentioned above that the impartial Englishman. would wish for an honest answer to the question, 'Why is it that some of the States, in literacy, industrial· development, etc., show so marked a superiority to most of British India?' There is no hard and fast answer to this question. The Congress answer, of course, is that the rule of the States, bad as it may be, is at least better than the rule of the British, on the principle that a bad Indian despot is better than a good British Civil Servant. This is a travesty of the facts; the true answer is far more complex and, if given in its entirety, would involve us in a long-drawn-out historical survey. Speaking generally we may say that the States, when they show any special excellence, owe it to a period of benevolent autocracy. Mysore is a case in point. The British treaty with this State dates from 1799 and during the most crucial years of its development the rulers were minors. By a fortunate circumstance their British tutors happened to be men of exceptional enlightenment; not only did they personally mould the policy of the State during the minorities but by imprinting their ideas on the minds of the young Maharajahs, they extended their influence through their whole lives, so that the so-called 'despots', when they came to rule for themselves, ruled more like old-fashioned liberals than oriental tyrants.

Again, the suggestion that Mysore's advanced industrial progress reflects unfavourably on the backwardness of British India will not bear serious examination. To a very large extent it is due to a series of happy natural accidents, of which the two most notable are the temperate climate — the finest in India — and the existence of water-power on a scale that has made possible an immense development of hydro-electric power.

What has been said of Mysore is also true, by and large, of Baroda, whose late Gaekwar was a man of brilliant parts, who showed a passionate interest in his people's welfare throughout his long reign.

Travancore and Cochin are often quoted, by Congress propagandists, as examples of what might be done in India if only the British would quit, for the literacy of these States is respectively

55 per cent and 35 per cent, compared with 12½ per cent for British India. We shall be touching on the educational problems in a later section, but for the moment we may note that the prowess of Travancore and Cochin is again explained by exceptional circumstances. Partly because both these States are the most orthodox in India and contain an enormous proportion of Brahmins, and partly because a series of historical accidents has implanted in them a very high percentage of missionaries, Travancore and Cochin have *always* been far ahead of the rest of India in literacy, long before education was seriously tackled in India — or, for that matter, in England itself.

Literacy figures, in India, can be made to prove anything or nothing, according to the personal bias of the commentator. Most of the writers who quote them do so without the smallest attempt to acquaint themselves with the historical and geographical background against which the figures are set. They lift up their hands in horror at the backwardness of Orissa, which has the lowest standard in India, apparently unaware that this State is largely composed of impassable jungle inhabited by aboriginals. They talk of the illiteracy of 'Bombay' as though only the city were concerned, whereas the figures are taken for the whole province, which contains a bewildering assortment of tribes and languages living in districts which are inaccessible by any modern form of transport.

v

What of the future?

Presumably, in the course of time, the States will either have to go or to effect such considerable modifications in their institutions that their functions will be practical rather than picturesque. On the whole, it is probably desirable that they *should* go, if only for economic reasons. They form a series of artificial barriers to the free development of commerce, and they represent a large reservoir of wealth which should be more profitably employed. It is ludicrous, for example, that the Nizam of Hyderabad should be allowed to sit, like an immovable idol, on a mountain of gold that is never put into circulation. Men of wealth so fabulous should be taxed like ordinary mortals. Again, it is undeniable that in a few of the smaller States there are grave abuses of the peoples' rights, and monstrous perversions of justice, to say nothing of private debaucheries which defy description. The British, of course, step in when 'things have gone too far', but the general feeling is that they do not step in soon enough. The lurid melodrama of more than one Maharajah should have been nipped in the bud during the first act instead of being allowed to run its course of murder and intrigue.

British policy towards the States is, on the whole, realistic. We have indicated to the rulers that if they wish to survive they must bring their institutions up to date. We have constantly urged the revision of the treaties in a modern direction and occasionally we have succeeded in winning our point. But after all, the treaties do exist, and have existed for a hundred years; many of the signatories to these treaties have been loyal and active subjects of the Empire; with the exception of foreign policy they have been confirmed in rights which they naturally guard with jealousy and pride.[1] To tear up the treaties as though they were so many scraps of paper would not only be an act of perfidy but it might set in train a disastrous series of commotions and civil disturbances. Some of the Princes have well-trained armies who would follow them to the death. In the absence of an overruling British power, and in the event of a precipitate British withdrawal, there is no knowing what these armies might do, nor when they might march. The soil of India — till the British came — had been stained through the centuries with the blood of countless civil wars; there seems no justification for assuming that history may not repeat itself.

However, facts are more important than speculations, and in this section we have adduced enough facts to indicate that the true story of the States is very different from that which Congress would have us believe. We have deliberately refrained from dwelling on the decorative side of the States, although even the most ardent Congressman, presumably, would regret the extinc-

[1] George V reaffirmed Britain's promises to the Princes in the most uncompromising words ... 'Ever to maintain the privileges, rights and dignities of the Indian Princes, who may rest assured that this pledge is inviolate and inviolable.'

tion of some of the amazing fêtes and carnivals with which they
still entertain their subjects, who take endless delight in these
affairs. But the States, as we have seen, have a higher function
than as purveyors of circuses. It may be salutary, in these days,
to recall what Lord Curzon said about them. There have been
many changes in the world since he was Viceroy, but not so many
changes that his words have lost their weight. Curzon was not
exactly a fool, nor was he an alarmist, and he knew his India as
few Indians, let alone Englishmen, have ever known it. This was
his judgment:

'The Princes of India sustain the virility, and save from extinc-
tion the picturesqueness of ancient and noble races. They show
in their persons that illustrious lineage has not ceased to implant
noble and chivalrous ideas, fine standards of public spirit and
private courtesy. With the loss of these, if ever they be allowed to
disappear, *Indian society would go to pieces like a dismasted vessel in a
storm.*'

EDUCATION

To discuss this subject in all its ramifications would require
many volumes; the best we can do is to indicate a few of the 'high
spots'.

There are two schools of thought about education in India; the
first contends that it should play handmaiden to economics on the
principle that it is useless to preach to children with empty
stomachs; the second maintains that it should have priority over
all other charges, since only by raising the peasant's standard of
intelligence can you teach him the sort of things which will enable
him to raise his standard of life. Actually, of course, the two
problems are one and indivisible; to discuss which should be
tackled first is as unprofitable as the old wrangle about the hen
and the egg ... education costs money and in order to have
money you must first have education — a truism that applies to
nations as well as to individuals.

Very few people have any conception of the astronomical sums
which will have to be expended before India, as a whole, attains
even a moderate degree of education. After all, to teach letters
to one-fifth of the human race is a task which cannot be under-

taken in any spirit of levity. 89 per cent of the population live an entirely rural life ... in other words, approximately 340 millions, or twice the population of the U.S.A., live in villages, each of which would require at least one teacher apiece. Taking an aggregate of 500 for a village, that means that you would have to begin with enlisting nearly three and a half million school marms. These figures are so gigantic that they may pass before the reader in a sort of blur; let us therefore write them in the form of an advertisement:

SITUATIONS VACANT

WANTED — 3,500,000 School Marms, willing to live alone in isolated districts. Salary, 60 Rupees a month.

60 rupees a month is about 25 shillings, or 6 dollars, a week. In India it is a living wage though it can hardly be described as a luxurious one. If we were to give it to our legions of school marms we should be involved, at the outset, in an annual charge of £210,000,000 a year, which is not only ten times the amount at present expended, but is considerably more than the total revenue of India itself![1] And all this for salaries only, without any thought of the equally staggering sums which would be required for buildings and equipment.

However, even if we had the money to pay our school marms, or could devise some scheme of financial juggling by which it could eventually be raised, where ... oh where ... are we to find the ladies themselves? We cannot stamp our heels on the ground and expect them to spring from the earth, fully armed with pencils, rulers, and india-rubber; we should be optimists to assume that we could discover even one-fiftieth of the required number, as things are at present. ·And assuming that we found our fiftieth, they would need something a good deal more substantial than pencils and rulers to protect their lonely persons in

[1] Actually, the Sargent scheme, which will probably form the basis of post-war education in India, contemplates the eventual annual expenditure of 313 crores of rupees, which is approximately £235,000,000, and even this, in the vast majority of cases, would not take the school age beyond 14. This huge annual charge is to have more modest beginnings, and will not reach the £235,000,000 mark till after the lapse of 50 years.

the sort of districts to which they would be obliged to penetrate. Regrettable as it may seem, the mofussil[1] is not a salubrious resort for unprotected females; it bears no sort of resemblance to the Middle West or the Home Counties. The arrangements needed to guard our school marms might well involve an expenditure even larger than their own salaries. The profession of school marm is held, by the Indians, in low repute, like the profession of nursing. It carries an apparently ineradicable association of loose morals.[2] And so, apart from the problem of finding the money, and the problem of finding the ladies to whom we are to pay the money, we are faced with yet another problem, which is nothing less than a total revolution in the attitude of the entire male population, Hindu and Muslim alike, towards the status of the school marm herself.

It is not really quite so simple as our theorists would have us believe!

'But all these troubles would be avoided,' you may say, 'if instead of school marms we engaged male teachers.' Not quite all. We might find, say, a whole fortieth of our staff instead of a mere fiftieth. And presumably the young men would be able to guard their virtue without extra assistance. Even so, that does not solve the problem of where we are to find the money nor — which is more important — how we are to persuade the young men to go 'back to the land', for that is what teaching in India really implies. It means isolation, desolation, and a long good-bye to the city or anything resembling a city; it means walking miles on foot to a rough track where a bus passes twice a week, and at the end of the bus route there is just another village, only a little bigger, a little less dirty than the one he has left behind.

The Congress propagandist, of course, will tell you that the moment British rule is finished the young men will pour away from the cities and bury themselves in the deserts, forgetting all their acquired tastes for the bright bustle of the city. The reply

---

[1] The interior of an Indian province, generally used to describe the country as opposed to the town.

[2] It is difficult for the Englishman or the American to understand the suspicion with which Indians regard any woman who shows a desire to do anything more ambitious than cook and have babies. For instance, in Bengal, the fact that a girl had a good voice or a fondness for songs was until recently a serious drawback to her marriage prospects (see Dr. Dhurjati Mukerji's *Modern Indian Culture*, p. 191).

that suggests itself to this propaganda is 'Oh yeah?' For it is an unfortunate fact, more marked in modern India than in any other part of the world, that once you have taken a young man away from his village you will need a good deal more than wild horses to get him back again. He would rather starve, and frequently does.

These scattered notes are, of course, entirely negative, and are only intended as a corrective to the airy nonsense which is so often talked at home, particularly by young schoolmasters themselves, who appear to labour under the delusion that it is a penny bus-ride from Srinagar to Trichinopoly.

On the positive side volumes might be written; I will content myself by expressing a purely personal opinion . . . namely, that the problem will have to be tackled by revolutionary methods, in which the radio and the cinema will be predominant and will, indeed, largely replace the school-teachers themselves. Needless to say, such schemes would be only temporary. No machines could ever usurp the role that must eventually be played by human teachers, but machines could at least serve the initial purpose of breaking up the thick crusts of ignorance which have accumulated, through the centuries, over the minds of the Indian masses.

LANGUAGE

Nothing more violently annoys the Congressman, with his 'One India' complex, than the reiteration of the simple fact that there happen to be 225 languages in India. It is, admittedly, a misleading fact, as we shall see, but it drives him to invent replies that are even more misleading, such as the fantastic statement, quoted above, that 'a speaker in Hindustani can go anywhere in India and make himself understood'. He *might* 'make himself understood' with his feet, or his hands, or the contents of his pockets, but most certainly not with his tongue (unless, of course, he put it out).

There are 225 languages in India, but a large number of them are local and unimportant, such as the tribal dialects of the Tibeto-Chinese speech-family, which are found only on India's north-eastern fringes. For all practical purposes the main Indian languages number fifteen. Try as you may, the Congressman cannot reduce the figure lower than that.

Of these languages the most important is:

Urdu ⎫
Hindi ⎭ Spoken by 150 millions.

We have bracketed these two together for reasons which we
will explain in a moment.

After this comes Bengali, a totally distinct language spoken by
55 millions.

And then the languages of the south — Tamil, Telegu, Kannada,
and Malayan, again totally distinct from the others, though sometimes bearing faint resemblances to one another, and spoken by
another 55 millions.

The two other principal languages are Marathi (20 millions)
and Gujerati (15 millions).

Of all these languages Urdu and Hindi are obviously the most
important, since they are spoken by three times as many people
as any other language. They are not one and the same, for Urdu
is plentifully interlarded with Persian and Arabic, but they resemble one another closely enough for their speakers to make
themselves mutually understood. Gandhi wants to lump the two
together under the common name of 'Hindustani', and to force
this compound down the throats of the remaining 200 million
Indians. But at the very outset he is faced with a grave difficulty —
and it is, as usual, a communal difficulty. For though the two
languages are similar in sound, they are totally dissimilar in
script; Hindi derives from Sanskrit and is written from left to
right in Nagari characters, whereas Urdu derives from Persian
and is written from right to left in Persian characters. Most important of all, the Muslim bible — the Koran — is written in
Persian script. And so the Muslims bitterly resent any attempt to
tamper with their script or to 'Indianize' their speech.

These grave cleavages are naturally poo-poo'd by Congress;
according to their propagandists they are merely British inventions, and they paint the Indian Tower of Babel as though it were
really a Temple of Harmony. However, sometimes they let the
cat out of the bag — usually from sheer irritation at the recalcitrant
Muslims, who staunchly refuse to be 'absorbed'. The passionate
determination of the Muslims to cherish Urdu as a separate language and not merely as a sort of echo of Hindi has been well

illustrated by a distinguished Hindu scholar, Professor Amarnatha
Jha. In a recent article in *The Leader*, Allahabad, he writes, under
the title of 'The Bubble of Hindustani':

'It is best to be frank. Go to any hostel of Hindu students;
there will always be some Urdu magazine in the reading room.
Go to a Muslim hostel, you will not find a Hindi magazine there
even by mistake. Look at the list of Hindu students of Urdu at
university examinations—contrast the number of Muslims offering
Hindi or — unless there is a miracle — Sanskrit. One must regret
having to write in this strain, but until we find that our Muslim
friends have a less contemptuous attitude towards Hindi we must
decline to consider the possibility of a coalition.'

Gandhi would like us to believe that, as soon as the British quit
India, all these ancient animosities will melt away like the mists
at dawn, that Hindus will write love letters to Muslims in the
hated Urdu and that Muslims will write love letters to Hindus in
the despised Sanskrit (though it is impossible to discover what
really *are* Gandhi's views on the language question, even after
reading every page of the book which he has devoted to the
subject).[1]

However, even if you could bring Hindi and Urdu together
under the common title of Hindustani (which is 10 to 1 'against'),
and even if you could decide upon a common script (which is
1000 to 1 'against') what about the rest of India? You cannot
suddenly inform language groups larger than the entire population of France that they are to go back to school, to sacrifice their
literature and start their mental life all over again. It is not even
as though you could say to them 'we must be bi-lingual' — you
would have to say 'we must be tri-lingual', for English is already
an absolutely essential secondary language in all affairs of commerce and government. History has seen to that, and even the
Congress propagandists are compelled to admit it, though with
much grinding of teeth.

And so the problem remains, and is likely to remain until the
modern world has been transformed by a great many miracles too

[1] The interested student in Gandhi's mental convolutions should read *Our
Language Problem*, by Mahatma Gandhi (Hingorani, Karachi). Another Congress
publication, which ties itself up in the most entertaining knots, is *National Language
for India* (Kitabistan, Allahabad).

startling to be envisaged even by Mr. H. G. Wells. In the meantime, the chief point to be noted is that the Congress suggestion
that 'a speaker in Hindustani can make himself understood all
over India' is a blatant lie. In vast tracks of the country he could
not even ask the way nor order a cup of tea, let alone express
complicated thought-processes such as 'give me the pencil of the
aunt of the gardener'. Perhaps that is just as well, for if he did
get hold of the pencil, he would only write more nonsense with it.

INDUSTRY AND AGRICULTURE

It would be obviously grotesque to attempt to tackle this
leviathan of a subject in a footnote; these few paragraphs are not
to be regarded as any attempt to do so; they are merely an endeavour to suggest the lines along which the interested student
would most profitably pursue his research.

Britain's industrial and agricultural policy is and always has
been the least creditable part of her Indian record. When Congress shoots at it they are shooting, for a change, with live ammuni-
tion instead of a lot of noisy blanks. It may be true that any other
imperialist power would have behaved worse, that our exploitations have been tempered by occasional outbursts of humanity
and that our inefficiency has been the result of ignorance rather
than of malice; the fact remains that the exploitations have been
gross and the inefficiency widespread.

It is monstrous, for example, that at Delhi the Department of
Lands — which is an agricultural country like India is of vital
importance, dealing as it does with such primary problems as
afforestation and irrigation — should be crowded into a single
small office with the Department of Health and the Department
of Education. It is like entrusting the Ministry of Information to
an office boy (though some office boys would provide a happy contrast to some Ministers of Information). It is equally monstrous
that in the fifth year of war, after rivers of ink have flowed in
celebration of India's development as an 'arsenal of democracy',
there should not be in the whole country a single factory capable of
producing anything but a few spare parts for one or two of the
more primitive war machines. When Congress proclaims that
Britain has deliberately kept India in a state of industrial back-

wardness, Congress is telling nothing but the truth. It may be a fact that a few industries — notably cotton, steel, cement, and paper — have grown rapidly in the last twenty years, but all the heavy industries — automobiles, shipbuilding, locomotives, and armaments, to say nothing of chemicals — have remained in a state of stagnation. Attempts to establish an Indian chemical industry, such as the ill-fated Morarjee scheme, have been destroyed by British efforts, with more than a suspicion of Government connivance. The infant Indian match factories were squashed in the interest of ostensibly Swedish but really British factories. It is the same story with cement, and, of course, with automobiles, over which some Anglo-American friction has been caused by our reluctance to allow American firms to establish Indian branches.

The British apologist may talk of a 'new spirit' and quote statistics to prove that India is making giant strides in industry. The 'strides' are illusory and the 'new spirit' is eyewash. For instance, a great deal of press publicity has been given to 'the Bevin boys' — the batches of Indian youths who have been sent over to Britain, under government auspices during the war, to be trained in British industrial methods (the first batch left India early in 1941). It sounds grand, and in theory it is. But how many Bevin boys are going? On an average, 50 every three months. So that if the war goes on till 1946, and if the flow continues uninterrupted, Britain will have given training to a thousand of India's youth — a whole thousand out of 400 million! If that is a 'new spirit' it does not suggest itself as strong enough to go to anybody's head. Reluctantly, we are obliged to admit the justice of Congress's complaint, which is proved by the conclusive fact that after 150 years of rule by the world's most highly industrialized power, only 4.4 per cent of the Indian people are themselves industrially employed.[1]

[1] In justice to Britain, however, it should be noted that Indian capitalists have consistently shown a strange reluctance to invest money in their own country, particularly in any transaction which has an element of risk. The railways are a case in point; in spite of every effort to collect Indian capital 92 per cent of the money had to be found in London. To-day, as the result of progressive 'Indianization', 51 per cent of the capital of new companies must be in Indian control. If, on account of the reluctance of the Indian investor, the remainder of the capital is of necessity provided by the British, and if the company happens to be a success,

Which brings us to what is really the paramount Indian economic problem — the condition of agriculture. We have seen that nine out of every ten Indians live an entirely rural life and, of these, eight are directly employed in agriculture. However rapid may be India's industrial development it is obvious that for many years to come it must remain primarily an agricultural country, so that every progressive scheme must begin with the land.

You must plan for the peasant or you might as well not plan at all, for until you have raised *his* purchasing power you will only be building castles in the air.

Of course most of the planners, particularly the British planners, *are* building castles in the air, with enviable rapidity and *élan*, merely because as usual they refuse to acquaint themselves with the facts. The India of fact is, indeed, precisely the opposite of the India of fancy — of most men's fancy, that is to say, including Milton's when he wrote of 'the wealth of Ormus and of Ind'. They think of her as a country with an almost inexhaustible supply of land; actually she is cramped and overcrowded. They think of this land as stocked with an equally inexhaustible supply of natural wealth; in reality nearly a third of it is useless waste and there are numerous grave deficiencies, for instance in coal.[1] This rich lush land of the popular imagination, in terms of cash, is worth on an average only 56 rupees an acre, which is a quarter of the English value and a third of the Japanese.

Whose fault is this?

It is certainly not entirely Britain's; but equally certainly it is not entirely India's.

The great majority of Indian agriculturists are still living in terms of the middle ages, apparently in total ignorance of the simplest rules which have become second nature to workers, on the soil, in most other countries. Their tools are antediluvian; they know nothing of the rotation of crops; and the prime need of the Indian soil — fertilizers — goes up, literally, in smoke.

[1] Fantastic estimates of India's 'potential' coal supply are often made, but they appear to be mostly wishful thinking. At the moment India produces barely one-tenth of the coal produced in Britain.

there are loud protests about 'British Exploitation' from all the Indian capitalists who had turned down the opportunity to 'come in on the ground floor'.

Cow dung, which is in many ways the richest of all natural manures, is carefully collected, moulded into flat cakes, plastered on the wall to dry, and then burned as fuel. Scarcely an ounce of it goes into the soil, with the result that the land becomes poorer and poorer, more and more starved.

This state of affairs, let us be frank, is discreditable to the British. Granted the immensity of the task, the religious and communal difficulties with which it is beset, the innate conservatism of the peasants and the mulish obstructionism, in late years, of the nationalists, we should somehow or other have surmounted these problems or at least shown a more determined effort to do so. We should have said to ourselves, years ago: 'We are faced with mass poverty; the poverty is largely due to the inefficiency of agricultural methods; we must tackle that inefficiency with every ounce of our energy.' For instance, in this vital matter of fertilizers, we should either have provided the peasant with some other form of fuel than cow dung (which would have meant gigantic schemes of afforestation), or we should have made other fertilizers available to him — whereas, in fact, we have exported them in large quantities, notably groundnut cake and bones.

Admittedly, in some respect we *have* shown ourselves worthy of our great traditions. Perhaps the happiest example, on our credit side, is irrigation — a prime problem in a country like India where for months in the year there is not a drop of rain. The British have given India the largest irrigation system in the world — the area brought under cultivation is nearly 55 million acres.

But our very success in this instance only shows up our other failures in sharper relief. To consider the matter from another angle, we have shown no really serious effort to tackle the social evils which choke the whole Indian agricultural system like rampant weeds. You cannot fertilize the earth by legislation nor bring crops into existence by the stroke of a pen, but you can — if you have the physical strength, as we have — pass laws which will break the shackles binding the limbs of the workers on the soil. It does not matter that the shackles are of Indian manufacture, nor that any attempt to remove them would cause uproars and protests — the business of a ruler is to rule, and this is one of the occasions where we have not done our business.

For instance, the worst pest of Indian agriculture, the blight that ravages his crops, poisons his soil and destroys, year after year, his most patient efforts to drag himself a few inches above the level of slavery, is an exceptionally virulent insect known as the 'banya'. Banya is Hindu for money-lender and a nastier specimen of blood-sucker will not be found in the whole insect kingdom. You find him in every village, demanding his pounds of flesh from bodies already so weakened that they could scarcely spare an ounce. The money-lender is the real owner of the Indian land; generations of indebtedness have placed the peasants in a tragic position where the combined labour of their families is only just sufficient to meet the interest on transactions so ancient that they are lost in the mists of history. 'It is estimated that the farmers of India pay more to the money-lender by way of interest than to the Government as taxes. The average rate is 35 per cent per annum on a compound basis; 50 per cent is common and sometimes 75 per cent is charged.'[1]

This is an abuse that we should have eradicated at all costs. We have only trifled with it. In the Punjab, legislation has restricted the rate of interest on unsecured debts to 18 per cent, and the Provincial Ministry in Madras passed a Rural Indebtedness Act which was admirably designed. Otherwise the situation stands much as it has stood for many centuries.

There are three main stumbling blocks in the path of those who wish to eliminate the banya.

The first is — as usual — vested interests. There are big men behind the banyas; they are sitting pretty, and they will be sitting even prettier if the British leave. The second is administrative; an army of inspectors with widespread powers of search and inquiry will be needed to see that any reforms which may be passed are actually carried out. The third is the traditional lethargy and 'live-for-the-moment' character of the peasant himself. Some may find physical reasons for this lethargy; others may attribute it to the Hindu doctrine of Karma, which can be twisted to mean more or less anything the believer wants, and is the best excuse yet invented by man for avoiding the unpleasant realities of the passing hour. Whatever the reason, the peasant must be

[1] *The Story of India*, by F. R. Moraes (Noble Publishing House, Bombay).

saved from himself and in spite of himself, and if the British do not do it, nobody else is likely to try.

In one vital department of agriculture, the British can emphatically plead 'not guilty', while the Hindu stands in the dock, condemned by world opinion and apparently quite unmoved by the verdict. That department is the cattle industry.

Pages of tedious statistics could be quoted about the livestock situation in India; the main facts may be summarized as follows:

India has about a third of the world's cattle — an absurdly excessive proportion. These vast numbers are largely useless. For instance, there are twice as many cattle per acre as in Denmark, which is . . . or used to be . . . the dairy of Europe. Yet in India you can very seldom find a decent glass of milk, even if you are able to pay for it.

The stark and disgraceful reason for this paradox is the Hindu religion, which forbids cattle to be killed. They can die by the inches, yes, they can starve to death, they can stagger about in a state of disease which is sickening to men with even the remnant of pity, but put them painlessly out of their misery? Oh no! As the Congressman Minoo Masani says, without a touch of irony: 'Why is this so? Because we are such a *kind* people!'[1] In consequence, the unfit cattle make life impossible for the fit; out of 100 cattle, 70 give no milk at all. And there is so little food left for the remaining 30 that they give an average of $1\frac{1}{2}$ lb. a day, which is less than a third of the amount they would be giving in a normal country.[2] That is the price the Hindus pay for allowing the elephant god to give orders in the farmyard.

This, it must be insisted, is a *contemporary* problem, and the British cannot be blamed for not solving it. It is quite beyond solution as long as the Hindu religion remains what it is. Gandhi might possibly bring about a change of view, but as always, when confronted with a concrete problem, he retires like a squid and confuses the issue by surrounding it with clouds of ink pumped

[1] *Our India*, by Minoo Masani (Oxford University Press). In spite of the apparent evidence to the contrary I do not think it is just to describe the Indians as deliberately cruel to animals. Unfortunately, however, their combination of ignorance and religious fanaticism produces results which are worse than the most devilish cruelty.

[2] The German gets the same amount of milk from one cow as the Indian from nine.

out at random. His attitude is summarized in the reply he sent to the manager of the goshala (cow asylum), who had written to him for advice. The facts, as given by this man, were as follows:

'There are in my charge 500 head of cattle. They are all utterly useless for any purpose and are simply eating their heads off. Out of these from 350 to 400 animals on the average are constantly at death's door, destined to die off one by one. Now tell me what I am to do?'

If Gandhi had replied with the three words 'Shoot the lot' he would have paid a greater service to India than a thousand non-resistance campaigns; he might have started a revolution in thought which in its turn would have started a revolution in agriculture and given the peasants their first impetus to rise above the servitude of their lot (He would, incidentally, have greatly endeared himself to writers of books on India by saying something which it was possible for them to understand without reading it sixteen times and going into a trance — only to discover that he had contradicted himself on the next page).

But Gandhi did not say 'Shoot the lot'. The phrase is far too direct, too blatantly Anglo-Saxon, apart from the fact that it runs counter to his much advertised worship of the cow. He got out of it very cleverly — firstly, by completely evading the issue, and secondly, by throwing the blame on somebody else, in this case, the management. He wrote:

'It is incumbent upon them (the management) and upon the organizers of all simply placed institutions to devise the most effective means of nursing and ministering to the needs of diseased and ailing cattle.'

For which bright and practical words, the dying beasts, the cancerous cows, the calves with broken legs, doubtless murmured a grateful 'moo'.

CHAPTER VII

TO QUIT OR NOT TO QUIT

AFTER a whole year it was still there — the big 'Quit India' sign outside the railway station — a little faded, perhaps, because the monsoons had washed away some of the chalk, but still easily legible. I greeted it as an old friend; it had given me my first shock, and all over India it had served as a constant reminder of the main argument, when I was in danger of wandering into unprofitable by-paths. To quit or not to quit? That was the question. And it is one which we must attempt to answer before we say good-bye.

It resolves itself into three parts.

1. *Should* we quit? This is fundamentally a moral question.
2. *Can* we quit? This is largely a physical question, involving considerations of defence.
3. *Will* we quit? This is, unfortunately, mostly a question of expediency, and is dependent on so many incalculable factors that the best answer we can give will only be an intelligent guess.

Let us consider these three questions in their order, remembering that to some extent the answers must inevitably overlap.

The first — 'Should we quit?' — is of special concern to the British electorate, who may be personified as Mr. and Mrs. Smith. Most of the Smith family, when they think of India at all, which is seldom, have a vague and generous feeling that we should quit, and they will probably vote accordingly. The word 'feeling' is used rather than the word 'opinion', because an opinion is — or should be — a point of view attained after a study of the facts, and the vast majority of the Smiths have neither any knowledge of the facts nor any inclination to study them. They prefer to trust to their emotions. They are warm-hearted people; they believe in 'freedom' in the same way that they believe in being kind to animals; they can find India on the map and they know that at any rate it *looks* like a single country, and they have a sneaking affection for Gandhi — 'after all, he must be a plucky old blighter', they say to themselves, 'not much of an oil-painting to look at, of course, but still he's got guts and anyway it's hard luck on him being in gaol and all that'.

This analysis of the minds of the Smiths may be considered as an insult to the bright new electorate of Britain. But is it? I have talked to many hundreds of young British serving men in India who should have been at least as well informed about the country as their brothers and sisters at home, and very few of them had even the most rudimentary ideas of the history, economy, or geography of the country, and scarcely one had ever heard of any Indian personality but Gandhi. They did not know the difference between a Hindu and a Muslim, nor which community was in the majority, they had no conception of the methods by which the country was governed, and though they knew—most of them! — that Lord Wavell was the Viceroy, they had no idea either of his powers or his limitations. Their ignorance was boundless — officers as well as men — yet *they*, remember, in comparison with their relations at home, are *authorities* on the India question! It was an illuminating sidelight on the workings of democracy, and it made one wonder, not for the first time, if there was really much point in having popular elections at all.

The curious thing about the apathy of the Smiths, and of their sons and brothers in India, is that they never for one minute ask themselves how quitting India is going to affect them, in their homes and their pockets. They have been told by Mr. Churchill that two out of every ten Englishmen gain their living, directly or indirectly, from the Indian connection, and they have an uneasy recollection that on more than one occasion in history Mr. Churchill has hit the nail on the head rather more squarely than some of his contemporaries. Yet the Smiths, through their representatives in Parliament (particularly in the working-class districts) blandly applaud the catchword 'Quit India' — on the assumption that it is somehow or other connected with 'progress' — the 'new world' — Sir William Beveridge, Professor Laski, J. B. Priestley, old Uncle Tom Driberg and all.

Mind you, I believe that if the Smiths really made up their minds that we *ought* to quit, on purely moral reasons, they would vote for quitting, even though they knew that they were voting against their own interests. It would not be the first time in

British history when the Smiths had done what they felt to be the right thing in the full knowledge that it was going to hurt them. The abolition of the highly profitable slave trade was a case in point. However, the Smiths have *not* made up their minds on this question, they have merely given an exhibition of amiable and apathetic ignorance. And so we cannot hand them any moral bouquets on this occasion; they have done nothing to earn them.

I am not so presumptuous as to imagine that this book can make up the minds of any very large number of Mr. and Mrs. Smiths, but since a personal opinion does help to clarify the issues, if it is sufficiently clear-cut, I will give my own answer to the question.

Should we quit?

On moral grounds the answer must be an emphatic 'yes'. If the Atlantic Charter means anything, if the whole war means anything, the answer must be 'yes'.

And equally on moral grounds, the 'yes' must be conditional on the recognition of the equal sovereignty and independence of the two great Indian nations — the Muslims and the Hindus.

The 'yes' is a farce and a fraud if it is not accompanied by this condition. We should be giving freedom with one hand and taking it away with the other. We should be letting 250 million Hindus out of what they are pleased to regard as gaol in the morning and shutting up 100 million Muslims in what they are quite *certain* is gaol in the afternoon.

We need not labour this point; it was made clear enough in the chapter on Pakistan. But it is quite vital that the intellectuals, the leaders of public opinion, and in particular the younger members of the labour party, should study the facts, instead of echoing the parrot-cries of Congress propaganda, and face the real issue, which is summed up in the phrase 'Divide and Quit'. There can be only two reasons for opposing that policy. The first is ignorance, the second is a denial of the principal of self-determination.

So much for the moral side of it. Now for the phy

II

Can we quit?

Of course we can. But only a wildly irresponsible person would suggest that we can quit overnight; India would be left almost completely defenceless from aggression.[1]

This quite fundamental matter of defence has received scant consideration from the so-called 'friends of India' at home, largely because they have been so bemused by Congress propaganda. It is dinned into their heads that 'India is eager to defend herself, if only she gains her freedom'. This apparently innocuous sentence is untrue and — apart from that — meaningless. On the one hand, India — at least Hindu India — is still sworn to non-violence, and although this dangerous sham has been somewhat discredited, it will never be completely eradicated from the Hindu mind. 'India is eager to defend herself' means, in the Gandhi philosophy, 'India is eager to play the role of doormat to any aggressor who chooses to wipe his feet on her.' On the other hand, to those who have rejected the creed of non-violence, 'India is eager to defend herself' is simply an empty slogan, flung out at large, to impress the world. 'Defend herself with what?' one may reasonably inquire. 'With catapults? With barge poles? With rotten eggs?' It is a legitimate question, but it seldom receives a legitimate answer, for the propagandist is too adroit to be caught napping; before you know where you are he has countered with another question ... 'And whose *fault* is it that India is so weak? Whose *fault* is it that we have no navy, no air force, no munition factories?' The applause which greets these rhetorical questions usually drowns any attempt to give a reasoned answer to them.

Of course, they really do not require an answer at all, for the question 'Whose fault is it?' is entirely irrelevant. However, let us be generous; let us grant the Congressman his point and say to him 'All right, have it your own way, it's all our fault.' So what? The hard facts of the situation are in no way altered, and those facts are of a nature to give pause even to Miss Pearl Buck. To take a very simple example, there is practically no such thing as an Indian navy. At the beginning of the war the entire Indian navy

[1] For the sake of simplicity I have deliberately avoided any consideration of the probability of civil war. The grant of Pakistan would, of course, remove the main danger; even so, it would seem fairly certain that large parts of India would revert to their traditional anarchy. It is inconceivable that all the States would vote themselves out of existence without a fight. It is equally inconceivable that the North-West Frontier would not flare up again in a bonfire of tribal warfare which might spread far beyond the frontiers.

consisted of a few *small patrol ships*.[1] This toy navy would have been totally, inadequate for a country the size of Denmark, let alone a continent the size of England, France, Germany, Scandinavia, Italy, the Balkans, and then some!

Well, what precisely is it suggested that we do about *this*? Leave these small ships to face the next combination of aggressors? No? Then what? Leave it to the United Nations? But surely that is a matter that demands somewhat lengthy discussion? If the United Nations are to shoulder so large a responsibility they will be entitled to ask what they are going to get out of it, and ... which is more important ... they will be entitled to demand that Gandhi does not start any anti-recruiting drives ... which, according to his life-long professions, he would be bound to do.

Pray do not shelve the question, nor cloud it with a lot of vague and idealistic talk. A navy does not drop from the clouds. It is a miraculous and delicate instrument, a creation of nerves as well as steel, united with blood, as well as rivets; it is in some ways the greatest expression of a nation's genius. Has India the genius to create a great navy? Let us again be generous, and take a deep breath, and gulp 'yes' ... whatever may be our misgivings. Even so, the craziest optimist could hardly suggest that such a navy could be built, recruited and inspired in a space much under twenty years.

And in the meantime? Is the British navy to carry on? Unpaid and unthanked? Is the British taxpayer to foot the bill? The answer, judging from the rantings of some British politicians, is 'yes'. But would it be the same answer if the warm-hearted British working classes, who are so eager to vote themselves down the rapids, realized even a shadow of the truth?

The same argument applies to the Indian army. Nobody would be so churlish as to deny the bravery which Indian troops have displayed in the present war, but it would be ludicrous to suggest that these same troops are capable of undertaking, on their own, the defence of one-fifth of the human race. Apart from the paucity of trained men, in proportion to the vastness of the territory and the richness of the interests to be protected, there are, at the time of writing, only a small handful of Indian officers who have

---

[1] Since the war a few corvettes, mine-sweepers, and sloops have been added.

ever been entrusted with any wide powers either in the field or in the office. Once again, let us grant that this may be our fault, that we have deliberately kept in our own hands the reins of power. That may be so, but whether it is due to British selfishness, or Indian reluctance to assume responsibility, is neither here nor there. The facts are all that matter, and the facts show us that as far as its officers are concerned the Indian army would have to start almost from scratch.

Is it suggested that these officers will suddenly drop from the skies, fully armed, miraculously endowed with the powers of discipline and command which must be theirs if they are to be worthy of their trust? From the declarations of Congress, this apparently *is* the suggestion. But to the realist it must surely appear doubtful whether so vast a *cadre* of highly trained men, with all the technical knowledge needed by the modern officer, can be created in the space of less than one generation, even under the most favourable circumstances.

What is to happen while this army is being created? Is India to be defended by an international army of Poles, Free French, Americans, Russians and Chinese? (Presumably the services of the hated British will not be required.) And is it going to be so simple, let as say, for a Czech lieutenant or a Norwegian sergeant to teach a bunch of non-violent Madrasis the elements of tank warfare — particularly when there happens to be no tanks available? Which reminds us of another little difficulty—the absence of an armament industry. Is there going to be another race among these international blood suckers to arm India — or rather, the two Indias? Are we going to see another breed of Zaharoffs trotting backwards and forwards across the borders of Pakistan and Hindustan, selling fifty machine guns to the Muslims on Monday and sixty machine guns to the Hindus on Tuesday?

These questions may be regarded as a *reductio ad absurdum*; but then the problem that they are probing is in itself absurd. It is absurd to imagine that India can dispense with an army; it is absurd to suggest that she has an army; it is absurd to believe that this army can be created in less than twenty years; and it is trebly absurd to underrate the dangers and difficulties with which any effort at international control will be beset.

Perhaps after a consideration of these competing absurdities the reader may have a faint inkling of the paramount absurdity of the generalization which hitherto he has been inclined to accept at its face value — 'India is eager to defend herself if only she is free.' The Mad Hatter never said anything quite so muddle-headed as *that.*[1]

III

Will we quit?

This is by far the most difficult question to answer, because it depends — and always has depended ever since the dawn of Indian freedom — on the attitude of the Indians themselves.

If the Cripps proposals had been accepted, we should be very much nearer the exit than we are to-day. Our bags would have been packed, most of our good-byes would have been said, and the taxi would have been waiting at the door. But the Cripps proposals were not accepted, and so everybody is in an uneasy state of transition. It is like living in suitcases, waiting for a telegram.

There is no point in rehashing the controversy which raged round the Cripps proposals. Their details are tedious, and in any case they are as dead as mutton, because the psychological atmosphere in which they were put forward can never be recreated. Only two points about them need concern the general reader. Firstly, they were regarded by both the great Indian minorities as a capitulation to the Hindus. The Muslims and the Untouchables cried with equal passion, 'You have sold us to the Hindus!' And the Muslims and the Untouchables — 160 million all told — were both quite right.

The second thing to realize about the proposals is that the vast majority of the Hindus bitterly regret their folly in rejecting them. All over India, if you listen carefully, you can hear the sound of Brahmins gnashing their teeth at the thought of the paradise they

---

[1] Pakistan would, of course, present a very much simpler problem of defence than Hindustan, partly because of its smaller area and comparatively insignificant coast-line, but principally because the Muslims are, and always have been, the warriors of India; they have a natural capacity to command (as they proved for 800 years) and in the present war they have contributed by far the larger proportion of men to the services. Apart from these considerations, Pakistan would lose no time in forging defensive links with the rest of the Muslim world.

so lightly spurned. For a paradise, potentially, it really was; in the Cripps offer was the essence of everything a Fascist dictatorship could possibly desire. Now it is too late — for as every day goes by the Muslim nation opens its eyes a little wider and the Untouchables raise their heads a little higher. Most important of all, more light floods the stage, and the world audience begins to realize that the Indian drama is not quite as simple as it has been persuaded to believe.

And yet — presumably — in one way or another, we shall quit. Maybe in haste, which would be an unredeemed tragedy, maybe in comparative leisure, which would at least give ourselves and the world a chance to adjust itself to the immense changes — racial, strategic and economic — which our withdrawal will inevitably entail.

I V

But whether it is to-morrow, or a day a little more remote, there will be one sense in which the British will never quit India, and that is a spiritual sense. With all our faults of omission and commission, our occasional outbursts of temper, our frequent lack of imagination, we gave India peace, and it was not the peace of the desert; we gave India law, and it was not the law of the strong; and — in the final judgment, we gave India liberty, for it was the ideals of Milton, of Locke, of Wilberforce, Mill, Bright and Gladstone that first kindled the Indian mind to an understanding of what liberty really is. Long after we have left, the students of the future will be opening the golden pages of the *Areopagitica*, and thrilling, as all young men should thrill, to the revolutionary music of Shelley. The ghost of Byron will brood in the quadrangles of universities yet unbuilt, and in the council chambers there will be heard the echo of the distant cadences of Burke. These things we gave to India, as we gave them to the rest of the world, and maybe it is in India that they will have their finest flowering. In the fulfilment of such a hope lies much of the future happiness of mankind.

Bombay
Spring, 1944